# MIRAGE IN THE WEST

### A HISTORY OF THE FRENCH IMAGE OF

### AMERICAN SOCIETY TO 1815

# Mirage in the West

## A History of the French Image
## of American Society to 1815

BY DURAND ECHEVERRIA

Foreword by Gilbert Chinard

1966
**OCTAGON BOOKS, INC.**
*New York*

*Reprinted 1966*
*by special arrangement with Princeton University Press*

## OCTAGON BOOKS, INC.
175 FIFTH AVENUE
NEW YORK, N. Y. 10010

LIBRARY OF CONGRESS CATALOG CARD NUMBER: 66-17509

*Printed in U.S.A. by*
NOBLE OFFSET PRINTERS, INC.
NEW YORK 3, N. Y.

# FOREWORD

THE field of study chosen by Mr. Echeverria is the most significant period in the history of Franco-American relations. During the second half of the eighteenth century one could witness the development of the American mirage above the horizon—its sudden surge and intensification, its subsequent equally abrupt collapse. This account of the rise and fall of an ideal presents a striking dramatic unity; it is also very timely.

Despite the innumerable books and articles published every year in both France and America, often by well-informed and well-meaning writers, the complaint is still commonly heard that the French fail to understand the Americans while the Americans evidence a similar lack of understanding. To many of the French America is still *terra incognita.* "L'Amérique cette inconnue" is a title which could be prefixed to hundreds of accounts written by would-be discoverers. In spite of the almost instinctive sympathy existing between the two peoples, half-truths, hasty judgments, preconceived notions, and traditional misconceptions at times befog the vision of the best observers. This curious phenomenon has sometimes been called the American mirage. It is composed of many different elements, but on the whole it presents certain ingredients which seem to have a permanent character and which have persisted for more than a century and a half. If, as we believe, the American mirage still exerts a very real but not always recognized influence, it is of prime importance for students of foreign relations to trace its origin historically. Such is the aim of this book.

The elements of the eighteenth-century mirage were various: nostalgia for the Golden Age and the Lost Paradise, tropical or semitropical dreams and exoticism, the myth of the Good Savage, an imaginary locus for the utopian constructions of philosophers and critics of society, the well-established tradition that "America" was a place where men could live "free and happy" in the midst of bounteous prosperity. From the days of the discovery of America these images were projected against a society which already showed signs of aging if not of senescence.

As a first result, the discovery of America brought to the fore a problem of civilization. It created the possibility of founding somewhere outside of Europe a new society. To the Old World America offered examples of peoples living without government or under a minimum of government, of colonies of religious refugees who had undertaken to establish an ideal republic. Most of all perhaps, America offered an unlimited territory where men could escape the restraints of a civilization growing every day more complicated. During the first half of the eighteenth century, this vision may have appeared as the "heavenly city of the philosophers"; in 1776 it seemed that the dream had suddenly become, if not a reality, at least an immediate possibility.

From the very beginning of the American Revolution two opposite reactions manifested themselves in the French public. It was recognized at once that the emergence of a new nation in the New World was "one of the major events of modern history," to quote the very terms used in October 1776 in a French periodical published under the supervision of the French foreign office. The United States appeared as a new force manifesting itself with explosive violence. It was a revolutionary force, for any new force introduced into an old society is necessarily considered revolutionary, that is to say, capable of operating radical changes. All the implications of the American Revolution were not realized at first, but they were confusedly felt—dreaded by some and enthusiastically welcomed by others. To cite only one instance, it was generally admitted that the independence of the American colonies and their victory would ultimately mean the complete abolition of the European colonial system. Thus America by its very existence became, and has never ceased to be, an important political factor in the internal life of the European nations. Nowhere perhaps was this fact felt more keenly and more quickly than in France, in a nation where the *ancien régime* was rapidly deteriorating. The first and important consequence was that sometimes unwittingly, sometimes deliberately, the American phenomenon was utilized to advocate or deprecate programs of domestic reforms. To those who already called themselves "republicans," the image of America appeared embellished as in a magic mirror. To the others it appeared as a horrible example and a dire anticipation of what the future held in store.

Little need be said here about these two extreme positions; they are fully analyzed in Mr. Echeverria's book. The enthusiasm for the cause of the *Insurgents* was genuine and widespread. The outspoken critics of America, on the contrary, were few and they generally opposed France's participation in the war solely on the ground that such an operation would be ruinous for the kingdom and would prevent or delay the internal reforms which had become imperative. It is to be noted, however, that the misgivings expressed at the time were sufficiently serious to deserve careful and systematic refutation by the French friends of the United States and later by the American envoys, Franklin, Adams, and Jefferson.

One of the earliest and most important sources of French misgivings was the fact that, by comparison with many other undeveloped countries, the land occupied by the Anglo-Americans had failed to sustain a large aboriginal population. It was a very serious question whether the climate and soil as described by travelers were such as to permit Europeans to live, prosper, and multiply, or whether the settlers as well as the animals transported to the New World would be thwarted in their growth and rapidly degenerate. Such was the fear expressed not only by a cabinet philosopher like De Pauw, but by a scientific genius and exact observer like Buffon.

Even if these fears proved to be ill-founded, it remained to be seen whether the political structure erected by the

Americans would stand the test of time. Their governmental organization seemed to be very weak, although resting on undeniable and self-evident principles, and it did not come up to the expectations of America's transatlantic friends. The state constitutions were good enough, but the federal system, and particularly the limited powers of the central government, appeared as limitations preventing the formation of a strongly united nation. Despite their love of liberty, men brought up in an overcentralized society and fond of abstract reasoning and logical constructions were unable to conceive a society composed of units endowed with extraordinary independence and consequently they believed that such a society would be unable in times of crisis to decide upon a concerted action. Even such an apostle of Americanism as St. John Crèvecœur emphasized the divisions existing between the "Yankees" and the "Virginians." Having different interests and different mores, living in different climates under different governments, would they be able to maintain an artificial and temporary unity? They had risen against a common foe; they had consented to great sacrifices to win their independence. Would they accept the same sacrifices and display the same spirit of cooperation in time of peace? In other words, after experimenting with extreme decentralization, would they have to resort to a dictatorship in order to avoid complete anarchy? These preoccupations did not lessen the sympathy for the American cause, but the main question was to find out whether the federative system, as it was called, which worked in Holland and Switzerland, countries with an exceedingly limited territory and small population, could work when applied to a larger territorial and social unit like France. These misgivings, which were quite legitimate under the circumstances, did not imply any systematic disparagement of America. They mainly reflected the deep concern of the French political philosophers in the success or failure of the American experiment.

America had been set up as the ideal city of man; the city was not entirely built, its plans were not even completed, but it was at least a beginning and a hope. Thus a heavy responsibility was placed upon the American people, who were entrusted with the task of erecting, for themselves and also for Europe and more particularly for France, the model organization which would demonstrate that the speculations of the political philosophers and reformers were not idle dreams but were susceptible of practical and immediate realization. The American constitutions were scrutinized and sometimes criticized with the same eagerness and zeal as if they had been French political documents. To be fully successful the American experiment had to conform to the program of reforms which the French "republicans" were contemplating. Thus is explained the extraordinary undertaking of the Abbé Mably, who took upon himself, after reading the texts of the state constitutions published by Benjamin Franklin in 1783, to point out the defects he had detected and the dangers he feared and to indicate the remedies and modifications to be adopted by the citizens of the United States. To a certain extent this was also the attitude of a much more profound thinker than Mably, the Marquis de Condorcet, and even of Brissot. That they were bound to be disappointed was inevitable; their expectations were too high to withstand the shock of reality. The dream disintegrated, to use Mr. Echeverria's terms, but it must be noted that the collapse of the American dream coincided with the collapse of the revolutionary dream and was largely brought about by the political confusion which followed the heroic period of the French Revolution.

Far more serious and durable were the doubts raised about the possibility that the United States would create a civilization, or as some would say a culture, comparable to the culture of older nations. More than any other people in Europe, perhaps, the French were proud of a long cultural tradition. To them culture was more than a certain climate of society. It was an inheritance representing the accumulated efforts of many generations. It was also the product and the expression of a limited social group. The arts and the letters had been protected by the king and the court through institutions, academies, and colleges of long standing. During the eighteenth century artists and writers had become more independent; they had addressed a larger public; but on the whole French literature and French art had a distinctly aristocratic flavor. The essence of French culture was concentrated in Paris and Versailles. Neither Philadelphia nor Boston and even less New York could compare with the capitals of Europe. These doubts were confirmed to a large extent by the *Emigrés*, who came to America not as immigrants eager to start on a new life, but as exiles who had found in a crude if hospitable land a temporary haven.

Largely because of the extraordinary prestige of Benjamin Franklin, it was readily granted that the Americans could excel in the mechanical arts and that they would make discoveries which would enable them to tame a rich but hostile nature and to exploit their domain. But the very success which was anticipated would soon give rise, it was feared, to a new danger. They would try to emulate their mother country, engage in commerce, manufactures, and speculation. A new aristocracy would appear, an aristocracy founded on money and material success, whose dominating and corrupting influence would pervade all the activities of American society. Large cities would grow and with them would appear all the vices of city life. The simple virtues of the American farmers would not long resist the depravity of large agglomerations. Although a young nation, America would be afflicted with all the evils of the old civilizations without enjoying their social refinements and amenities. The disintegration of the political dream of the philosophers would soon be followed by the disintegration of the pastoral dream of St. John Crèvecœur and the Physiocrats.

Such were some of the pessimistic anticipations and misgivings underlying the enthusiasm for America generally expressed in France on the eve of the French Revolution. In most cases these reservations and criticisms sprang from a failure to admit that the American people had a right to develop a society of their own and to establish their own tradition. Here we touch what may be called a neuralgic point in the relations between the two countries. The French were perfectly satisfied to accept their European neighbors as they were. They would never have dreamed of changing the so-called national characteristics of the Italians, the Germans, the Spanish, or the British. America was entirely different: any American shortcoming, any failure to fulfill the mission the young country had assumed, was felt by the French as if it had directly affected their national life and their own possibilities of changing their own order. To what degree this prejudice has lasted cannot be discussed here; it may not be out of place to submit that like a weed it has never been completely eradicated. Undoubtedly it influenced Tocqueville and, were we to mention contemporaries, we would find it stronger than ever in the too famous and misunderstood book of Georges Duhamel. Occasionally it even crops up in the books and articles of such a keen and sympathetic observer as André Siegfried. Its survival is not due to any lasting and fundamental antagonism, but to the fact that it reflects two of the main problems which have troubled French society during the last hundred and fifty years.

The first is a problem of government, and more particularly of democratic government, to which no definite and final solution may be found, since in the last analysis it depends upon the "eternal vigilance" of the individuals and not upon any ready-made formula. The American experiment, which was brought to the attention of the world in 1776 and 1787, is still going on; it still arouses almost the same reactions as it did at the start. The least that can be said is that in the eyes of the conservatives America still appears as a revolutionary force capable of bringing about sudden and consequently unwanted tranformations.

The second is essentially a social problem or corollary: it rests upon the preservation and formation of the elites and primarily upon the definition of the term itself. The resistance offered by certain elements of the French people to the American way of life is to a certain extent a modern expression of the criticisms of the American society analyzed in this book.

A study of this nature, therefore, has an immediate and general importance. At the end of the eighteenth century and during the first decades of the nineteenth our predecessors were confronted with problems which we are still striving to solve. On both sides of the Atlantic they felt that they were engaged in the tremendous undertaking of remaking the world; they hoped that it would be a better world and they believed that the experiment in which they were engaged transcended national boundaries. They worked in an atmosphere of passion, enthusiasm, and fever. The lesson to be derived from their failures as well as from their successes can help us in some degree to understand the perplexed world in which we live.

GILBERT CHINARD

# PREFACE

ONE of the most difficult of the many problems facing modern man is the fact that as the various peoples of the world have been drawn closer together by technological progress they have failed to grow in sympathy and tolerance. They have found no way to share more fully one another's fears and aspirations or to tolerate unfamiliar values and beliefs. Each nation is shocked and dismayed by the distorted image of itself it sees reflected in other eyes, and is outraged to hear its idols mocked and its fears derided. How, each people asks, can we work and live with these strange brothers? What can be done, if not to understand one another (for perhaps that is hopeless), at least to discover some areas of sympathy, to learn to tolerate ways and values not our own, and to instill like sympathy and tolerance in others?

Americans perhaps more than any other people suffer from a feeling of frustration and resentment from the world's incomprehension, and we have been searching in our pragmatic way for a solution. But if we are to find a solution we must first know more than we now do about the nature of our predicament. Obviously something more is needed than just an analysis of a current crisis, for international misunderstanding is a historical, continuing phenomenon. Prejudices are as durable as stone and mortar; antipathies grow from seeds planted centuries before. Only by going back to the moment of first contact, by catching the first glimpse of that other self which others have fashioned of us, by following its growth and evolution through the years, by seeing the unsuspected events and ideas which have disguised that strange image of ourselves in undeserved virtues and vices, by watching the image grow until it arrives at the moment of today—only in this way can we hope to comprehend our own incomprehensibility.

The full histories of these other selves by which each nation is haunted are still to be written. This book is merely an attempt to relate a few chapters in one such history. After the British, the French have been the people with whom Americans have had the longest and most intimate contact. Moreover the French, more than the British, stand in a central position in the complex of Western culture. Their image of us has had a unique importance among the images created by all others.

These pages, then, are the history of another United States, the nation which existed in the minds of the French from their first awareness in the seventeenth century of the momentous new civilization arising across the Atlantic, down through the years of the American Revolution, the French Revolution, the Undeclared War of 1798, and the tragedy of the First Empire. They are a partial account, leaving the later chapters still to be written. But it was necessary to begin at the beginning, and perhaps they will provide the foundation for a better understanding of European attitudes to the United States in the nineteenth and twentieth centuries. In addition, they may serve as a sort of case history. By recreating the mirage that the French saw glowing in the West we can more easily understand the nature of all the mirages which deceive the peoples of the world.

In writing this book I have been aided by many friends, but I should like to extend my special thanks to Dr. Lawrence C. Wroth of the John Carter Brown Library, to Professor Ira O. Wade of Princeton University for his criticisms and counsel, and finally to Professor Gilbert Chinard, who first suggested the subject to me and who has offered so generously his learning, wisdom, and kindness. In addition, I must express my gratitude for the support of a Fulbright Grant and a Brown University President's Fellowship, which made possible the completion of this work.

D.E.

*Brown University*
*Providence, R.I.*
*August 1956*

# CONTENTS

# MIRAGE IN THE WEST

## A HISTORY OF THE FRENCH IMAGE OF

## AMERICAN SOCIETY TO 1815

CHAPTER I

## THE *PHILOSOPHES* DISCOVER AMERICA

IN THE three-year period from 1767 to 1770 occurred an event which was to turn out to be of considerable importance in the history of European thought. This was the discovery of a wondrous new nation taking form in the thin line of colonies strung along the coast of British North America. It was evident even then to the clearest thinkers that this first nation to arise out of European colonialism was destined for eventual independence and for the economic, political, and cultural domination of the New World, and consequently that it was a potent new force to be reckoned with in the balance of world power. Secondly, these Americans, in their struggle with England, appeared to be forcing, with a freedom and decisiveness impossible elsewhere, the immediate application of most of the controversial social and political ideas under discussion in Europe. America was suddenly "the hope of the human race," as Turgot was to say, or conversely the threat of the world, because it was to be the first practical trial construction of the Heavenly City of the *Philosophes.*

Though the French had been aware for over thirty years, ever since Voltaire's *Lettres philosophiques,* of William Penn's famous experiment in toleration and brotherly love, the British colonies had, before 1767, suggested no more than the curious but limited example of Pennsylvania. But now, with the Stamp Act crisis, which drew the attention of all Europe, and with Franklin's two visits to Paris in 1767 and 1769, the French learned that in the fate and future of these colonies were involved not merely the practical possibility of religious toleration, but also many fundamental questions

*3*

in political and economic theory, in social morality, and in the progress of the human mind.

At the same moment, however, that the French became aware that the American example might be of the greatest relevancy to the future of Europe, a sharp difference of opinion (which has yet to be settled) appeared as to the essential nature of these new creatures, the Americans. Were they Europeans strengthened and liberated by the opportunities and challenges of the New World and hence the precursors of a new era, or were they Europeans transformed and debased by transplantation and hence useful only as warnings of the dangers of colonialism?

It was a Hollander named Cornelius de Pauw (or de Paw) who in 1768 precipitated the bitter debate over how to interpret the American example. He asserted that the climate of the New World was so unfavorable to all forms of life that animals and men, whether indigenous or transplanted from Europe, inevitably degenerated, and that, consequently, colonials born in America tended to become with successive generations physically, morally, and intellectually inferior to their European ancestors. If this were true, then obviously no argument for the perfectibility of mankind could be drawn from any American example.[1]

This pessimistic idea, which attracted wide belief and which was to persist well into the nineteenth century, had been taking shape for a half century, and was compounded of a number of currents in eighteenth-century thought.

It was based, of course, on the theory of climate, the belief that man's physical, mental, and moral character is determined by relative temperature and humidity, an idea which Montesquieu had popularized in his *Esprit des lois* (1748). He had postulated "that the nature of men's minds and passions are extremely different in the various climates," and consequently that the legislator must draw up the laws of the

[1] On the theory of American degeneration, see G. Chinard, "Eighteenth Century Theories of America as a Human Habitat," *Proc. Amer. Philos. Soc.*, XCI (1947), 27-57; and my "Roubaud and the Theory of American Degeneration," *French American Rev.*, III (1950), 24-33.

state so that they will be relative to these differences.[2] But the idea was not new with him. It went back at least as far as Plato; it had been employed by political theorists of the Renaissance, such as Jean Bodin and Louis Leroy, and it had appeared in Montaigne, in travelers of the sixteenth and seventeenth centuries, and even in literary critics such as Dubos.[3] By the second half of the eighteenth century the theory had been made a commonplace by Montesquieu's authority and by the diffusion of his ideas in Diderot's *Encyclopédie* and in the works of lesser writers. Furthermore, corroboration had been given by the sensualistic psychology of Locke and Condillac. If it were true, as Condillac said, that not only our ideas but our faculties as well are produced entirely by sensory experience, then environment could be the only factor determining the nature of man. To the eighteenth-century mind it was obvious that if American climate were so unlike that of Europe, American civilization must differ in like degree. So while the theory of climate was not, in its simplest principle, a new idea, it was given a new meaning as an expression of the century's faith in the universal force of natural law operating upon the destiny of mankind. For this, men like Fontenelle and Bayle were directly responsible, though of course they owed their inspiration to Newton and Bacon.

That the American climate must be different was suggested not only by the striking variations in mean temperature between corresponding North American and European latitudes, but also by the belief that the New World was actually new. At an early date, probably in the sixteenth century, the semantic confusion inherent in the epithet *nouveau monde* had begun to cause the idea of a newly created world to overlap that of a newly discovered world. Montaigne, for

<hr/>

[2] *Esprit des lois*, Bk. XIV, Ch. 1.

[3] Jean Bodin, *Methodus ad facilem historiarum cognitionem* (1566), Ch. v, and *Les Six livres de la république* (1576), *passim*; Louis Leroy, *De la vicissitude* (1577), Bk. I; Montaigne, *Essais*, "Apologie de Raimond Sebond"; Gabriel Sagard, *Histoire du Canada* (1636), p. 256; Baudelot de Dairval, *De l'utilité des voyages* (1686), I, ii; Jean Chardin, *Voyage en Perse et aux Indes Orientales* (Amsterdam, 1711), II, 8; Jean-Baptiste Dubos, *Réflexions critiques sur la poésie et sur la peinture* (Paris, 1719), II, 141.

instance, had called America an infant to whom the Old World was still teaching its ABC's,[4] and by the eighteenth century scientists such as Buffon and Engel were stating a later geological and biological formation of America as an accepted fact.[5]

This newness of the New World was in large part suggested by the primitive level of Indian culture. Parallel to the idealization of the "Good Savage," the innocent child of nature, there existed, especially among explorers and colonials, a less literary disposition to consider the Indians as an inferior breed in the Great Chain of Being halfway between men and beasts. Pope Alexander VI had found it necessary to decree to the Spaniards, who hunted the natives of Santo Domingo with dogs as a species of game, that the Indians were human enough to receive the Catholic faith. French explorers were usually equally contemptuous, and Cartier called the Indians of Canada "the most miserable people there can be in the world."[6]

At the same time the Spanish developed a strong popular prejudice against their own colonials. Cervantes called America the refuge for all the scum of Spain,[7] and Coreal, in a work translated into French in 1732, described bitterly the corruption, ignorance, and cruelty of the colonial administration.[8]

The conclusion was obvious that the corruption of the colonials and the primitiveness of the Indians were the result of an unfavorable climate, which in turn might be explained by the newness of the New World. French writers were all the more ready to seize such a hypothesis because of the widespread prejudice against colonialism suggested by the obvious evils of the inflation caused by the importation of gold, the

[4] *Essais*, "Des coches."

[5] Buffon, *Histoire naturelle*; J. Engel, *Essai sur cette question: Quand et comment l'Amérique a-t-elle été peuplée d'hommes et d'animaux?* (Amsterdam, 1767).

[6] *Les Français en Amérique pendant la première moitié du XVIe siècle* (Paris, 1946), p. 104. See also Thevet, *Singularitez de la France Antarctique* (1557).

[7] *Novelas ejemplares*, "El Celoso Extremeño."

[8] *Voyages aux Indes Occidentales* (Paris, 1722), I, 133, 140-141.

supposed introduction of syphilis from America, and the failure of France's colonial ventures, particularly Law's disastrous scheme to colonize Louisiana.

"Men," Montesquieu was saying as early as 1721, "should stay where they are." The ordinary effect of colonies, he explained, was to weaken the mother country without populating the new land. The mere change from one climate to another could cause sickness, and if the change were to a wilderness, which had to have a bad climate if it had remained uninhabited, the result would be fatal.[9]

In 1748 Benoît de Maillet's curious book *Telliamed* gave a different twist to the idea. Adapting Oriental transformism to Western science, De Maillet, who had lived in the Near East, propounded the theory that the earth had once been entirely covered by water, and that as the land masses had gradually emerged from the seas animal life had evolved from fishes. Consequently, he argued, life on the "newer" lands must be the more primitive.

Voltaire ridiculed De Maillet's hypothesis, preferring to believe that the baffling seashells found on mountaintops had been dropped by pilgrims on their way to Santiago de Compostela rather than that the Alps had ever been under water;[10] but in his *Essai sur les moeurs* (1753-1756) he went along with De Maillet's conclusions. Voltaire was a polygenesist, believing that the various races had been separately created and were inherently inferior or superior to one another; but he stated that the New World was a younger continent, that the Indians were an inferior species created later than the white race, and that the climate and physical environment of America were unfavorable to human life. Voltaire, of course, was a strong anti-colonialist and he ridiculed the costly wars France had fought over "a few acres of snow."

It was the natural scientist Buffon who gave the theory of American degeneration scientific respectability. In contrast to Voltaire, he based his monumental *Histoire naturelle*

[9] *Lettres persanes*, Lettre 121.
[10] *Oeuvres* (Molland ed.), XXI, 330-334; XII, 380.

on the theory of monogenesis, namely, that each genus had originated from a single species which later was modified and differentiated in the various regions of the earth by climate, diet, and physical conditions. Hence man too had come from a single prototype, and in spite of his greater power to resist the effects of environment, he had likewise been modified into the present different races.[11] In a volume of the *Histoire naturelle* published in 1761 treating the animals of the New World, Buffon claimed that from all available evidence it appeared that animal species in America were less varied, smaller, and less vigorous than those of the Old World, because of the unfavorable cooler and more humid climate, natural to a continent which had "remained longer than the rest of the globe under the waters of the sea." This same degeneration from "something contrary to the development of living nature in this New World" was to be seen in the native Indian, "a mere animal of the first rank," and in domestic animals transplanted from Europe, which tended to grow smaller and less vigorous.[12]

Buffon did not take the logical step of arguing that European settlers must degenerate in like manner, for his belief in man's power to overcome an unfavorable environment led him to predict that the settlers would succeed in clearing and draining the land and thus make it fertile and healthy. This reservation, however, was overlooked by most of his contemporaries and his authority was repeatedly misused, in spite of his protests, to prove the degeneration of European settlers.

In the same year, 1761, the theory of American degeneration received the support of firsthand evidence from the Swedish naturalist Peter Kalm, whose widely read *Travels* were published in Swedish in 1753-1761 and partially translated into French in 1761.[13] Kalm had spent two and a half

11 *Histoire naturelle* (Paris: Imprimerie Royale), III (1749), 529-530 and IX (1761), 125.

12 *Ibid.*, IX, 103-104, 111, 114, 125.

13 The *Journal étranger* published in July 1761 a long paraphrase of Kalm's passage on the degeneration of Americans; Rousselot de Surgy's *Histoire naturelle et politique de la Pensylvanie* (1768) was an abridgement and adaptation of the *Travels*.

years traveling through the colonies from Pennsylvania to Quebec and from the Atlantic to the Blue Ridge Mountains. He was a reputable scientist and a careful observer, but he appears to have been extremely gullible. He soberly reported a tale told him by Bartram, the American botanist, that American bears killed cows by biting a hole in their sides and blowing them up until they died of over-inflation. Though Kalm felt no prejudice against Americans and greatly admired the prosperity, learning, and good government of the colonies, he wrote on the degeneration of the settlers several pages which were to become famous. He said that though they were generally healthy and robust, the native colonials matured earlier and died younger than Europeans. The woman ceased bearing children sooner than in Europe and American soldiers did not have the stamina of English troops. Similarly, the cattle imported from Europe grew smaller in successive generations. Climate, he suggested, might be the reason.[14]

Nevertheless, no one up to this point had specifically stated that there was a necessary cause-and-effect relation between climate and the inferiority of colonials to Europeans. This was the contribution of De Pauw. Born in Amsterdam in 1739, he had taken minor orders and as a young man had spent eight months at the court of Frederick the Great at Potsdam as the representative of the Prince-Bishop of Liége. Upon his return he wrote, while still in his twenties, his controversial *Recherches philosophiques sur les Américains,* published in Berlin in 1768. The work caused much discussion and was attacked the following year in a lengthy *Dissertation sur l'Amérique et les Américains* by Dom Pernetty, and ex-Benedictine monk serving as Frederick's librarian. De Pauw replied with a lengthy *Défense,* which was also answered by Pernetty.[15] De Pauw became, as a result of his

14 *Peter Kalm's Travels in North America,* ed. A. B. Bensen (New York, 1937), I, 56.

15 De Pauw, *Défense des Recherches philosophiques sur les Américains* (Berlin, 1770); Pernetty, *Dissertation sur l'Amérique et les Américains contre les Recherches philosophiques de M. de P . . .* (1769); Pernetty, *Examen des Recherches philosophiques sur l'Amérique et les Américains et la Défense*

publications, the authority on American questions, and in 1776 he was asked to write the nineteen-page article on American for the new supplement to the *Encyclopédie* to replace the half column on the subject in the original edition.

De Pauw's thesis was nothing more than a rigid application of Buffon's principles to the specific problem of the American Indians and the colonial settlers, copiously documented by evidence from Kalm and a host of other travelers. He claimed that the American climate was cooler and more humid than that of the Old World because of the continent's more recent emergence from the waters of the Flood and because of the dense forests and swamps. This climate, as Buffon had said, produced animals "degenerate, small, cowardly and a thousand times less dangerous than those of Asia and Africa."[16] As both Kalm and Buffon had reported, domestic animals imported from Europe suffered a similar degeneration. The most important effect of this climate, however, was on man. The Indians were physically, morally, and intellectually inferior to Europeans. They lacked vigor and endurance, were sexually frigid and perverted, unprolific, hairless, insensitive to pain, short-lived, and afflicted by a list of ills and perversions ranging from irregular menstruation to the eating of iguanas. Morally they were cowardly, indolent, and devoid of the most basic moral sense. Mentally, they lacked intellectual ambition and curiosity and were incapable of reason. Indian children, he said, seemed to show some progress under instruction until they were sixteen or seventeen, but after that age they inevitably lapsed into brutal stupidity.

All this was no more than a documentation and amplification of Buffon's theories. But De Pauw was more logical than his master in insisting that in spite of civilized man's greater power to combat an unfavorable environment, the same factors which affected the animals and Indians must

---

*de cet ouvrage* (Berlin, 1771). Up to 1799 there appeared eleven editions of De Pauw's *Recherches*, nine of his *Défense*, seven of Pernetty's *Dissertation*, and two of his *Examen*. Most of these editions were published in the 1770's.
16 *Recherches*, I, 8-9.

also operate on the colonials.[17] White children born in America, like the young Indians, lost all interest and receptivity to learning after an early precociousness, so that "they were already blind when other men are just beginning to see." "This phenomenon," as Kalm had testified, "has been observed among the colonials of the north just as much as among those born in the southern provinces."[18] The universities of America had not produced a single man of reputation, not a single individual capable of writing even a bad book, not a single teacher, philosopher, doctor, physicist, or scholar whose name had ever reached Europe.[19] It might be supposed, he remarked sarcastically, that this failure could be blamed on the ignorance of the Jesuit teachers, but no: "It has not been observed that the professors of the University of Cambridge in New England have educated any young Americans to the point of being able to display them in the literary world." Something might be accomplished by the exercise of great gentleness and understanding, "but is it from American merchants, from adventurers guided in all their actions by the most burning avarice that we may expect the necessary effort? Alas! We greatly doubt it."[20]

Such reasoning was a good example of the eighteenth-century *esprit de système*, of the elaborate documentation of a priori hypotheses. The vehemence of De Pauw's arguments revealed the intensity of his faith in two negative ideas: the evils of colonialism and the falseness of the "Good Savage" myth.

De Pauw's sojourn in the Prussian court had brought him under the influence of Frederick, one of whose key policies was the prevention of emigration. He was engaged in a highly organized and subsidized effort to attract settlers into his own realm, and consequently he strongly and actively opposed any flow of population in the opposite direction, even to the extent of establishing a special agency at Hamburg to stop emigrants preparing to sail for America. De

[17] *Ibid.*, II, 164-165.    [18] *Défense*, p. 8.
[19] *Recherches*, II, 167.
[20] "Amérique," *Supplément à l'Encyclopédie*, I (1776), 351.

Pauw supported this political policy with an impressive barrage of arguments and testimony. He opened by flatly postulating that the discovery of America had been the most important and most disastrous event in the history of civilization, and that a second such catastrophe would bring the extinction of mankind. Economically, the American trade sapped Europe's strength by drawing off commodities such as wheat, clothing, and wine essential to her standard of living and returning only useless luxuries like gold and tobacco. At the same time the high mortality rate of the settlers forced a constant drain on the population of Europe to maintain the colonies. He claimed that England had taken more than 500,000 men and women from the various German states to send them to die as slaves in Pennsylvania.[21]

Just as the degeneration of the Creoles was a powerful argument to prevent emigration for political reasons, so the degeneration of the Indians served the ideological purpose of destroying the myth of the "Good Savage." Rousseau in his First and Second Discourses had advanced the revolutionary (but not original) idea that man's stage of greatest happiness, virtue, and well-being had been in a hypothetical semi-savage state before he had been enslaved by the institutions of property and government. He then had cited certain American Indian tribes as living examples of his man of nature. De Pauw, who, like Buffon and Voltaire, was on the side of civilization, hoped to destroy this primitivistic argument by showing that the so-called "Good Savage," the child of nature, was in reality a degenerate race. "It has been claimed," he wrote, "that, in spite of their ruthless character, these savages are not barbarians, but that civilized people are." This was the judgment of a misanthrope or a madman. "If crimes are frequent among the most civilized nations, it is not science nor the arts which are to be blamed."[22] It was beyond argument that societies which had produced men like Newton, Locke, Leibnitz, Descartes, Montesquieu, and 'S Gravesande were infinitely superior to hordes of degenerate bar-

21 *Recherches*, I, v-vi; *Défense*, Ch. xxiv and pp. 118, 119.
22 *Recherches*, I, 125-126.

barians who could neither read nor write nor count beyond their fingers and whose so-called philosophy consisted in mistreating their women, getting drunk, smoking tobacco, waging war, taking scalps, torturing prisoners, practising cannibalism, and spending their days in stupid indolence in smoke-filled hovels. "Perfectibility," De Pauw said, "is the greatest gift that Nature has bestowed upon man," and it was man's duty to cultivate it.[23]

For De Pauw's purposes, the physical, moral, and intellectual degeneration of man in the New World had to be proved to refute Rousseau and discourage colonial ventures. It was only, we see, an intermediary proposition in the demonstration. The curious consequence, however, was that while De Pauw's final arguments were lost in the triumph of Rousseau in the French Revolution and of colonialism in the nineteenth century, his secondary theory of American degeneration, particularly of intellectual and cultural degeneration, continued to appeal to certain segments of French thought, right down to such modern writers as Duhamel.[24] It was a plausible deterministic argument, incapable of being either proved or disproved, which could be made to serve any doctrine of European cultural hegemony.

Although the theory was to be counteracted and momentarily submerged by the triumph of the pro-Americanists in the 1770's and 1780's, it became widely diffused in the fabric of French thought. The vulgarization of the idea was the work less of De Pauw himself than of another writer, the Abbé Raynal, whose *Histoire philosophique et politique des établissements et du commerce des Européens dans les deux Indes* appeared in its first edition in 1772. This lengthy and extremely influential work, which went through thirty-seven editions between 1772 and 1820, was a sort of encyclopedia of the non-European world, to which a large number of *Philosophes* contributed and for which Raynal did not hesitate to draw and even plagiarize verbatim from a variety

[23] *Défense*, p. 228.
[24] G. Duhamel, *Scènes de la vie future* (Paris: Mercure de France, 1939), pp. 113-114.

of sources. By a constant process of revision and addition, the work grew from edition to edition until Raynal's death. This method of composition naturally occasioned many ideological inconsistencies and contradictions, but it made of the work an arsenal of arguments for liberal reformers of the last years of the *ancien régime*.[25]

Since one of the work's main arguments was against colonialism, which Raynal said was "contrary to nature," it was inevitable that in the first edition Raynal would reproduce De Pauw's theory of American degeneration. He made only two modifications. The first was to go back to Montesquieu's suggestion that part of the degeneration might be caused by the difficulty of adjusting to an alien environment. The other was to lay the charge of intellectual degeneration more specifically and in stronger terms than ever before against the English settlers in North America. They had "visibly degenerated," he wrote, and were physically weaker than Europeans. Under alien skies, "their minds have been enervated like their bodies. Quick and penetrating at first, they grasp ideas easily; but they cannot concentrate nor accustom themselves to prolonged reflection. It is amazing that America has not yet produced a good poet, a capable mathematician, or a man of genius in a single art or a single science. Almost all have some facility in everything, but none has a marked talent for anything. Precocious and mature before us, they are far behind when we have reached our full mental development."[26]

Raynal was soon to be forced to retract these words, for if the degenerate American was a useful demonstration of the evils of colonialism, the noble American was, it soon became evident, an even more valuable demonstration of the blessings of the Enlightenment. The theory of American degeneration ran headlong into the countercurrent of thought which idealized Americans as the exponents of religious, economic, and political liberty.

25 See A. Feugère, *Un Précurseur de la Révolution, l'abbé Raynal* (Paris, 1922) and *Bibliographie critique de l'abbé Raynal* (Paris, 1922).
26 *Histoire philosophique et politique* (Amsterdam, 1770), VI, 376.

Until 1767 this countercurrent had been weak, mainly for the simple reason that so little was known in France about the British colonies. In 1755, just before the outbreak of the Seven Years War, it was being said that in France all but a few individuals were "almost completely ignorant of conditions there."[27] This lack of information is confirmed by the infrequency with which even the best informed writers referred to the British possessions. Of a list of 200 authors cited as authorities on the New World by the various contributors to the *Encyclopédie*, only eight dealt specifically with the British colonies in North America.[28] Every writer referred to by Buffon in his description of the animals of the New World either was Spanish or wrote about Spanish America or the West Indies.

Nevertheless we find, from the end of the seventeenth century, a few writers who identified the British colonies with the ideas of religious freedom and political liberty. The Quakers had attempted to make converts in France as early as 1656, and when William Penn received his charter for Pennsylvania from Charles II in 1681 he caused his agent in Rotterdam, Benjamin Furly, to distribute on the continent tracts in French as well as in Dutch and German in order to recruit colonists.[29] Furly's pamphlets are of interest as probably the first work in French identifying the British colonies with political and religious liberty. Pennsylvania, he told the French, was a haven where a man could live in plenty and peace, an asylum for the poor and oppressed of Europe, a refuge for "ingenious spirits of low estate." But he offered them something more than escape, for he also promised liberty, representative government by secret ballot, taxation only by their own consent, the right to make their own laws, and, above all, religious freedom.[30] Furly was an influential

[27] G. Butel Dumont, *Histoire et commerce des colonies angloises dans l'Amérique Septentrionale* (Paris, 1755), p. v; see also J. I. Delaville, *Etat présent de la Pensilvanie* (1756), p. 3.

[28] B. H. Swigart, *The Americas as Revealed in the Encyclopédie,* unpublished doctoral dissertation, Univ. of Illinois, 1939.

[29] See J. F. Sachse, "Benjamin Furly," *Penna. Mag. of Hist. and Biog.,* XIX (1895), 277-306.

[30] *Recueil de diverses pièces concernant la Pensylvanie* (The Hague, 1684).

figure and a friend of such men as Leibnitz and Jean Le Clerc. That he had an influence on representatives of the critical, skeptical, and rationalistic thought of the first decades of the century is indicated by Le Clerc's eulogy of Pennsylvania in 1712. He wrote of its fertile lands, its rapid growth, its religious freedom, and its virtuous and industrious inhabitants. Of New Jersey, then Quaker territory, he told an amusing incident. "A man one day asked one of the proprietors of New Jersey if there were any lawyers there. The other replied no. Then he asked him if there were any doctors. The other answered no. Finally he asked whether there were any theologians, and the other said no again. 'Happy land!' exclaimed the man. It deserves to be called 'paradise.' "[31]

Furly's pamphlets were addressed principally to the French Huguenots who had been forced to flee France by Louis XIV's revocation of the Edict of Nantes, and in them he offered lots at half price "to the poor French Protestants." Apparently he failed to attract many to Pennsylvania, though a considerable number did eventually emigrate to the other provinces, mostly to New England, New York, Virginia, and South Carolina.[32] It would be false, however, to attribute this migration to the identification by the Huguenots of America with religious freedom. The British colonies were to them simply another Protestant land in which they could expect to be welcome, as they had been in England, Germany, and the Netherlands, and the reports sent back by their advance agents and explorers dwelt mainly on the fertility of the land and the hospitable welcome to be expected.[33] Economic opportunity was probably the main attraction. Beverley's widely read *History of Virginia*, of which there were four French editions in 1712, likewise stressed such material inducements as cheap land, good climate, abundant game, and a hospitable reception.

31 *Bibliothèque choisie*, 1712, XXV, 130-131.
32 See G. Chinard, *Les Réfugiés huguenots en Amérique* (Paris, 1925).
33 Durand de Dauphiné, *Voyages d'un François exilé pour la religion* (The Hague, 1687); *Nouvelle relation de la Caroline* (The Hague, c. 1685); *Plan pour former un établissement en Caroline* (The Hague, 1686).

John Locke's *Fundamental Constitutions of Carolina*, drafted for the Earl of Shaftesbury in 1669, were more important ideologically and were second only to the legislation of Penn in identifying in the French mind the British colonies with enlightened government. The *Constitutions* were repeatedly cited by Voltaire as a successful application of the principle of religious toleration; but even before Voltaire ever mentioned the Carolinas a group of 370 French-Swiss, attracted by promises of religious freedom and representative government as well as of economic opportunity, had founded in 1731 a small colony in South Carolina.[34]

Voltaire's *Lettres philosophiques* (1734), which marked the real beginning of the legend of the "Good Quaker" in French literature of the century, was the first widely read work to identify Pennsylvania with religious toleration.[35] In the first four letters, "Sur les Quakers," Voltaire, though he did not spare the Quaker eccentricities, expressed great admiration for the sect's Early Christian simplicity and its preference of morality over theology, which corresponded so well to his own deism. The fourth letter, on Penn and Pennsylvania, described Philadelphia as a city so prosperous that it even attracted citizens from the other colonies. The laws framed by Penn were, he said, so wise that none had ever been changed, and the just treatment of the Indians had made of these "so-called savages" devoted and grateful friends. Most of all, he stressed the spirit of equality, the religious freedom, the peace, and the absence of priests which blessed that happy land. "William Penn could boast," he wrote, "of having brought to the world that golden age of which men talk so much and which probably has never existed anywhere except in Pennsylvania." All this was of course merely a literary device to express effectively his own pacificism, deism, and anti-clericalism.

Montesquieu shared Voltaire's admiration for Penn as a

[34] Jean Pierre Purry, *Mémoire présenté à Sa. Gr. Mylord Duc de Newcastle . . . sur l'état présent de la Caroline* (London, 1724) and *Description abrégée de l'état présent de la Caroline Méridionale* (Neufchâtel, 1732).
[35] See E. Philips, *The Good Quaker in French Legend* (Philadelphia, 1932).

legislator and called him "a veritable Lycurgus."[36] The
*Encyclopédie* further contributed to this picture by including three articles on Pennsylvania, Philadelphia, and the
Quakers, all by De Jaucourt, which were drawn almost entirely from Voltaire and Montesquieu. Thus, in the first half
of the century Pennsylvania became established in the minds
of French liberals as a land where *bienfaisance*, the spirit of
benevolence and humanitarianism, reigned as an operative
political principle.[37]

During his years at Cirey with Mme du Châtelet, Voltaire
seems to have lost interest in the Quakers, but with the beginning of the second period of his life at Les Délices and
Ferney (1755) and his vigorous championship of toleration
and justice, he again took up the useful example of Pennsylvania. In the *Essai sur les moeurs* he once more eulogized
that "land unique in the world" for its just treatment of the
Indians, its simple equalitarian society, its perfect religious
freedom, its pacifism, and its freedom from lawyers and
doctors.[38] From this time until his death his writings contained increasingly frequent references to Pennsylvania as
an example of the successful practice of toleration and civil
liberty. As the years went by, the American Quaker became
to Voltaire less a historic phenomenon worthy of investigation and more and more a sort of idealized symbol of what
he was himself preaching for France. Pennsylvania was in
his hands a lever by which he could prove that dogma and
ritual had nothing to do with happiness and virtue, and
that liberty and toleration produced, not anarchy, but peace
and prosperity.[39] He even confessed that if the sea did not
make him suffer "an unbearable discomfort" it would be to
Pennsylvania that he would go to end his days, for in that
fertile, prosperous land, blessed by a favorable climate,
eternal peace reigned and crimes were almost unknown. "A
man can, for a dozen guineas, acquire a hundred acres of

36 *Esprit des lois*, Bk. IV, Ch. 6.
37 E.g., Lévesque de Pouilly, *Théorie des sentiments agréables* (Paris, 1747).
38 *Oeuvres* (Molland ed.), XII, 417 ff.
39 E.g., *Traité sur la tolérance* and *Dictionnaire philosophique, ibid.*, XXV,
36; XVIII, 498-501; XIX, 27; XX, 311-313; XX, 523.

very good land; and on these hundred acres he is in truth king, for he is free and he is a citizen. He cannot harm any one, and no one can harm him; he thinks what he pleases and he says what he pleases without being persecuted."[40]

French interest in the British colonies in these years was to a large extent a by-product of the Anglomania of the century, exemplified by such works as the *Lettres philosophiques* and the *Esprit des lois* and created by the influence of Newton, Locke, Hume, the English Deists, and the English constitution. The French were at first aware of the colonies only as a part of the British dominions, and only later and gradually as a nation with a distinct destiny.

The outbreak of the Seven Years War, many of whose battles were to be fought in the New World, excited considerable curiosity about the British colonies. Three books were published to profit by this interest: Palairet's *Description abrégée des possessions anglaises et françaises* (1755), Butel Dumont's *Histoire et commerce des colonies anglaises* (1755) and Delaville's *Etat présent de la Pensilvanie* (1756), the last a translation of William Smith's *A Brief View of the Conduct of Pennsylvania*. All emphasized the phenomenal growth and prosperity of the colonies. During the course of the war the public naturally had the opportunity to learn more of the new region across the seas and its inhabitants through the newspapers and the pamphlets published on the occasion of French victories in America.[41] It was at this time that the name of Washington was first heard in France, as the alleged murderer of De Jumonville, a young French officer killed under a flag of truce.

After the Treaty of Paris in 1763, there were various indications of an increasing though still modest interest in the British colonies. On April 30, 1764, for instance, was performed Chamfort's successful drama *La Jeune Indienne*, the first appearance of the American Quaker on the French stage.

[40] *Ibid.,* xx, 312.
[41] E.g., *Relation de la prise des forts de Choueguen ou Oswego* (1756); *Relation de la prise du Fort Georges* (Paris, 1757); *Relation de la victoire remportée sur un corps de troupes commandé par le général Braddock* [1755].

Chamfort, who was later to be a friend of Franklin and to call the United States "the place in the universe where the rights of man are best understood,"[42] offered his audience a curious mixture of primitivism, bourgeois morality, and a popularization of Voltaire's symbol of the "Good Quaker."

It was also apparently in the 1760's that citizens of the French and American cultures first came into direct contact and communication. Dr. William Shippen of Philadelphia was in Paris in 1762 and paid a visit to Jardin du Roi to see Buffon, who was in correspondence with the American botanist John Bartram.[43] American artists too were becoming known. Benjamin West, who had studied in Rome from 1760 to 1763, was in London as one of the leading lights of the British neo-classical school of historical painting. Though none of his paintings left England and few French artists ventured to cross the Channel, West was known through engravings and was much admired. Reproductions of his "Death of Wolfe" were selling in Paris for 25 to 30 louis, and Renou copied his "Agrippina with the Ashes of Germanicus" and Lépicié his "Regulus Leaving Rome." Moreover West was identified by admiring French critics as an American, not an Englishman, and opponents of De Pauw were to point to him and Copley as proof that America could produce talented artists.[44] The works of American writers were also now appearing for the first time in France, and 1767, the year of Franklin's first visit, saw translations of William Smith Jr.'s *History of the Province of New York*, a work of considerable merit, and of Anthony Benezet's *A Caution and Warning to Great Britain and Her Colonies*, an anti-slavery pamphlet important as the first link between French and American abolitionists. In this same year appeared the translation of Edmund Burke's *An Account of the European Settlements*

[42] *Oeuvres* (Paris, 1824), I, 443.

[43] W. F. Falls, "Buffon, Franklin et deux académies américaines," *Romanic Review*, XXIX (1938), 37-47.

[44] See J. Locquin, *La Peinture d'histoire en France de 1747 à 1785* (Paris, 1912), pp. 152-157, and "La Part de l'influence anglaise dans l'orientation néo-classique de la peinture française entre 1750 et 1780," *Actes du Congrès d'Histoire de l'Art* (Paris, 1924), II, 391-399.

*in America,* which was to do much to supply the French lack of factual information.

The government of Louis XV in these years was beginning to take an increasing interest in the British colonies. As soon as the ink was dry on the Treaty of Paris, Choiseul, the prime minister, started scheming to restore France's power. Besides reforming the army, rebuilding the navy, and reorganizing the colonial system, he developed a widespread system of intelligence, sending agents to Africa, the Indies, the Baltic, and to America to feel out England's weaknesses in preparation for a renewal of the struggle. Naturally the news of the troubles in England's American colonies aroused his special interest and he sent at least three spies successively to report on the political and economic situation: De Pontleroy in 1764,[45] a second, whose name is unknown, in 1765,[46] and in 1767 the Baron De Kalb, who later was to serve as a volunteer in the American Revolution and die in the Battle of Camden. All three reported in amazement the prosperous, energetic nation they discovered. The climate was healthful, the land fertile, natural resources were abundant, the shipyards were launching 150 ships a year, the fishing fleet was large, and a surprising active and growing foreign trade filled the harbors with ships. The people were healthy and vigorous and were reproducing at such a rate that the population was doubling every twenty years. On all sides they saw "children swarming like broods of ducks in a pond." "Whatever may be done in London," De Kalb wrote to Choiseul, "this country is growing too powerful to be much longer governed at so great a distance."[47] It was, incidentally, a curious fact that long before independence became a political issue in America French observers like the Marquis d'Argenson and Montesquieu had been predicting the separation of the British colonies in North America from the mother country.[48]

[45] G. Bancroft, *History of the United States* (Boston, 1852-1874), VI, 25-26.

[46] "Journal of a French Traveler in the Colonies, 1765," *Amer. Hist. Review,* XXVI (1921), 726-747; XXVII (1921), 70-89.

[47] F. Kapp, *The Life of John Kalb* (New York, 1870), p. 63.

[48] *Journal et mémoires du Marquis d'Argenson,* ed. E. J. B. Rathery (Paris, 1859), I, lv-lvi; Montesquieu, "Notes sur l'Angleterre," *Oeuvres complètes,* ed. Laboulaye (Paris, 1875), VII, 194.

So it was not surprising that in 1767 the government was eager for Franklin, then serving as the colonies' representative in London, to visit Paris. Durand, of the French legation in London, pushed the idea and offered, as Franklin remarked, "letters of recommendation to the Lord knows who."

Everything favored the generation in France of sympathetic interest in the colonies. Pennsylvania and the Carolinas were by now firmly associated in the minds of the *Philosophes* and their disciples with religious toleration and enlightened legislation. To a nation worried lest its population might be decreasing and troubled by serious economic problems, a region with so rapidly expanding an economy could certainly have lessons to teach. Finally, if these colonies should rebel and break from England, as seemed a real possibility, France would be well revenged for the Seven Years War, her latest humiliating defeat, and would reap political, military, and possibly economic profits. All that was needed was a catalyst to start the fermentation of Americanism in Paris; that catalyst was provided by Benjamin Franklin.

Franklin was of course already a familiar name to French scientists. In 1751 Buffon had been so impressed by his *Experiments and Observations on Electricity* that he suggested a French translation, published the next year.[49] Then De Lor, Dalibard, and Buffon on May 10, 1752 successfully performed for the first time the experiment Franklin had suggested of drawing electricity from the clouds by means of an iron rod. To a century intrigued by its discovery of the experimental method and bemused by man's hitherto unsuspected power to decipher the secrets of the universe, this astounding achievement of chaining the thunderbolt was extremely exciting. Dalibard wrote a report to the Academy of Sciences, and the king after witnessing the experiment had his compliments transmitted to Franklin through the Royal Society in London. The theories and discoveries of Franklin were discussed at length by the Abbé Nollet in his *Lettres sur l'électricité* (1753-1760) and by the scientific contributors

[49] J. A. Nollet, *Lettres sur l'électricité* (Paris, 1753, 1760), I, 4-5; Franklin, *Expériences et observations sur l'électricité* (Paris, 1752).

to the first volumes of the *Encyclopédie*, which were just appearing. Franklin became overnight a peer among the major scientists of Europe. Dalibard wrote him in March 1754, "All our philosophical friends, Messrs. Buffon, Fonferrière, Marty, &c., charge me to make you their best compliments, and M. Dubourg also. We are all waiting with the greatest eagerness to hear from you. I beg that you will let me have letters as soon and often as possible. Your name is venerated in this country as it deserves to be."[50] When Diderot sought that same year for the best example of an experimental scientist, he could think of no name more fitting than Franklin's.[51] This was the highest compliment a *Philosophe* could pay.

So Franklin would have arrived in France already famous even if he had not been the official spokesman for the colonies. But he had now acquired a new stature. His dramatic defense of the rights of the colonies before the bar of Parliament in February 1766, in which he had defiantly declared that there was no power on earth which could force a man to change his opinion, had both dramatized the crisis and had raised him in the eyes of all Europe to the position of the champion of the cause of the gallant Americans.

There was undoubtedly a political aspect to the trip. Durand's eager encouragement and the king's gracious reception of Franklin at Versailles were obvious indications of Choiseul's wishes "to blow up the coals between Britain and her Colonies" (Franklin's own words). But Franklin was perhaps the wiliest diplomat of the age. Instead of allowing French flattery to aggravate the situation, he made use of the opportunity to establish in Paris a nucleus of friends and supporters from which was to expand the powerful wave of Americanism of which he would later make so effective political use.

Dalibard and his attractive wife entertained Franklin during this first visit and introduced him to many *Frank-*

[50] *Works of Franklin* (ed. Sparks), VI, 194.
[51] "Pensées sur l'interprétation de la nature," *Oeuvres*, ed. Assézat and Tourneux (Paris, 1875-1877), II, 39.

*linistes* among the physical scientists, including Joseph-Etienne Berthier, Jean-Baptiste Le Roy, and the Abbé Chappe. "All the *savants* are rushing to see him and confer with him," one observer wrote.[52] Of the *Economistes*, a politically powerful group advocating free trade and the encouragement of agriculture, he met François Quesnay, the founder of the school; the elder Mirabeau; Barbeu Dubourg, his future disciple and translator; and he just missed seeing Du Pont de Nemours, who was so disappointed that he wrote a note to Franklin after his departure expressing his regret. The second visit in the summer of 1769 served to strengthen and widen these friendships.

Franklin had, it seems clear, a definite purpose—the creation in France of a climate of sympathetic interest for the political and philosophical advantage of his own country. The methods he used were both simple and effective. He worked by establishing between the intellectual leaders of France and of his own country the maximum of mutual interests and common purposes. The *Philosophes*, who were relatively free to theorize but who had few opportunities to put their proposed reforms to practical tests, were eager to find justification and proofs in the experience of other nations. China had hitherto been their favorite example, but it was rather a remote one. Franklin saw that if he could identify the cause of America with the ideas of the French *Philosophes*, with their plans for the new Heavenly City of Men which was to replace the moribund City of God, then he would have won the support of the intellectual leaders of Europe. This he clearly intended and successfully achieved.

Franklin's key move was to subscribe to the economic doctrines of the *Economistes*, who were at their point of greatest influence. They proudly announced that he had "adopted the principles and doctrines of our French Economists,"[53] and he publicly proclaimed his adherence not only in informal conversations but also in a number of contributions to their

[52] Bachaumont, *Mémoires secrets* (London, 1777-1788), III, 266 (Sept. 19, 1767).
[53] *Ephémérides du citoyen*, 1769, IX, 68.

official journal, the *Ephémérides du citoyen*, edited by Du Pont de Nemours.[54] Among these was his important "Positions to Be Examined." Moreover he carefully explained to his French friends both that the conditions in the colonies were a striking confirmation of the truth of their doctrines and also that the American opposition to English commercial restrictions and tax policy was based upon their own economic principles. The foundation of Physiocracy, as their system was to be named, was that the soil is the only true source of national wealth and that the key to prosperity is the encouragement of agricultural production. Obviously the colonies, whose economy was almost entirely agricultural, whose prosperity was one of the wonders of the age, and whose population, Franklin announced, was doubling every twenty years, proved this point.[55] The *Economistes* taught that trade in grain must be unrestricted, and so it was, Franklin assured them, in the colonies.[56] They believed that the maximum population should be on the farms and the minimum in the cities, and Franklin told them that the colonies were a land where cities were almost unknown.[57] The protests against the Navigation Acts were in accord with the principles of free trade. The slogan "No taxation without representation" agreed with the Physiocratic principle that taxes, derived from the soil, must be returned to the land which produced them. England's position was fundamentally wrong, for the belief that colonies and colonial trade enriched a nation was a fallacy.

Franklin did not ignore the political issues involved. For this purpose he chose the work of America's most convincing advocate, John Dickinson. He had already published

[54] "On the Price of Corn and Management of the Poor," 1767; "Positions to Be Examined," 1769; "Mythology of the Iroquois," 1769; a prospectus for Dalrymple's expedition to New Zealand, 1772. See A. O. Aldridge, "The Debut of American Letters in France," *French American Review*, III (1950), 1-23.

[55] D. Blackford, *Précis de l'état actuel des colonies angloises* (Milan, 1771), p. 44; John Dickinson, *Lettres d'un fermier de Pensylvanie* (Amsterdam [Paris], 1769), p. iv; *Ephémérides*, 1776, III, 60.

[56] *Ephémérides*, 1768, I, 137.

[57] *Journal de l'agriculture, du commerce, des arts et des finances*, 1771, II, 42-43.

Dickinson's *Letters from an American Farmer in Pennsylvania* in London, and now he asked one of his new *Economiste* friends, Barbeu Dubourg, to translate it into French. Dubourg undertook the task with enthusiasm, and the book was a great success.[58] In February 1769 young Dr. Benjamin Rush, who had just completed his medical studies at Edinburgh, set off for a Paris vacation with his pockets stuffed with letters of introduction from Franklin. One of the first persons on whom he called was Dubourg, whom he found at his desk working on the translation. When Rush mentioned that he knew the author of the *Letters* personally, Dubourg "broke out into many fine encomiums upon them and said 'that in his opinion the Roman orator Cicero was less eloquent than the Pennsylvania Farmer.'" Then Dubourg took Rush to be introduced to Mirabeau's coterie. The marquis shook him warmly by the hand and welcomed him as a friend of Franklin. The conversation turned on "economics, liberty and government," and Rush was eagerly questioned about Dickinson, whose letters were "praised with enthusiasm" by the company. Rush met Le Roy, Augustin Roux, Antoine Baumé, Pierre-Joseph Macquer, Jean-Joseph Sue, the Abbé Nollet, Bernard de Jussieu, and Diderot, and returned to England and America another convert to the theories of the *Economistes*.[59]

No doubt Franklin had his reasons for seeing that the brilliant young doctor from Philadelphia met important people in Paris. One of the prime articles of faith of this Age of Reason was the progress of the human mind, *le progrès de l'esprit humain*. Franklin wished to assure Europe that the Enlightenment was shining just as brightly on the far side of the Atlantic as on the banks of the Seine and the Thames. He sought not only to ensure the prestige of his own nation but also to obtain for his countrymen seats in the cosmopolitan symposium of philosophers.

[58] *Op.cit.* On the relations of Barbeu Dubourg and Franklin, see A. O. Aldridge, "Jacques Barbeu-Dubourg, a French Disciple of Benjamin Franklin," *Proc. Amer. Philos. Soc.*, xcv (1951), 331-392.
[59] Benjamin Rush, *Autobiography* (Princeton, 1948), pp. 66-69, and "Journal" in *Selected Writings* (New York, 1947), pp. 391-394.

Franklin's own genius was of course the most potent argument. Publications of his works in France multiplied: two editions of his *Experiments* in 1752 and 1756, five separate publications of his testimony before Parliament, a translation of his *Observations on the Increase of Mankind* included with Dickinson's Letters, his contributions to the *Ephémérides*, and finally in 1773 a handsome two-volume quarto edition of his works translated by Dubourg, selections from which were reprinted in the *Journal de lecture* in 1775.[60] In 1772 he was elected as one of the éight foreign associates to the Royal Academy of Sciences, and the verses beneath the handsome portrait which served as frontispiece to the *Oeuvres* expressed the universal admiration:

> Il a ravi le feu des Cieux,
> Il a fait fleurir les Arts en des Climats sauvages,
> L'Amérique le place à la tête des Sages,
> La Grèce l'aurait mis au nombre de ses Dieux.[61]

The third line referred, no doubt, to his presidency of the American Philosophical Society, a position which Franklin exploited skillfully for his purposes. The first volume of the Society's *Transactions*, published in 1771, was a fine proof that America contained more sages than himself, Dickinson, and Rush. He sent copies to academies, universities, and influential figures throughout Europe, and he was rewarded by the most flattering reception. The *Journal des savants* said that the *Transactions* was worthy to take its place among the memoirs of the leading academies of Europe,[62] and the *Journal de l'agriculture* declared that the society had clearly proved that the colonies were extending and continuing the rationalism and enlightenment of the century—which was just the reaction Franklin desired.[63]

The European success of the first volume of the *Transac-*

[60] II (1775), 106-113.
[61] "He stole the fire of the Heavens and caused the arts to flower in savage climes. America has placed him at the head of her sages. Greece would have set him among her gods."
[62] 1773, février, pp. 87-89.
[63] 1773, I, février, pp. 156-165.

*tions* came less from the brilliance of the various contributions than from the spirit in which they were written. There
was a happy consonance between the frontier-engendered
practicality of the American mind and the French philosophic
faith in the social utility of knowledge. The preface to the
*Transactions* postulated that "knowledge is of little use when
confined to mere speculation," and dedicated the society to
the application of "speculative truths" to the "common purposes of life," to the improvement of agriculture and trade
and the increase and happiness of mankind. It was this utilitarianism which drew the most applause in France. The
*Journal encyclopédique,* in its review of the *Transactions,*
declared that the only societies truly deserving the title
"philosophic" were "those which, neglecting all discussions
which are more abstruse than useful and of which the solution can scarcely interest a very small number of persons,
devote their learned investigations to the various problems
vital to the general welfare."[64]

It was not enough, however, merely to display the genius
of America. It was necessary to affirm the partnership of European and American scientists, philosophers, and reformers.
To this end Franklin proposed the election of a great many
foreign members, especially Frenchmen, to the society. Buffon was the first in 1768; he was followed by Le Roy in 1773
and by the Abbé Rozier, Raynal, Condorcet, Lavoisier,
Daubenton, Dubourg, Pierre-Joseph Roux, and Augustin
Roux in 1774. During the American Revolution Franklin
added many more names. These men were flattered by the
honor, and, as Franklin had hoped, they entered into correspondence with their American colleagues. In 1773 the Abbé
Rozier wrote the society requesting "an abstract of the most
essential articles of their proceedings" for inclusion in his
*Observations sur la physique,* which was designed to be a
sort of clearing house for international science. The next
year Franklin forwarded from Buffon four handsomely bound
volumes of the *Histoire naturelle,* and a request for "some

[64] 1773, janvier, pp. 240-251.

natural productions of Pennsylvania for the King's Cabinet,"
together with a memoir of Daubenton's on the preservation
of birds. The same year came requests from Raynal and Condorcet for information on the colonies (for which the society
appointed committees to draft suitable replies) and also a
letter from Lavoisier expressing his pleasure in corresponding "with a famous society which has carried the torch of
truth into a new world and which has contributed more than
any other to extend the empire of philosophy."[65]

Franklin was at his best, however, not in these public
tradings of honors and compliments but in private conversations, when he could pour his message into his listener's
attentive ear. He was a veritable Johnny Appleseed, plant-
ing seeds of the American Dream back and forth across the
fields of Europe. In almost every page written on the British
colonies during these years can be heard echoes of Franklin's
conversations and letters. He described to everyone he met
Philadelphia's excellent college, libraries, schools, and newspapers, so that America sounded to the French like a nation
where every citizen was a philosopher.[66] "The famous Franklin has told us," one of his friends wrote, "that there is no
working man in Pennsylvania who does not read the newspapers at lunch time and a few good works of philosophy or
politics for an hour after dinner."[67]

This picture of the philosophic American was in direct
contradiction to De Pauw's gloomy picture of the degenerate
American. Franklin quickly recognized that the theory of
American degeneration had to be refuted. On his trip to
Germany in 1766 he had learned of the damage done by
Kalm's *Travels* and he had attempted to correct some of the
false notions the Swedish botanist had propagated.[68] Now

[65] G. Chinard, "The American Philosophical Society and the World of
Science," *Proc. Amer. Philos. Soc.*, LXXXVII (1943), 7. See also "Old Minutes
of the Society, from 1743 to 1838," *ibid.*, XXII (1885), Pt. 3, No. 119; W. F.
Falls, *op.cit.*; J. G. Rosengarten, "The Early French Members of the American
Philosophical Society," *Proc. Amer. Philos. Soc.*, XLVI (1907), 87-93.

[66] E.g., D. Blackford, *op.cit.*, pp. 35-36; William Smith, *Relation historique
de l'expédition contre les Indiens*, tr. C. G. F. Dumas (Amsterdam, 1769), pp.
viii-ix; Franklin, *Oeuvres*, tr. B. Dubourg (Paris, 1773), I, i.

[67] *Ephémérides du citoyen*, 1771, XI, 74-75.        [68] Blackford, *op.cit.*, p. 4.

he turned his attention to the harm done by Buffon and De Pauw. He gave Pernetty material for his polemic with De Pauw,[69] and in June 1772 wrote one of his friends in Paris a letter (now lost) in which he claimed that the Indians were not inferior to Europeans in strength or courage or intelligence, but that it had been the lack of iron and other natural resources which had prevented them from rising to the same degree of civilization.[70]

The *Economistes* gladly carried the burden of the polemic, and the bitterness of their attack revealed how essential the American had become to their doctrine. The *Ephémérides* berated Buffon for his "very specious arguments" and pointed out that "the inhabitants of the English colonies of North America, who form one great people, are both physically and morally perhaps the healthiest of all the peoples in the world." The examples of Franklin and Dickinson were ample proof that "a good government has a far greater influence on the nature of man than does climate."[71] The strongest critic of De Pauw was the Abbé Roubaud, the editor of the *Journal de l'agriculture*, since 1771 a Physiocratic paper, who published in 1773 a violent article lambasting De Pauw for filching his ideas from Buffon, for falsifying his evidence, and for sheer ignorance.[72] Two years later in his *Histoire générale* he wrote a long and more temperate refutation, using as his clinching arguments the examples of Franklin, Dickinson, and the *Transactions*, and predicting that the colonies were destined to be "the capital of humanity."[73]

All this was most persuasive, and the *Economistes* were carried away in their enthusiasm for the wisdom of the newly discovered Americans. "We have been accused," wrote the editors of the *Ephémérides*, in their review of Dickinson's *Letters*, "of being prejudiced in favor of these Americans.

[69] D. Pernetty, *Examen des Recherches philosophiques sur l'Amérique* (Berlin, 1771), II, 584.

[70] P. J. Roubaud, *Histoire générale de l'Asie, de l'Afrique et de l'Amérique* (Paris, 1770-1775), V, 90.

[71] 1769, X, 46-48.

[72] 1773, I, février, pp. 15-30. See also *ibid.*, pp. 156-157.

[73] V, 72.

As justification we shall recall the noble and wise testimony which Franklin gave before the English Parliament, and we shall offer these Letters to be read. We dare to believe that those who have considered these two works will share, not our prejudice, but our esteem and our veneration for men whose wisdom is so vigorous and whose courage is both so firm and so temperate. The character of this flourishing nation, of this beautiful land peopled by three million happy men, can give us some idea of the dignity of which the human race is capable."[74]

Others than the *Economistes* were impressed. Raynal, in spite of what he had said of the degeneration of man in America, acknowledged that the best hope for a rebirth of learning lay in the British colonies. Boston was fully the equal of London in its polished society and commodious living, and Philadelphia, thanks to Franklin, was famous for its library and college. "A new Olympus, a new Arcady, a new Athens, a new Greece will perhaps give birth on the continent, or on the neighboring islands, to new Homers, new Theocrituses, and especially new Anacreons. Perhaps there will arise another Newton in New England. It is in British America, let there be no doubt on this, that the first rays of knowledge are to shine, if they are at last to dawn under this long obscured sky."[75] Even De Pauw acknowledged grudgingly that learning would begin to appear sooner in North America than in the southern regions.[76]

At the same time that this Physiocratic image of the American rural philosopher was developing, there also began to take shape the legend of the American as the rural man of virtue and simplicity. The origins of this idea are less clear. It probably was to some extent suggested by Voltaire's "Good Quaker." The century, however, was intensely preoccupied with ethical problems, and it was impossible for the eighteenth-century mind not to see moral implications in the character of the American.

[74] 1769, X, 44-45.       [75] *Op.cit.*, VI, 377.
[76] *Défense*, pp. 8-9.

A certain ideological alliance existed between the *Economistes* and the disciples of Rousseau. Both groups advocated a return to the soil, to the simple life of the peasant and the paternalistic landowner, though one did so on economic grounds and the other on moral. Moreover, both agreed that the rural life favored the cultivation of the human mind. Rousseau had made this point in his *Lettre à d'Alembert*, and Dubourg made sure to point out, in his preface to Dickinson's *Letters*, that the eloquence of "this good farmer" proved that in America "the cultivation of the soil has not harmed the cultivation of the mind."[77] A further parallelism existed in the common opposition to De Pauw and the defense of primitivism. The Abbé Roubaud, in his attack on De Pauw, defended not only the American colonists but also the American Indians, denying their degeneration and repeating the primitivistic argument that in his simple and virtuous society the savage was morally superior to the cultured European corrupted by civilization.[78]

So it was not surprising that the Rousseauists were led to endow the *Economistes'* wise and equalitarian American farmer with all the virtues that Rousseau had extolled in the *Nouvelle Héloïse*.

The best example was Gaspard de Beaurieu's *Elève de la nature*, a sort of ultra-*Emile* avowedly inspired by Rousseau, in which the child was preserved from all corrupting contact with civilization by being raised in a box to be deposited eventually on a carefully prepared "Isle of Peace," where he was allowed to discover his Julie and found a Rousseauist Utopia. In the 1771 edition of this work (first published in 1763), Beaurieu added a "Dedication to the Inhabitants of Virginia": "In that land which you inhabit and which you cultivate, there are to be found neither cities nor luxury nor crimes nor infirmities. Every day of your lives is serene, for the purity of your souls is communicated to the skies above you. You are free, you labor, and bring forth all about you, besides your abundant crops, a harvest of all the virtues. You

---

[77] *Lettres d'un fermier de Pensylvanie*, pp. xiv-xv.
[78] *Histoire générale*, v, 56-57.

are as Nature would wish us all to be. I therefore dedicate to you this portrait of a man whom I have conceived as formed by nature alone."[79]

This new dedication was explained by an episode which the author had added to the end of the second volume. Ariste, Beaurieu's child of nature, providentially receives from a passing ship a bundle of the latest numbers of the *Ephémérides*, in which he comes upon two letters which are promptly copied into the account of his life, because, as he says, "We lead here a life as innocent and as imperturbably happy as that of the inhabitants of Virginia."[80] These letters actually had appeared in the *Ephémérides*, probably contributed by Beaurieu himself. The first, addressed to Du Pont de Nemours, announced that the Physiocratic dream of a purely rural society did in fact exist in America, in a province named New York, in which dwelt a race of wise but simple countrymen. "In no country in the world can one find women more beautiful, even at an advanced age, men handsomer or stronger, minds more lofty, characters more gentle, or hearts more intrepid."[81] The second letter advised the editors that Franklin, during his recent visit in 1769, had informed the writer that the picture was not wholly accurate for New York, but that Virginia better fitted the description of a colony without cities. So Arcadia was transferred south to Virginia, where existed, Beaurieu then added, the additional blessings of economic freedom, fraternity, and equality.[82]

Raynal did far more than Beaurieu to propagate the Arcadian myth of America. In his first 1770 edition of his *Histoire philosophique*, in spite of all he had said of the degeneration of the American mind, he described Americans as frugal farmers leading lives of simple virtue. "The inhabitants of the Colonies," he wrote, "lead that rustic life for which the human race was originally intended and which most favors health and fecundity. There man enjoys all the

[79] *L'Elève de la nature* (Amsterdam, 1771), III, i-ii.
[80] *Ibid.*, II, 239.
[81] *Ephémérides du citoyen*, 1769, II, 76. Aldridge, *op.cit.*, attributes these letters to Barbeu Dubourg.
[82] *Ibid.*, 1769, VIII, 39-52.

felicity which is compatible with the frailty of humankind."[83]
Dubourg called Philadelphia the city of "three fair sisters,
wealth, knowledge and virtue."[84] He might well have applied
the image to all the colonies, for it exactly expressed the myth
which the *Economistes* and Rousseauists had created.

Only a few years later the word "America" was to be
synonymous in Paris with "Liberty," yet this political idea
remained curiously subordinate in the first stage of the
American myth. This is a confirmation of De Tocqueville's
remark that the idea of liberty did not become politically
potent in France until about 1770. One obvious reason was
that the *Economistes* advocated a state of aristocratic landowners under a paternalistic and benevolent but centralized
and absolute monarchy. When they spoke of liberty they
meant economic liberty.

Nevertheless, particularly after 1770, there were increasing signs that America was coming to be associated with the
civil and political liberty of the individual citizen. There
was of course the long-standing tradition, created by Penn,
Voltaire, Montesquieu, and Locke, which identified the
colonies with religious liberty and representative government. Frequently writers attributed American prosperity to
the practice of religious toleration.[85] Moreover the *Economistes*, in spite of their absolutist politics, favored a number
of liberal and humanitarian reforms, particularly religious
liberty, freedom of the press, public education, and the abolition of slavery. For their argument for emancipation they
found support in Franklin and especially in Rush, who in
August 1769, after his return to Philadelphia, wrote to Dubourg of the Quakers' decision to free their slaves. The letter
was proudly printed in the *Ephémérides* as an indication of
a general abolitionist movement in the colonies.[86]

An interesting example of the growing realization that the

[83] *Op.cit.*, VI, 390.
[84] Franklin, *Oeuvres* (Paris, 1773), I, i.
[85] Blackford, *op.cit.*, p. 4.
[86] 1769, IX, 172. See also Rush's letter to Dubourg on the anti-slavery movement in Pennsylvania, April 29, 1773, in *Letters of Benjamin Rush*, ed. L. H.
Butterfield (Princeton, 1951), I, 176-177.

colonies might offer political as well as economic and moral lessons is the "Lettres d'Abraham Mansword," which appeared in the *Ephémérides* in 1771, presented as a translation from the Philadelphia *Chronicle* but undoubtedly the work of a French pen, probably Dubourg's. These letters were nothing less than a proposal for a liberal representative constitution for an independent government of the colonies, and were a surprising anticipation of the interest of a few years later in American constitutionalism.[87]

The climate of opinion was changing fast in these years, and the America which was to inspire the men of 1789 was beginning to emerge from the Physiocratic America. "Who could not experience a thrill of pleasure," Chastellux wrote in 1772 in *De la félicité*, "in thinking that an area of more than a hundred thousand square leagues is now being peopled under the auspices of liberty and reason, by men who make equality the principle of their conduct and agriculture the principle of their economy?"[88] It was some time before the revolutionary implications of Dickinson's *Letters* were to be fully appreciated, but there were a few who from the moment of their publication perceived their import. "I have been somewhat surprised," Diderot wrote, "to see the translation of these Letters appear here. I know no work more capable of instructing the people in their inalienable rights, and of inspiring in them a love of liberty. Because Dickinson was writing for Americans they did not conceive that his Letters were addressed to all men. . . . They allow us to read things like this, and they are amazed to find us ten years later different men. Do they not realize how easily noble souls must drink of these principles and become intoxicated by them?"[89]

Too much could easily be made of the importance of the British colonies in French thought in the early 1770's. Even though the Americans had attracted the interest of influential

[87] 1771, XI, 75-112 and XII, 6-45. See also A. O. Aldridge, *op. cit.*
[88] *De la félicité* (Amsterdam, 1772), II, 97.
[89] "Sur les Lettres d'un fermier de Pensylvanie," *Oeuvres complètes*, IV, 88-89.

thinkers like Raynal, Diderot, Voltaire, and the Physiocrats and had been freely used as examples in the major economic, political, and ethical discussions of the moment, nevertheless, quantitatively, they still occupied only a minor place in the literature of these years. Furthermore, there is no evidence, apart from the genuine legend of the "Good Quaker," that the Physiocratic and Rousseauistic idealization of the American was as yet a popular concept familiar to the general literate public.

On the other hand, the almost complete ignorance of the British colonies which had existed ten or twenty years before was gone forever. The Stamp Act crisis was a political event of international importance. As one French journalist wrote in 1769, "All Europe has its eyes fixed upon the quarrel which now divides England and her colonies."[90] France, the traditional enemy of Great Britain, could not fail to be sympathetic to the rebellious colonials. From the beginning of the troubles, the French papers had printed London dispatches describing the parliamentary debates on the American question and also a great many political documents of American origin, copied from English newspapers. Historians have probably paid too little attention to the possible influence on European political thought exerted by the quantities of American political writings published in continental newspapers after 1765. As one example, the *Journal de l'agriculture* published in 1768 a series of twenty-two items, consisting of the circular letters sent to the other provinces by the Massachusetts Assembly in 1768, the replies of the various other provincial legislatures, the correspondence between the Massachusetts Assembly and Governor Francis Bernard, and a number of other related documents.[91] As the situation grew more critical from 1773 to 1775, newspapers like the *Gazette de France*, the *Gazette de Leyde*, and the *Mercure de France* gave more and more space each month to American news, until each issue contained at least one such item and sometimes several. The news was printed as received, but

[90] *Journal de l'agriculture*, 1769, III, 151.     [91] 1768, IV, 123-183.

*36*

the American point of view was well expressed by translations of the various petitions and resolutions issued by the colonies. Certainly the cause of the Americans was presented fairly and sympathetically. The *Gazette de France* reported under a London dateline (April 4, 1774), "Those of our mariners who know North America well claim that a certain innate spirit of liberty is inseparable from the soil, the sky, the forests and the lakes of that vast and virgin land, and that this spirit of liberty marks it off from all the other parts of the universe."

The outburst of enthusiasm for America in France which was to follow the news of Lexington and Concord can be understood only if it is realized that the literate Frenchman had been well prepared for the American Revolution by reading not only the speeches of Burke and Chatham but also a multitude of American political documents ranging from the petitions of the Continental Congress to the resolutions of the town of Abington, Massachusetts. Moreover, however much Anglophobia prompted the sudden enthusiasm for American rebellion, also significant was the idealism of those *Philosophes,* who for nine years had been repeating that the Americans were the precursors of a new era of liberty, equality, fraternity, prosperity, and virtue.

All France was not to be carried away by the new Americanism. There was a powerful body of Europe-centered thought in France, forcibly championed by De Pauw, which faced the expanding universe and the unknown and dangerous forces of the non-European world with fear and distrust. It was in the year 1776, when the Americans proclaimed to the world their faith in the inalienable rights of man, that De Pauw summed up his theory of American degeneration in his long article on America for the supplement to the *Encyclopédie.* Moreover the American *Insurgents* and their magic word "Liberty" were frightening to the many who clung to the principles of French absolutism. So it was by no means a simple picture. The important fact, however, is that in the years from 1767 to 1775 the Americans had somehow come to symbolize the dream of a new order, in which men would escape from poverty, injustice, and corruption and dwell together in universal liberty, equality, and fraternity.

CHAPTER II

# LIBERTY, VIRTUE, PROSPERITY, AND ENLIGHTENMENT, 1776-1783

"THE shot heard round the world" sounded as sharp and clear in the Gardens of the Tuileries as if it had been fired on the Place Louis XV. The Age of Revolutions had begun, and the literary symbol of America fashioned by the Physiocrats and *Philosophes* was transformed almost overnight into a popular enthusiasm which fired all of France. The spark of ignition was the news that Washington had forced General Howe to evacuate Boston. The Count de Ségur was spending that summer of 1776 in Spa, and he witnessed the impact of the achievements of the *Insurgents* on international society gathered there: "Their courageous audacity electrified everyone and excited a general admiration, especially among the young, who always were in search of something new and eager for a war. In that little town of Spa, where there were so many tourists, accidental or voluntary deputies, as it were, from all the monarchies of Europe, I was particularly struck to see burst forth in everyone so keen and universal a sympathy for the revolt of a people against their king. The serious English card game whist was suddenly replaced in all the salons by a no less sober game which was christened 'Boston.' "[1]

Nor was the enthusiasm confined to the nobility and the fashionable. One observer wrote the following December, "We have fanatics here of every sort—even women who are mad about the *Insurgents*."[2] A story went around Paris of an attractive young lady who dreamed of nothing but Phila-

[1] Louis Philippe, Comte de Ségur, *Mémoires, souvenirs et anecdotes* (Paris, 1859), I, 51.
[2] F. Métra, *Correspondance secrète, politique et littéraire* (London, 1787-1788), III, 68 (Dec. 27, 1776).

delphia and the *Insurgents*, spending her days reading books about America and turning a deaf ear to the calls of love. The *petit maître* who was campaigning for her favors succeeded at length only by the stratagem of disguising himself as an American and introducing himself as a Quaker "burning with love for Liberty—and for Madame." That winter the writers of popular songs took up the theme, and Parisians were singing "Les Insurgents," of which the first stanza went

> Pour amuser notre loisir
> Sans blesser la décence,
> Il est naturel de choisir
> Ce que l'on aime en France:
> Il faut donc sur un nouveau ton,
> Comme notre musique,
> Ne Parler ici que du con-
> Tinent de l'Amérique.[3]

The fad, both in its frivolous and serious aspects, hit the provinces as hard as Paris. When two Boston ladies appeared in Bordeaux in the first weeks of May 1777, they were welcomed by local society, and when they strolled in the Allées de Tourny dressed in a curious mixture of Boston and French styles they were surrounded by all the fashionable ladies and beaux of the city, who showered courtesies upon them.[4] On December 13, 1777 thirteen citizens of Marseille, "in admiration for the heroism of the *Insurgents*," formed a coterie to hold thirteen banquets each year in honor of the thirteen United States, at which exactly thirteen toasts were to be drunk to the Americans and a specially composed song of thirteen verses was to be sung.[5]

Yet this enthusiasm was much more than just a fad. It permeated the army and sent Lafayette and the other adventurous volunteers to suffer with the Americans at Valley

---

[3] "To while away our hours without wounding the ears of decency it is natural that we should choose what we love best here in France. So to a new note shall we sing here of nothing but the continent of America." *Recueil Clairambault-Maurepas* (Paris, 1879-1884), IX (1777), 119-120.

[4] *Journal encyclopédique*, July 1, 1777.

[5] *Courier de l'Europe*, Feb. 10, 1778.

Forge. It was stronger than ever before among the *Philosophes*, who carried it into the circles of Free Masonry, the Academy of Sciences, the various salons, and the Court. It filled the newspapers and burst forth in verse, in plays, in novels, and in a flood of new books on America.

This new Americanism was different from that which had existed before the war. America was no longer a mere parable for philosophers; it had become a popular movement spreading down into the lower classes and out to those members of the bourgeoisie who were usually little interested in the polemics of the Physiocrats and *Philosophes*. Americanism now had a new emotional content which revealed that it had somehow caught the imagination of the people and had become identified with certain powerful social drives within the nation. Yet the anatomy of this enthusiasm was complex and its origins various.

Nothing could have more easily excited the interest of the public than a revolt against England. The humiliation of the Treaty of Paris of 1763 was recalled with undiminished rancor in 1776, and the Americans, as bold challengers of the despotism of hated Albion and as underdogs in an unequal struggle, aroused spontaneous sympathy in the French. To the young men particularly, the American war seemed an exciting opportunity to win honor and advancement. The romantic adventure of Lafayette, who attracted from all sides admiration and sympathy, contributed to this atmosphere of chivalric fervor; it was no wonder that suddenly a crowd of young men and adventurous nobles were trying by every means possible to follow his example. The thrill of something new and different appealed to everyone, especially to the women. Thus some of the motives were superficial, though nonetheless effective.

Real political forces, however, lay behind the support of America, for both the royal government and the *Philosophes* had strong reasons to hope for American victories. In spite of an initial reluctance to make official commitments and a definite distrust of American republicanism in the Court, Vergennes' ministry was very pleased to see a revolution which would bleed England militarily and economically, whatever its outcome, and which, if successful, would throw open to French trade the rich American market. Consequently, the government furnished secret aid through Beaumarchais, winked at the volunteers, and later, when Burgoyne's defeat at Saratoga made the gamble worth while, joined the Americans in a military alliance which rendered war with England inevitable.

For their part, the liberals and intellectuals identified the American struggle against British oppression with their own battle against autocracy. The word *liberté* was a constant refrain in every panegyric of America, and to a great extent the American example was used as an excuse to express ideas which otherwise could not have been voiced. As Condorcet, the philosopher and mathematician, later recalled, "Men whom the reading of philosophic books had secretly converted to the love of liberty became enthusiastic over the liberty of a foreign people while they waited for the moment when they could recover their own, and they seized with joy this opportunity to avow publicly sentiments which prudence had prevented them from expressing."[6] The American war was for the *ancien régime* a sort of Pandora's Box out of which poured a cloud of books and articles advocating equality, republicanism, liberty, and constitutionalism, and attacking both the aristocratic principle and monarchical absolutism. Unquestionably the popular support of the United States was in large part actually a disguised demand for reform of the existing French social and political order.

The new nature and new dimensions of this interest in the United States naturally implied a revised picture in the French mind of American civilization. Not only were there shifts in interest from one aspect to another, but also the public demanded, and received, information in quantities far greater than had been available before. All the newspapers devoted a large share of their space to the war, printing long reports of the battles and campaigns, a great variety

[6] "Eloge de Franklin," *Oeuvres* (Paris, 1847), III, 406-407.

of American political and military documents, and extracts from American papers and articles by American writers.[7] The number of books on America increased at an almost geometric rate, indicating graphically the rise in public interest. Antoine Hornot's *Anecdotes américaines* appeared in 1776, Paul Dubuisson's *Abrégé de la révolution de l'Amérique anglaise* in 1778, Raynal's *Révolution de l'Amérique* in 1780, Hilliard d'Auberteuil's *Essais historiques et politiques sur les Anglo-Américains* in 1781, Joseph Mandrillon's *Précis sur l'Amérique Septentrionale* in 1782, and there were many others.[8] The new supplement to the *Encyclopédie* gave a revised and much fuller treatment to the United States and the *Dictionnaire universel des sciences* (1777-1783) likewise contained many articles on the new nation. The poets of the day—Voltaire, Dorat, Parny, D'Alembert, Lebrun, and many lesser figures—found inspiration in the *Insurgents*. There appeared even an American epic, Chavannes de la Giraudière's *L'Amérique délivrée* (1783).

Practically all, however, of these French reports and interpretations published during the war were composed from second-, third-, or fourth-hand information and were usually written in haste and with little critical evaluation of the facts. Volunteer officers returning from America occasionally served as such sources and themselves published a minor item or two, but during the war years whatever influence their impressions had on public opinion was exerted directly through the spoken rather than the written word. In the case of Lafayette, this influence was important, but the reports of the others appear, from all evidence, to have had little effect. This was because most of those who returned were

[7] See especially *Les Affaires de l'Angleterre et de l'Amérique*, which was devoted almost exclusively to news of America and of the war; *Le Courier de l'Europe*, which contained excellent coverage of military events, long articles on the United States, anecdotes on Franklin, works by American authors, and poems and songs on America; the *Journal historique et politique;* the *Courrier d'Avignon*; the *Gazette de Leyde*; the *Gazette de France*; the *Journal politique de Bruxelles*; and the *Journal encyclopédique*.

[8] E.g., Barbeu Dubourg, *Calendrier de Philadelphie* (Paris, 1777, 1778, 1779, and 1785); Brion de La Tour, *Almanach intéressant* (Paris, 1780); *Histoire de la guerre d'Amérique* (Paris, 1783); Poncelin de la Roche-Tilhac, *Almanach américain* (Paris, 1783).

disgruntled by Congress' failure to accept their services, and their bitter and critical comments were overwhelmed by the din of pro-Americanism.

English publications contributed an important share to the total picture. Translations of works written before the war generally presented a favorable picture of life in America. A new translation of Burke's *Account of the European Settlements in North America* appeared in 1780, and French versions of Burnaby's *Travels* appeared in 1778 and of Cluny's *American Traveller* in 1782. A flood of hostile political propaganda pamphlets, however, also came from across the Channel, answered by an equal amount of pro-American political literature from the Continent.

Although these English translations and the secondary works of French writers like Raynal had, apparently, fairly wide circulation, the significant new contributions to the picture were those provided, directly or indirectly, by the Americans themselves.

Aside from the many Franklin items, the number of American books published in France remained relatively small. Paine's *Common Sense* was translated in 1776, and there were five French editions in 1782 and 1783 of his *Letter Addressed to the Abbé Raynal*. John Adams's *Memoir to Their High Mightinesses the States General of the United Provinces* appeared in 1781, and there were a few additional minor titles.[9] It was in the newspapers that the greatest variety of American writings appeared, and *Les Affaires de l'Angleterre et de l'Amérique* and the *Courier de l'Europe* published selections and letters by Washington, Paine, Franklin, John Adams, Samuel Adams, Richard Henry Lee, Samuel Cooper, John Hancock, and Benjamin Rush, as well as innumerable extracts from American newspapers, some of which gave interesting glimpses of American life.[10]

The war brought Americans to France for the first time in

[9] *Lettres de Jonathan Trumbull et William Livingston* (1779); Anthony Benezet, *Observations sur les Quakers* (Philadelphia, 1780 and London, 1783); William Smith, *Voyage historique et politique* (Paris, 1778).
[10] E.g., *Courier de l'Europe*, Nov. 18, 1777; April 21, 1778.

appreciable numbers, both to Paris on diplomatic missions and to the various seaports on merchant ships, privateers, and naval vessels. John Adams seems to have been the only other diplomat besides Franklin to make a lasting impression on the French public. Though in far less accord with French ways than Franklin, he nevertheless was a respected figure. John Paul Jones, who held a commission in the French as well as the American navy, a far more colorful figure and better suited to the taste of Parisians, achieved a truly extraordinary popularity. The King received him, made him Chevalier of the Order of Military Merit, and presented him with a gold-hilted sword. He was greeted with applause at the Opera and in fact wherever he showed his face in Paris. In the spring of 1780 he was initiated into the Masonic Lodge of the Nine Sisters, which commissioned Houdon to make a bust of him and held an elaborate fete in his honor. He even enjoyed the reputation of being a talented poet, especially, it was said, in the eclogue and elegy, and he passed into the realm of mythology as the supposed author of a series of burlesque prophecies.[11]

It is difficult to estimate how many Americans arrived in the various coastal cities, but they could not have been few and the impression they made was frequently reported in the papers. For instance, the *Courrier d'Avignon* published on April 11, 1777 the following typical item: "The Bostonians that we see here are dressed with a simplicity which offers a singular contrast with the elegance of our *petits maîtres.* Their hair is cut round, no curls, no gold lace on their clothes. Consequently they are not yet taking any fashionable goods, but they are buying up at any price our coarse cloth. The simplicity and sincerity of this new, free people is a spectacle as touching as it is rare."

But the sum total of all these various American contacts were less important than the pervasive influence of Benjamin Franklin. As America's first and most successful cultural

[11] See L. Amiable, *Une Loge maçonnique d'avant 1789* (Paris, 1897), p. 150; *Correspondance littéraire, philosophique et critique par Grimm, Diderot, Raynal, Meister, etc.*, ed. Tourneaux (Paris, 1877-1882), XII, 394; *Paul Jones ou prophéties sur l'Amérique* (Basle, 1781).

ambassador, he produced an incalculable effect on French opinion, both directly as a living symbol of Americanism and indirectly as an assiduous and efficient purveyor of information.

The key to his tremendous influence was his extraordinary popularity with all classes of the French people. He had been eagerly awaited as an old friend of France, and his recent trip to Canada and his interview with General Howe and Lord Howe had been well reported in the French papers. On December 3, 1776 he landed at Auray in Brittany, wearing his tall fur cap and his spectacles, spent the night at an inn on the river front which still stands today, stopped for the next night at Vannes, and left the following day for Paris. Within a few weeks his arrival was the sensation of Paris.[12]

Franklin was very secretive about the motives of his coming and he gave out only that he intended to live henceforth in France. Everyone was debating whether he had really crossed the Atlantic merely to pass his old age in peace and comfort, or whether he was on some secret diplomatic mission.[13] For several weeks he lodged with Silas Deane, who had preceded him, in a hotel where he received a steady stream of visits from savants and *Philosophes*, all eager to meet him, to discuss his theories of electricity, and to invite him to their homes. By the middle of January it had become the fashion to have an engraving of the sage over one's mantelpiece, and the prints published of Franklin were practically numberless. There were canes and hats à la Franklin, and his likeness appeared on medallions, snuff boxes, rings, watches, vases, clocks, dishes, handkerchiefs, and even pocketknives. Many hours of the summer of 1777 he was forced to spend sitting for portraits, and he wrote his daughter, "Your father's face [is] as well known as that of the moon, so that he durst not do anything that would oblige him to run away, as his face

12 On Franklin in France, see especially E. E. Hale and E. E. Hale, Jr., *Franklin in France* (Boston, 1887-1888); and C. Van Doren, *Benjamin Franklin* (New York, 1938). To these sources I am indebted for many of the following details.

13 F. Métra, *op.cit.*, III, 86 (Dec. 27, 1776).

would discover him wherever he should venture to show it."[14]
The best known of these paintings were those by Cochin,
Duplessis, Greuze, and J.-F. de l'Hospital. Houdon did a bust
of him in 1778. The poets too were busy, especially composing verses to be printed under the engraved portraits. Lebrun
wrote

> Triomphe, ô divine Uranie,
> Et dans ton disciple vanté,
> Reconnais la double génie,
> Des arts et de la liberté.[15]

Feutry, Dalibard, and others wrote similar quatrains; one,
ending with the line "Qui désarme les dieux peut-il craindre
les rois?" was forbidden by the censor as "blasphemous."[16]
All the poets, professional and amateur, apparently tried
their hands at tributes to Franklin, and their efforts ranged
from Feutry's polished "Envoi au docteur Benjamin Franklin"[17] to the "Chanson faite dans un souper où se trouvait
Monsieur Franklin à Auteuil," which began

> Monsieur Francklin que j'estime,
> Bien qu'à Londres il soit pendu,
> Veut que je m'exerce en rime
> Sur le nom si répandu
>> De Washington
>> Tontaine, tontaine,
>> De Washington
>> Tontaine, tonton.[18]

Evidences of the great and universal esteem the American
envoy enjoyed were many and various. For instance, the

---

14 *Writings of Benjamin Franklin*, ed. A. H. Smyth (New York, 1905),
VII, 347.

15 "Triumph, O divine Urania, and in thy vaunted disciple recognize the
double genius of the arts and liberty." *Courier de l'Europe*, June 2, 1778.

16 "Can he who has disarmed the gods fear the power of kings?" *Correspondance par Grimm, Diderot* . . . , XII, 3 (Oct. 1777). The author was
Barbeu Dubourg.

17 *Nouveaux opuscules* (Dijon, 1779), p. 20, and *Courier de l'Europe*, Nov.
18, 1777.

18 "Monsieur Franklin, whom I esteem, though they are hanging him in
London, asks me to make a rhyme on the famous name of Washington,
Tontaine. . . ." *Courier de l'Europe*, April 18, 1777.

Comédie Française on July 31, 1777 gave special productions of Molière's *Amphitryon* and *Monsieur de Pourceaugnac* merely because Franklin had expressed regret that he had never seen these plays.[19] But Franklin's fame was by no means limited to the learned and fashionable. John Adams, who usually had a good Yankee distrust of superlatives, wrote, "His reputation was more universal than that of Liebnitz or Newton, Frederick or Voltaire, and his character more beloved and esteemed than any or all of them. . . . His name was familiar to government and people, to kings, courtiers, nobility, clergy, and philosophers, as well as plebeians, to such a degree that there was scarcely a peasant or a citizen, a *valet de chambre*, coachman or footman, a lady's chambermaid or a scullion in a kitchen, who was not familiar with it, and who did not consider him as a friend to human kind. When they spoke of him, they seemed to think he was to restore the golden age."[20]

Somehow Franklin seemed to fit every qualification for the popular hero which the French had long been awaiting. Voltaire had embodied the reason, the scientific spirit, and the humanitarianism of the century; Rousseau the *sensibilité*, the return to nature, simplicity, and goodness. But each had lacked the qualities of the other; Franklin miraculously seemed to fuse the virtues of both. He was the complete and perfect *Philosophe*. What could be more Rousseauan than his long white hair, his spotless linen, his plain brown coat, and his tall fur hat? What more Voltairian than his shrewd common sense, his devotion to liberty and tolerance, and his lightning rod? He dressed and lived like Rousseau, he thought like Voltaire, and he loved the ladies like both.

Moreover Franklin had done what no French *Philosophe* had accomplished: he had transformed theory into practice. Montesquieu, Voltaire, Rousseau, Mably, Helvétius, and Raynal had all produced fine theories on political liberty and equality, but the theories had remained merely theories. Franklin had—at least in the French mind—transformed

19 *Ibid.*, Aug. 12, 1777.
20 *Works* (Boston, 1850-1856), I, 660.

these ideas into political reality, for they believed him to be the instigator of the American revolt against tyranny and the author of the American constitutions. Thus he combined for them not only reason and sentiment but also the man of ideas and the man of action.

Still, this is not the whole explanation of his influence. To be enduringly popular, a man must love his public, and Franklin loved the French. "I find them here a most amiable people to live with," he wrote his friend Josiah Quincy. There is nothing wanting in the character of a Frenchman that belongs to that of an agreeable and worthy man. There are only some trifles surplus, or which might be spared."[21] Moreover, like every great leader, Franklin had a discreet dash of the actor, even of the charlatan. He had worn his fur hat on shipboard because the weather was cold, but when he saw it was greeted in France as a "badge of transatlantic philosophy," he wisely kept on wearing it. When he was received by the King, along with Silas Deane and Arthur Lee, after the conclusion of the Treaties, he was fully conscious of the dramatic contrast of his plain brown coat in the midst of the brilliantly dressed courtiers. Madame Du Deffand, writing her friend Horace Walpole, wondered whether the white hat he carried under his arm was a symbol of liberty.[22]

Most important of all was Franklin's undeniable charm, his civilized taste, his broad humanitarianism. Perhaps his old and dear friend the Abbé Morellet expressed it best when, upon learning of Franklin's death, he wrote, "His friendship was delightful: a perfect good nature, a simplicity of manner, a rectitude of mind that made itself evident in the slightest matter, an extreme forbearance, and above all a sweet serenity that easily turned into gaiety. Such was the society of this great man."[23]

Significant as were Franklin's political achievements, his scientific discoveries and his writings, he was one of those

[21] *Writings*, VII, 290-291.
[22] Marie, Marquise Du Deffand, *Correspondance complète* (Paris, 1865), II, 648.
[23] *Memoires* (Paris, 1823), I, 299.

rare spirits, like Samuel Johnson, who make their imprint on history by the sheer force of personality. This was a lever which Franklin did not hesitate to use to move the world. His reputation and popularity did more than anything else to gain French support for the American cause and to establish American culture, at least for the moment, on an equal footing with that of France.

Much of Franklin's influence was exerted informally and intimately through his many friends, among whom were many charming and influential women. There was Madame Brillon, with whom he often dined twice a week and with whom he maintained a continual byplay of facetious gallantry;[24] the Countess Golowkin, Chastellux's *amie*, who sang him naughty romances and translated his German documents;[25] the Dowager Duchess of Deux Ponts, who gave him his famous crabtree cane; the Countess Diane de Polignac, who talked so incessantly about Franklin at Court that the King in desperation presented her with an elegant Sevres *vase de nuit* on the bottom of which he had painted Franklin's portrait surrounded by Turgot's motto "Eripuit fulmen coelo sceptrumque tyrannis";[26] and many more. Madame Campan, Marie Antoinette's secretary, recalled a fete "where the most beautiful among three hundred women was designated to place upon the white hairs of the American philosopher a crown of laurel and two kisses upon his cheek."[27]

This was all very frivolous and eighteenth-century, but the shrewd old man knew how to put frivolity to his nation's service. Among his most important friendships was that with Madame d'Houdetot, one of the most influential women of the time, who, besides organizing elaborate *fêtes champêtres* for her beloved philosopher, was the center of an important and powerful group of Americanists composed of

[24] Mme Vigée-Lebrun, *Souvenirs* (Paris, n.d.), p. 118; Van Doren, *op.cit.*, p. 641.

[25] G. Chinard, "Benjamin Franklin and the Mysterious Madame G———," *Amer. Philos. Soc. Library Bulletin for 1946* (Philadelphia, 1947), pp. 50-62.

[26] Jeanne Louise Campan, *Mémoires de la vie privée de Marie Antoinette* (Paris, 1822), I, 233-234.

[27] *Ibid.*

her lover the poet Saint Lambert, Louis de Lacretelle, editor of the *Mercure*, the Prince and Princess de Beauvau, and Jean Baptiste Target. She befriended stranded American sailors, encouraged St. John de Crèvecoeur to translate into French his *Letters of an American Farmer*, and continued to correspond with Franklin after his return to America, following with passionate interest the deliberations of the Constitutional Convention in Philadelphia.[28]

More important still was Franklin's friendship with Madame Helvétius, the widow of the *Philosophe*, who had established her famous salon in Auteuil, to which Franklin was introduced by Turgot and Malesherbes. Two or three times a week he used to walk from his nearby house in Passy to dine with "Notre Dame d'Auteuil," as he affectionately called her. She said she regretted she had not paid him, on his first call, the royal honor of coming to meet him at her gate, as she had greeted Voltaire, and she broke the rule she had kept since her husband's death by going out once a week to call on him in Passy. The parties at Auteuil were "very gay," as Morellet said, and Franklin's attentions frankly gallant. Once when she reproached him for failing to call he replied, "Madame, I am waiting till the nights are longer." He seriously proposed marriage, and when she refused out of loyalty to her late husband he replied with the most charming of his bagatelles, "A Madame Helvetius." At her salon he met, in addition to the Abbés de La Roche and Morellet, who helped her receive her guests, such men as Condorcet, Turgot, Chamfort, Volney (who had been introduced to Franklin by D'Holbach), and particularly Cabanis, to whom Franklin on his death left his dress sword. Into this circle, which was the birthplace of *Idéologie*, Franklin introduced John Adams and later Thomas Jefferson, William Short, and Charles Ingersoll.[29]

For all his social activity, Franklin was nonetheless a busy and highly effective diplomat. Besides achieving his

[28] See G. Chinard, *Les Amitiés américaines de Madame d'Houdetot* (Paris, 1924).
[29] See A. Guillois, *Le Salon de Mme Helvétius, Cabanis et les Idéologues* (Paris, 1894), pp. 42-43, 60.

primary purpose of enlisting French financial and military support and of negotiating the peace treaty, he was constantly occupied in strengthening the bonds between French and American minds. In this the American Philosophical Society continued to play its important part. The new French members elected during the war were all men serving in America—the officers Lafayette and the Chevalier de Chastellux, the diplomats Conrad Gérard, Anne César de La Luzerne, and François Marbois. But Franklin seems to have handed out memberships rather informally. The poet Feutry proudly proclaimed his election, and the philologist Court de Gébelin wrote the society a letter of thanks, though neither ever appeared in the list of members.[30]

Franklin was a subtle diplomat: while he enjoyed and cultivated his universal popularity, he always preferred to exert his influence privately, unobtrusively, and if possible anonymously. In innumerable private conservations and letters he kept explaining his country and bringing his American and French friends together. He understood how greatly the French were interested in the propagation of the Enlightenment, so he repeatedly emphasized, as he had on his first visits to Paris, such items as the fact that it was in America and not in London that his experiments in electricity had been made, and he told his friends of the rich libraries and the college established in Philadelphia. Recording one of these conversations, the Duke de Croÿ wrote in his diary that Franklin had pointed out "how remarkable it was that this colony established less than a hundred years ago had already attained this high degree of knowledge, power and wealth." His own observation was, "One sees from this how little time is necessary to form a great empire when it is founded by great and well educated men."[31]

Personalities were the favorite instruments of Franklin's diplomacy. He recommended his fellow Mason, the Abbé

[30] "Old Minutes of the Society, from 1743 to 1838," *Proc. Amer. Philos. Soc.*, xxii (1885), pt. 3, no. 119 (see minutes of Sept. 26, 1783); A. A. J. Feutry, *op.cit.*
[31] *Journal inédit* (Paris, 1906-1907), iii, 301.

Robin to Rochambeau, as a chaplain and gave him letters of introduction to Jonathan Williams of Boston and others, thus indirectly making possible Robin's book on America. To Chastellux, the most noted *Philosophe* in the French army and later the author of an important work on the United States, he gave a letter addressed to Joseph Reed, a letter which no doubt led to Chastellux's election to the American Philosophical Society. When John Adams arrived in April 1778, he met Turgot at Passy, dined with Franklin at the Brillons' and the De Chaumonts', and became a friend of Madame Helvétius. Though Adams knew no French and was inclined to be somewhat suspicious and reserved, Franklin saw to it that he met everyone of note. After the war Franklin found many more opportunities to introduce to his French friends his compatriots, including such men as Thomas Paine and of course his successor Thomas Jefferson. He aided President Eleazar Wheelock in his efforts to raise funds in France for Dartmouth College, and wrote Court de Gébelin on American linguistics and the Abbé Soulavie on American geology. He served as the most important link between the European press and America, receiving requests for information on the American market for European publications and queries on sources of information about America and on possible American correspondents. Thus in countless and varied ways Franklin was an ever-active agent, bringing French minds into contact with American civilization, and American minds into contact with French civilization.

In the eighteenth century cultural nationalism was still unknown and there existed in its place a spirit of genuine cosmopolitanism which had created a supra-national philosophical state that ignored political boundaries. European scientists, writers, and philosophers were frequently members of academies and learned societies in a number of different countries; they collaborated closely by correspondence; they accepted ideas from each other without any nationalistic reservations; their works were published simultaneously in two, three, or even four languages. Into this fraternity Americans could be accepted, as a matter of course, as individuals capable of contributing their share to the enlightenment of mankind. Franklin had already made a start toward integrating his countrymen in this philosophic republic of Europe, and now he succeeded in completing the task. Moreover this cultural integration had a very real political value. Franklin consciously and systematically employed his own prestige as a philosopher and the prestige with which he had endowed his nation to win support for his diplomatic and military ends.

Before 1776 his own reputation in France had rested on his scientific discoveries and to a less extent on his political and economic writings. Now he assumed the additional character of a moralist, as the result of the extraordinary vogue of his *Way to Wealth*, or *La Science du Bonhomme Richard*, as the title was translated. A few months after his arrival it had been printed, as a contribution from a Scottish subscriber, in the *Courier de l'Europe*.[32] Ruault, a Paris publisher, soon printed the first French edition in 1777 and from then on republications continued to appear at frequent intervals until the middle of the nineteenth century. The work had a tremendous and instantaneous appeal as a sort of gospel of the virtues of bourgeois thrift and common sense. Le Bonhomme Richard was one of those characters like Don Quixote who achieve an extra-literary existence in the popular mind. He reappeared in other works, like the *Calendrier de Philadelphie*, and he gave his name to John Paul Jones' famous ship. Nor was the work ignored by serious critics, for the authors of the Grimm-Diderot Correspondence thought highly of its "series of apothegms full of reason, energy and clarity," and advised that they knew of no book more worthy to be placed in the hands of everyone.[33] *La Science du Bonhomme Richard* was of course not the only work of Franklin's circulating in Paris during the war. His *Oeuvres* had been published only a few years before, and the newspapers frequently printed selections from his writings, such as his

[32] Mar. 28–May 30, 1777.
[33] *Op.cit.*, XII, 29 (Nov. 1777).

famous epitaph, published in the *Courier de l'Europe*[34] and cited by Marmontel in the Supplement to the *Encyclopédie* and later in his *Eléments de littérature* as a perfect example of the genre.[35] Moreover his own press at Passy was busy turning out in both French and English a considerable number of bagatelles, hoaxes, and propaganda pieces, as well as more serious works, such as his *Avis à ceux qui voudraient s'en aller en Amérique.*

In the latter work, as in his private correspondence, Franklin sought to correct French misconceptions of life in America and to discourage rash plans to emigrate. It was popularly believed, he said, that Americans were very wealthy, that there was a great lack of trained men in the various arts and professions, and that consequently any European with a modicum of talent could find lucrative opportunities. The reverse was true, Franklin warned; while there were few poor, there were also few rich. On the other hand, although there were plenty of educated men and persons of artistic and scientific talent, the lack of wealthy patrons had forced geniuses like West and Copley to go to London, and it would be the height of folly for French artists, scientists, government administrators, or military men to go to the United States in the hope of being richly welcomed. What America needed was industrious and skillful workmen, not sculptors.[36]

Franklin also engaged in a good deal of undercover political propaganda. In addition to producing items like *The Sale of the Hessians*[37] and his famous *Supplement to the Boston Independent Chronicle*, a spurious newssheet faking a report of wholesale deals between the British and Indians for the scalps of American women and children, he was also an active collaborator in the *Affaires de l'Angleterre et de l'Amérique*. This semi-clandestine periodical was published by La Rochefoucauld d'Anville, Court de Gébelin, and Jean

[34] Oct. 28, 1777.

[35] "Allégorie," *Supplément à l'Encyclopédie*, I, 302; Jean François Marmontel, *Oeuvres complètes* (Paris, 1818), XIII, 327.

[36] Hale, *op.cit.*, II, 256.

[37] See my " 'The Sale of the Hessians.' Was Benjamin Franklin the Author?' *Proc. Amer. Philos. Soc.*, XCVIII (1954), 427-431.

Baptiste Robinet from 1776 to 1779 to furnish news of the American war and to support the American cause. Using as news sources both English periodicals (principally Almon's *Remembrancer*) and American publications and documents furnished by Franklin, the *Affaires* provided detailed reports on the military and political progress of the war, forceful editorials in support of the American cause, writings by such men as Paine and John and Samuel Adams, and translations of the Declaration of Independence and of most of the American constitutions. La Rochefoucauld, who had already met Franklin in London, had called on him at his hotel soon after he arrived. When Franklin learned of the *Affaires* he immediately offered to collaborate, and he became, according to contemporary reports, one of the principal figures behind the enterprise. He contributed at least ten articles and was particularly valuable in obtaining documents and news from America.

Another example of his clandestine political activity was the affair of the Cincinnati. As an enemy of aristocratic government, Franklin strongly opposed the hereditary and quasi-aristocratic character of the Society of the Cincinnati, an American veterans' organization open to French as well as to American officers. Unable because of his official position to attack the society directly, he engaged two of his friends, Chamfort and the young Mirabeau (who had already produced American propaganda in his *Avis aux Hessois*), to translate an American attack upon the society, Aedanus Burke's *Considerations on the Society or Order of Cincinnatus,* and to incorporate into the translation an essay in letter form that Franklin had himself written to his daughter, which demonstrated mathematically the absurdity and moral and social evil of aristocracy or "descending honor." Mirabeau's book, *Considérations sur l'Ordre de Cincinnatus,* published in London in 1784 through the efforts of Franklin and later translated into English, created a great furor, for it attacked an organization headed by such respectable figures as Washington, Lafayette, and Rochambeau, and at the same time struck, convincingly and cleverly, at the foundations of the existing French social order. Meanwhile Franklin had his own letter-essay against the Cincinnati translated by Morellet.[38] Not daring to publish it, he caused it to be circulated clandestinely among his French friends, who finally published it in 1790 as a justification for the abolition of the nobility, in the *Journal de la Société de 1789*.[39]

The two most important French organizations to which Franklin belonged were the Masonic Lodge of the Nine Sisters (La Loge des Neuf Soeurs) and the Academy of Sciences, and both these groups were linked with the story of Franklin's friendship with Voltaire. The lodge, founded in July 1776, had been planned by Helvétius and established by the astronomer Lalande, for the purposes of uniting in a single lodge all the Masons distinguished in the arts, sciences, and learning. It was only natural that Franklin, a Mason ever since 1731 and Grand Master of the Province of Pennsylvania since 1749, would become a member. His actual decision to be initiated may have been prompted by his acquaintance with Voltaire. The Sage of Ferney had returned from his long exile to Paris in February 1778, and Franklin went immediately to call on him, taking along the other American envoys and his grandson Temple Franklin. It was difficult to say which of the two philosophers was the more impressed by the occasion. A crowd of about twenty people pressed into the room where the ailing philosopher received his American visitor. Voltaire tried to use his rusty English, but he was forced to slip back into French, saying regretfully, "I could not resist the desire to speak for a moment the language of Mr. Franklin." When Franklin asked him to give his blessing to Temple he replied with the words "God and Liberty!"[40] "All those who were present shed tears of emotion," Voltaire wrote later to a friend.[41]

[38] See B. Faÿ, "Franklin et Mirabeau collaborateurs," *Revue de littérature comparée*, VIII (1928), 5-28.

[39] July 24, 1790. See my "Franklin's Lost Letter on the Cincinnati," *Bulletin de l'Institut Français de Washington*, nouvelle série, no. 3, Dec. 1953, pp. 119-126.

[40] Condorcet, "Vie de Voltaire," in Voltaire, *Oeuvres*, ed. Molland (Paris, 1883-1885), I, 276.

[41] *Ibid.*, L, 372.

The two old men were next together on the morning of April 7, when with elaborate ceremony and in the presence of the highest French Masonic dignitaries Voltaire was initiated into the Lodge of the Nine Sisters. When he entered the crowded chamber Court de Gébelin supported him on one side and Franklin held his arm on the other. Immediately after Voltaire's initiation, Franklin joined the lodge, which honored him with a special ceremony in July at which he was presented with the apron which had belonged to Helvétius and which Voltaire had worn. In November took place a fantastic apotheosis of Voltaire, who had died the previous May. Franklin, whom Lalande hailed as "the noblest friend of this great man," took a leading part in the elaborate ceremony, which was held in a great chamber hung with black draperies and dimly lit by flickering lamps.[42] At the banquet which followed, attended by two hundred guests, the first toast paid tribute to the thirteen United States.

In May 1779 Franklin was elected *Vénérable* (Grand Master) of the lodge, and the following year he was chosen again. In November 1782, after the conclusion of the preliminary treaty with England, a delegation of fellow Masons waited on him to honor him as a great statesman and benefactor of humanity. The following March the Musée de Paris, founded by Court de Gébelin and other members of the lodge in 1780, held a grand celebration in honor of French victory and American independence. The moment Franklin entered the hall he was greeted by thunderous applause. De Carla gave a discourse on the American Revolution, the Abbé Brizard read his *Fragment de Xénophon*, and Houdon presented his bust of Franklin to the Musée.[43] After Franklin returned to Philadelphia the lodge offered a prize of 600 francs for the best eulogy in his honor.

The great importance of the lodge for Franklin was not the honors it paid him but the members with whom it brought him into contact and through whom he was permitted to exert his influence. A great many of them were

42 Amiable, *op.cit.*, p. 85.
43 *Mercure de France*, Mar. 22, 1783.

intimate friends and associates, and a significantly large number were active Americanists—the Abbé Robin, Court de Gébelin, Hilliard d'Auberteuil, Démeunier, Chamfort, Cabanis, Houdon, La Rochefoucauld d'Anville, Condorcet, the Marquis de Marnésia, Billardon de Sauvigny, Cadet de Vaux, Moreau de Saint Méry, Brissot de Warville, Dr. Guillotin, and, of course, Voltaire. The political, intellectual, and artistic quality of the lodge is indicated by such members as Camille Desmoulins, Danton, Marie Joseph Chénier, Fauchet, Sieyès, Rabaut Saint-Etienne, Bailly, Pétion, Parny, Lalande, Delille, Piccini, Greuze, La Dixmerie, and Montgolfier.

The Academy of Sciences, to which Franklin had been elected in 1772, was also a valuable point of contact with the scientific and intellectual life of Paris. In the midst of so many preoccupations, Franklin had little time for scientific investigations, but even during the semi-retirement of the first year at Passy he frequently attended sessions of the academy, where it was hoped that he would deliver a paper on electricity. His scholarly reputation was recognized throughout the world during these years by election to academic and learned societies in Padua, Turin, Boston, Madrid, Paris, Lyons, Orleans, Edinburgh, Manchester, and Rotterdam— all these in addition to his earlier memberships in the Royal Society of London, the Society of Arts in London, and the Royal Society of Sciences in Göttingen. Franklin apparently had time to deliver only one paper before his colleagues in Paris, that on the Aurora Borealis—in French—on April 14, 1779,[44] but he was frequently asked to sit on committees of the academy. For instance, he submitted in May 1778 with Le Roy, Condorcet, and Lalande a report on La Blancherie's Nouvelles de la République des Lettres et des Arts, an organization designed to promote international cooperation and correspondence between scholars and scientists.[45] Six years later, when the debate over the merits of Mesmer's theories on animal magnetism rocked Paris, Franklin was

[44] Louis de Bachaumont, *Mémoires secrets* (London, 1777-1788), XIV, April 15, 1779; Franklin, *Writings*, VII, 209-215.
[45] *Courier de l'Europe*, June 30, 1778.

put on the committee, which was set up at the King's request and included his friends Le Roy, Bailly, Lavoisier, and the mathematician De Bory, to report on the validity of the new doctrine.

Franklin's greatest moment was the session of the academy which he and Voltaire attended on April 29, 1778. John Adams wrote in his diary what was probably the best of the many accounts of the incident: "After dinner we went to the Academy of Sciences, and heard M. d'Alembert, as perpetual secretary, pronounce eulogies on several members, lately deceased. Voltaire and Franklin were both present, and there presently arose a general cry that M. Voltaire and M. Franklin should be introduced to each other. This was done, and they bowed and spoke to each other. This was no satisfaction; there must be something more. Neither of our philosophers seemed to divine what was wished or expected; the clamor continued, until the explanation came out. 'Il faut s'embrasser, à la française.' The two aged actors upon this great theater of philosophy and frivolity then embraced each other, by hugging one another in their arms, and kissing each other's cheeks, and then the tumult subsided. And the cry immediately spread through the whole kingdom, and, I suppose, over all Europe. 'Qu'il était charmant de voir embrasser Solon et Sophocle.' "[46]

Adams obviously did not approve of such goings on, but he did not miss the point. The embraces of Voltaire and Franklin were so dramatic because they were so symbolic. Franklin had succeeded in wedding American constitutional liberalism with French philosophic liberalism. Perhaps the wedding was based more on a sentimental identification of a common political vocabulary than on a fundamental compatibility derived from common traditions and purposes. Nevertheless Franklin stood for the moment as the leading political philosopher of Europe, and it is difficult to measure the great extent of his influence.

In spite of such activities as his instigation of the *Considérations sur l'Ordre de Cincinnatus*, Franklin was certainly

[46] *Works*, III, 14-17.

not engaged in revolutionary conspiracy. In fact, in a conversation with the Abbé Soulavie in. 1781, he scoffed at his friend's fears of revolution and declared that France was the most stable of all European states.[47] As a typical eighteenth-century thinker he believed in the beneficent evolutionary power of ideas and he did not suspect their explosive qualities. As a political philosopher he was interested in furthering the cause of democratic constitutionalism, in which he believed, but he never dreamed he was helping to prepare the death sentence of a king whom he sincerely regarded with admiration and gratitude. In the last months of his life, in 1790, the news of the violence and terror in Paris filled him with disquietude, and it is perhaps possible that he was dismayed to find flecks of blood on his own philosophic hands.

Franklin's many activities amounted to an impressive total. It is safe to say that his influence and example, directly and indirectly, was, after the war itself, the preponderant instrument for creating in French minds a consciousness of America and a fairly definite image of American society.

No opinion, however, is ever unanimous and we should not suppose that there existed no reactions or reservations in the face of the general tide of Americanism. The dissemination of foreign propaganda was difficult to control, and there circulated in Paris many pamphlets and books of English inspiration, printed usually in London or The Hague, which combatted the American arguments, libeled Franklin, and sought to avert a Franco-American alliance. Some, such as the anonymous poem, *L'Amérique* (1780), had literary pretensions; some were official white papers, for instance, the *Mémoire justificatif de la conduite de la Grande Bretagne* (1779); some, like John Lind's *Réponse à la Declaration du congrès américain* (1777), were serious essays on the political issues; and others were vitriolic satirical libels, of which Richard Tickell's *La Casette verte de M. de Sartine* (1779) was a good example.[48] An idea of the kind of publication

[47] Jean Louis Soulavie, *Mémoires historiques et politiques du règne de Louis XVI* (Paris, 1801), v, 183.
[48] See also, of the serious essays, Issac Pinto's *Lettre à Mr. S. B.* (The Hague,

being circulated is given by the following verses, which were printed under an unflattering engraving of Franklin published in London:

Renégat de son culte, infidèle à son Roi,
Sous-cape il se moqua du ciel et de la loi.
Vergennes et Maurepas crurent à ses sornettes,
Et le doyen de tous les charlatans
Trompa les bons avec ses cheveux blancs
Et les sots avec ses lunettes.[49]

The inner court circles, particularly the royal family, were decidedly lukewarm in their enthusiasm for the Americans,[50] and there were influential individuals like Madame Du Deffand, who, in spite of a visit from Franklin in his fur cap, refused to fall in with the popular sentiment.[51]

The most notable expression of anti-Americanism was made by a man named Simon Linguet, a strange and paradoxical figure who had been disbarred from legal practice and had been forced in 1776 to resign his editorship of the *Journal de politique et de littérature*. In 1777, in exile in London, he started a new journal called *Annales politiques, civiles et littéraires du 18e siècle*, which enjoyed a great popularity in Paris, and particularly in the Court, but which at the same time aroused violent hostility in other quarters.[52] That Linguet had both violent partisans and enemies is understandable, for he supported the thesis of a strong centralized monarchy and was bitterly against the *Encyclopédistes*

---

1776), *Seconde lettre* (The Hague, 1776), and *Réponse aux Observations d'un homme impartiale* (The Hague, 1776), and Dean Josiah Tucker's *Cui bono?* (London, 1782); of the satires, *Entretiens de Guillaume de Nassau* (London, 1776), Delauney's amusing *Histoire d'un pou français* (Paris, 1779), and the curious *Lettres iroquoises* (London, 1781), directed against Franklin and French aid.

[49] "Apostate to his religion, traitor to his king, he laughed up his sleeve at heaven and at the law. Vergennes and Maurepas swallowed his humbug, and this dean of all charlatans deceived the good with his white hairs, and fools with his spectacles." Métra, *op.cit.*, XI, 230 (May 3, 1781).

[50] See Campan, *op.cit.*, I, 233-234.

[51] Du Deffand, *op.cit.*, II, 584.

[52] See *Correspondance secrète inédite sur Louis XVI, Marie Antoinette, la cour et la ville*, ed. Lescure (Paris, 1866), I, 133 (Feb. 1, 1778).

and the *Economistes*. Quite naturally he aligned himself with those who distrusted the new liberalism emanating from America and who deplored the popular and official support of a people in rebellion against their legitimate sovereign. Though his paper was not actually an organ for British propaganda, his position in London and his prior falling out with French political and philosophic powers further strengthened his inevitable support of the British side of the quarrel.

Without faith in republicanism, he predicted that the United States would be torn by a multitude of factional and local interests and divided by the ambitions of individuals, "as in all aristocracies, in which patriotism is more a false show and less a genuine sentiment than it is in monarchies," and that the new nation would soon degenerate into a despotism ruled by petty local tyrants. He appealed to deep-seated European xenophobian and anti-colonial fears by predicting that American independence would draw from Europe a "horde of active spirits and restless minds" who would bring to America "their vices, their greed, their aversion for both leisure and useful work, and their willingness to try anything new," thus multiplying disorder and contributing to the power of the new tyrants. He believed that most of these new immigrants, forced to settle in the barren and mountainous regions, would be sure to perish, thus depopulating the Old World without adding numbers to the New. But an even more fearful eventuality, he warned, would be that the United States, taking advantage of its rich resources, might indeed grow and prosper. Economically independent and in a position to control the trade of the world, the Americans would then become the arbiters of Europe's destiny. Having gained power by a rapid revolution, they would lack that "elevation of soul" which older empires attain by a process of long and painful growth. They would have not only wealth and power but the energy and immaturity of youth, and "they would be all the more terrible." Eventually they would cross the Atlantic to crush and subjugate a weakened and impoverished Europe. If they did not, then "it will be Europe's poverty which will save her.

She will not be conquered by them, because she will not be worth the trouble, and because the barbarism into which she will have already sunk will inspire only disgust in these possessors of the most brilliant empire that history has ever produced." Such, Linguet predicted, would be the consequences of an American military victory, and he appealed to the powers of Europe to consider well before they lent support to this transatlantic catastrophe. Europe could be saved only by destroying the American cancer.[53]

Such opinions as these were symptomatic of a latent disquietude in France and in the rest of Europe, inspired by the rise across the seas of a rival power whose phenomenal growth threatened the comfortable balance of power and the European hegemony. Linguet was not the only continental with such views. The anonymous *Rêveries d'un Suisse* (1781), which Linguet republished in part in his *Annales,* in similar language warned that independence would bring to the United States a decline in population, economic ruin, and despotism. The Americans, the author said, had been seduced by the promise of a liberty "such as exists nowhere in the world." Raynal had predicted as early as 1770 that the English colonies, once independent, would become a military power which would conquer and appropriate the rest of the New World from the European colonial powers.

The theory of American degeneration by no means disappeared with the American Revolution. Buffon's words were still being read, the Raynal of the early edition was the *Guide bleu* for America which all the volunteers bought before setting out for Philadelphia, and De Pauw not only published a new edition of his *Recherches* in 1777 but also reaffirmed all his theories in his article on America in the Supplement to the *Encyclopédie,* published in 1776 and of course widely read and frequently consulted. Moreover, De Pauw's and Raynal's ideas were absorbed and diffused by other writers. For instance, the article "Sauvages" in the *Dic-*

[53] *Annales politiques, civiles et littéraires du 18e siècle,* I (1777), no. 1, pp. 11-16; and in *Mélanges de politique et de littérature* (Bouillon, 1778), pp. 7-12.

*tionnaire universel* was lifted directly from De Pauw, and Hornot, in spite of his support of the American cause, reproduced faithfully in his *Anecdotes américaines* De Pauw's and Raynal's thesis of the degeneration of the colonials.

But the powerful chorus of Americanism coming from the people, the *Philosophes*, and the government drowned out De Pauw's and Linguet's warnings. Buffon in 1777 disclaimed any responsibility for De Pauw's biased and specious arguments, and modified his own earlier statements by admitting that degeneration among the Indians occurred only in certain regions of South America and not at all in the northern continent. Quoting the authority of Franklin, he rejected Kalm's observations on the Americans by saying, "In a country where the Europeans multiply so rapidly and where the life span of the natives is longer than elsewhere, it is scarcely possible that mankind degenerates. I fear that this observation of M. Kalm's is as ill founded as the one he made about the snakes which, according to him, bewitch the squirrels into falling into their waiting jaws."[54]

Jefferson later told how Franklin had once refuted Raynal. The French philosopher was a guest at a dinner party at Passy during which the conversation turned to the theory of American degeneration. Franklin suggested that all the Americans present rise, and then all the French. As it happened, the Americans were all unusually tall and vigorous, while the French were unusually diminutive, and Raynal himself was, as Franklin said, "a mere shrimp."[55]

Raynal gracefully made his retraction in 1781 and admitted that the Americans suffered degeneration neither in their physical nor intellectual stature. It was because they had chosen to devote all their energies to improving the land, he said, that the Americans had given the false impression of intellectual stagnation. The rest of the passage is worth quoting:

"For this unjust prejudice to be dissipated, we had to wait

[54] *Supplément à l'Histoire naturelle* (Paris: Imprimerie Royale, 1777), IV, 530-531.
[55] *Works of Thomas Jefferson*, ed. W. C. Ford (New York, 1904), III, 458.

*65*

until a Franklin taught the physicists of our astounded continent how to master the thunderbolt, until the disciples of that illustrious man, organized into a society, cast a brilliant light upon several branches of natural science, until eloquence created in that part of the New World once more those strong and vivid effects which it wrought in the proudest republics of antiquity, until the rights of man and the rights of nations were firmly established by new documents which are to be the charm and consolation of far-off ages. Works of imagination and taste will not be long in following those of reason and observation. Soon perhaps New England will be able to point to her Homer, her Theocritus, and her Sophocles. There is no lack of encouragement, of masters, or of models. Education is being expanded and improved continually. In proportion one finds in the United States more men of breeding, more leisure, and more opportunity for the individual to develop his talents than exist in Europe, where so often the training of our youth is contrary to the development and progress of intelligence and reason. By a strange contrast with the Old World, where the arts spread from the south to the north, we shall see in the New World the north enlighten the south."[56]

Raynal also reversed himself by deprecating Linguet's fears of the American colossus, writing, "Some go so far as to fear that Europe may some day find her masters in her children. Let us dare to resist this flood of opinion."[57]

Such refutations multiplied. In the *Dictionnaire universel* the article "Amérique" took issue with De Pauw and Raynal on the inferiority of the Indians, and the article "Climat" contained an important denial of the idea that climate was the sole factor determining man's intellectual and physical nature. Hilliard d'Auberteuil denied Raynal's earlier pessimistic prognostications on the probable limited growth of American population.

So, while the pessimistic current, which condemned Americans to intellectual inferiority and at the same time feared

[56] *Histoire philosophique et politique* (Geneva, 1781), IX, 109.
[57] *Ibid.*, IX, 234.

American military and economic power, still persisted to a degree, it was Americanism which dominated French opinion and determined the course of events.

In analyzing the French image of American society, we must remember that there always exist strata of opinion. On a lower level exists the body of popular or public opinion composed of clichés, normally unexamined and vague in content and without any necessary consistency. On a higher level are the individual opinions of the intelligent leaders whose ideas are more definite and individualized and tend to form a consistent system. Such a stratification existed in France at this period when Americanism was both popular and intellectual. But the two levels interacted, and the general tendency of eighteenth-century thought to rationalistic simplification made popular diffusion and acceptance of upper-stratum concepts particularly easy.

The Americanism of the war years was composed of four dominant ideas: Liberty, Virtue, Prosperity, and Enlightenment. It is indicative of the continuing influence of the earlier Americanism of the Physiocrats and Rousseauists that these were the same four themes which they too had stressed. They formed for the eighteenth-century mind a naturally unified logical system. There existed a tendency to regard man as psychologically indivisible and to treat his various activities—political, moral, economic, spiritual, emotional, and intellectual—as merely so many phases of an essential unity. The idea of progress made the basic assumption that man advanced toward intellectual, moral, economic, and political perfection in simultaneous and interdependent processes. Therefore American political achievements necessarily implied parallel moral, economic, and intellectual progression. No one could have better substantiated such an assumption than did Franklin, who was at once a scientist, a moralist, and a politician, and who constantly preached the gospel of American prosperity and progress.

The idea of American liberty at first meant to the French merely the political independence of the colonies from England, and their support was at once an expression of Anglo-

phobia and a generous admiration for a small nation asserting its national integrity. It was a political, chauvinist, and
militaristic sentiment, which frequently motivated political
propaganda such as Beaumarchais' *Voeu de toutes les nations*
(1778).[58] The same feeling found expression in Hornot's
*Anecdotes américaines* and in popular songs and poems, as
when Dorat wrote in his "Aux Insurgents":

> Bravo, messieurs les Insurgents!
> Vainqueurs dans une juste guerre,
> Fiers de ravir à vos tyrants
> Les palmes de votre hémisphère,
> Vous donnez par vos sentiments
> Un peuple de plus à la terre.[59]

This was the kind of admiration which, in part at least, inspired the French volunteers of 1776 and 1777. Such French
support of American independence was reinforced by similar
sentiment elsewhere on the Continent, particularly in Holland, and even by English sympathizers whose arguments in
favor of American independence were occasionally translated into French.

But this championship of American liberty in the limited
sense of national independence soon broadened into a championship of the rights and liberties of man, into the philosophic idealization of America as a land of freedom, equality,

---

[58] See also N. Vincent, *Lettres d'un membre du Congrès amériquain* (Philadelphia [Paris], 1779), republished as *L'Amériquain aux Anglois* (Philadelphia
[Paris], 1780); A. M. Cerisier, *Le Destin de l'Amérique* (London, 1780); *Les
Bigarures d'un citoyen de Genève* (Philadelphia [Paris?], 1776); *Observations
d'un homme impartial* (London, 1776); *Quelques observations sur la seconde
lettre de M. Pinto* (1776); *Lettres de M. R ―――― Esq. au Lord Comte de D.*
(Amsterdam, 1779); *Pamphlet programatique* (Geneva, 1780).

[59] "Bravo, Insurgents! Victors in a just war, proud of having snatched from
your tyrants the palms of your hemisphere, by your greatness a new people
is added to the world." Quoted in Evariste de Parny, *Oeuvres*, ed. A. J. Pons
(Paris, 1861), p. 343. See also "Description des colonies anglaises," *Courier
de l'Europe*, Sept. 26—Nov. 14, 1777; "Le Chardonneret en liberté" and "Le
Chardonneret et l'aigle," two fables attributed to the Duke de Nivernais,
*Correspondance par Grimm, Diderot. . .*, XIII, 171, 253 (July 1782 and Jan.
1783); "Proclamation du général Burgogne," Métra, *op.cit.*, v, 388-392 (Jan.
15, 1778); "La Princesse Treize-Etats et la Princesse Albion," *Courier de
l'Europe*, Mar. 27, 1778; *L'Amériquiade, poème* (Philadelphia [Amsterdam?],
1780).

and toleration. Or, better said, the two concepts became inextricably and fatally confused. Turgot, it will be recalled, wrote to Dr. Richard Price in 1778, praising his defense of American liberty and saying, "It is impossible not to hope that this people may attain the prosperity of which they are susceptible. They are the hope of the human race; they may well become its model."[60] The anonymous *Pamphlet programatique* defended the American right to independence on the ground that England had broken the social contract. Brissot in 1783 described the United States as a union of democracies founded on the principle that all power emanates from the people.[61] Diderot called the new republic "an asylum for all the peoples of Europe from fanaticism and tyranny."[62] Parny wrote

> Quel droit avez-vous plus que nous
> A cette liberté chérie
> Dont vous paraissez si jaloux?
> L'inexorable Tyrannie
> Parcourt le docile univers;
> Ce monstre sous des noms divers
> Ecrase l'Europe asservie;
> Et vous, peuple injuste et mutin,
> Sans Pape, sans rois et sans reines,
> Vous danseriez au bruit des chaînes
> Qui pèsent sur le genre humain![63]

Raynal in his *Révolution de l'Amérique* was an authentic subversive when he argued from the concept of popular sov-

---

[60] "Lettre à Price," in Honoré Gabriel Riquetti, Comte de Mirabeau, *Considérations sur l'Ordre de Cincinnatus* (London, 1784), pp. 199-200.

[61] *Le Philadelphien à Genève* (Dublin, 1783), p. 46.

[62] "Essai sur les règnes de Claude et de Néron," *Oeuvres*, ed. Assézat and Tourneux (Paris, 1875-1877), III, 324.

[63] "What right have you more than we to that precious liberty of which you seem so jealous? Inexorable Tyranny sweeps through the unresisting universe. That monster under a multitude of different names crushes an enslaved Europe. Would you, unfair and unruly people, Pope-less, king-less and queen-less, would you dance amidst the clanking of the chains that weigh down the rest of the human race!" *Oeuvres* (Paris, 1861), p. 345. This poem also appeared in Bachaumont, *op.cit.*, x, Oct. 15, 1777; in the *Recueil Clairambault-Maurepas*, IX, 134-135; and in Métra, *op.cit.*, v, 187-189 (Sept. 27, 1777).

*69*

ereignty to the right of revolution and asserted that "there is no form of government whose prerogative is to be immutable."[64] He urged the Americans to found their liberty on constitutionalism, union, freedom of conscience, and the education of the people.[65] Joseph Mandrillon saw the spirit of tolerance as the basis of the American political system, and he emphasized the Americans' political maturity. He called American independence one of the great events of the century, and, like Condorcet, he saw it as the precursor of a more just world order.[66] The Abbé Gabriel Brizard declared in his *Fragment de Xénophon* that a golden age in very fact reigned in America, and he represented the United States as an asylum in which all the oppressed of Europe might escape tyranny and injustice and find liberty, "that idol of all mankind."[67]

Thus, early in the war, American liberty came to signify to most Frenchmen not merely an overthrow of British political and economic control, but a revolt of an entire people against the tyranny of absolute power, a mass assertion of the inalienable rights of man. This interpretation of the American Revolution as a social rather than a political revolution was a preparation for eventual French disillusion and bitterness; it was caused partly by the myth, originated by Penn, Locke, and Voltaire, of America as a libertarian utopia, but it was produced mainly by American political documents. The many pamphlets, constitutions, and bills of rights protesting against English interference and reaffirming already established and familiar rights and privileges sounded in French ears like the most radical and revolutionary utterances. For instance, a declaration of religious freedom in a bill of rights was no more an act of social revolution in Pennsylvania in 1776 than it would be today. But the same document, translated and published in Paris in 1777, was highly revolutionary. Most of all, this French misinterpretation of the

[64] *Révolution de l'Amérique* (London, 1781), p. 37.
[65] *Histoire philosophique et politique* (Geneva, 1781), IX, 238.
[66] *Le Voyageur américain, augmenté d'un précis sur l'Amérique Septentrionale* (Amsterdam, 1782), pp. 32-34, 64-67.
[67] *Fragment de Xénophon* (Paris, 1783), p. 16.

American Revolution was due to the fact that the French liberals, themselves working toward a social revolution, were too eager to see in America a harbinger of their own immediate triumph.

Consequently, the extensive publication in France of translations of American political literature constituted a historical event of considerable importance. The items were various in nature and included the writings of Dickinson, Paine, Franklin, and other American leaders, the many resolutions and acts of Congress and the state legislatures, and frequent reprints from American newspapers. The key documents, however, were the American constitutions. One of the early drafts of the Articles of Confederation was published, probably by Franklin, in Paris in December 1776, and early in 1777 the *Affaires de l'Angleterre et de l'Amérique* began the publication of the Articles of Confederation, the Declaration of Independence, and the constitutions and bills of rights of Delaware, Maryland, New Jersey, New York, Pennsylvania, South Carolina, and Virginia. All of these, with the exception of the constitution of New York, were reprinted, accompanied by notes which explained such matters as the writ of habeas corpus and the jury system, in a collection entitled *Recueil des lois constitutives des colonies anglaises* (1778). Later, in 1783, La Rochefoucauld and Franklin published the *Constitutions des treize Etats-Unis de l'Amérique*, which contained the bills of rights and constitutions or colonial charters of all the states, the Declaration of Independence, and the Articles of Confederation.[68] Moreover, the newspapers were extremely active in this work of propaganda, printing translations of the Declaration of Independence, the Articles of Confederation, and many of the state bills of rights and constitutions. Hilliard d'Auberteuil gave further diffusion to the documents published by the *Affaires* by republishing them in full or in summary form in his *Essais historiques et politiques*.[69]

[68] See G. Chinard, "Notes on the French Translations of the 'Forms of Government or Constitutions of the Several United States' 1778 and 1783," *Year Book of the Amer. Philos. Soc., 1943*, pp. 88-106.

[69] John Lind's *Réponse à la Déclaration du congrès américain* (1777) also

There is plenty of evidence that these documents were studied with intense interest in France, and they were to form the basis of the Abbé Mably's famous *Observations sur le gouvernement et les lois des Etats-Unis d'Amérique* (1784). As Regnier, the editor of the *Recueil des lois constitutives*, said, they could not fail to be of interest to every thinking man. "These laws," he wrote, "seem to me the finest monuments of human wisdom. They constitute the purest democracy which has ever existed; they already appear to be achieving the happiness of the people who have adopted them, and they will forever constitute the glory of the virtuous men who conceived them."[70] Thus American liberty was no vague slogan, but had a very definite, specific content—representative democratic government, religious toleration, trial by jury, freedom of speech, and freedom of the press. Through these translations, through Franklin, and through the Lodge of the Nine Sisters, which was more a political than a fraternal body, America became identified in France directly with democracy and constitutionalism.

The image of America also had a moral content. We have seen how before 1776 the Rousseauists and Physiocrats had pictured America as an egalitarian, rural, agricultural society in which men lived a bucolic life of simplicity, felicity, and virtue. During the war this part of the picture naturally had less appeal, but it still formed an important part of the total image. Mandrillon wrote, "There reigns so great a degree of order, decency and tranquility in Boston, Philadelphia, Charleston, Saint Augustine, etc. that there is no man who in all these respects would not prefer to live in these cities rather than in the best regulated city of the Old World."[71] "The golden age sung by the poets," the Abbé Brizard said,

---

contained a translation of the Declaration of Independence. Most of the editions of Franklin's *Science du Bonhomme Richard* of the years 1777-1783 included a translation of the constitution of Pennsylvania. On all these publications, see my "French Publications of the Declaration of Independence and the American Constitutions, 1776-1783," *Papers of the Bibliographical Society of America*, XLVII (1953), 313-338.

[70] *Recueil des loix constitutives* (Philadelphia [Paris], 1778).

[71] *Op.cit.*, p. 33.

"seems to be realized in that happy land. Dissension and war, which ruled the rest of the world, have respected those climes defended by the immensity of the seas and by the innocent lives of the inhabitants."[72]

A new idea, however, was now added to the earlier simpler image, namely, that both American liberty and virtue were the product of an equal distribution of property and the absence of *luxe*. Hilliard d'Auberteuil wrote in support of this egalitarian thesis, "In general the inhabitants of these colonies lived in happiness and innocence, occupied with farming, hunting and fishing, and the tranquil pleasures of rustic life."[73] But he warned that the changes brought by war and the introduction of wealth might destroy this virtue and felicity. In a very important passage Diderot likewise expressed the idea that American liberty and virtue were the product of this simple, modest, egalitarian life, and he warned Americans to guard their shores against the increase and unequal distribution of wealth, which would bring luxury, corruption of manners, ambition, and the eventual destruction of their freedom.[74] Raynal saw the American political system as a product of the morals of the people, and he wrote of Pennsylvania, "Never perhaps had virtue inspired legislation better designed to bring happiness to man. The opinions, sentiments and customs of the people corrected whatever might be defective and supplemented whatever was imperfect."[75] But he too warned Americans to profit by the example of Europe. "Fear the influence of gold, which brings luxury, corruption of morals and contempt for the law; fear a too unequal distribution of riches, which gives wealth to a few and leaves a multitude of citizens in poverty. . . . Seek well-being and health in labor; prosperity in the cultivation of the soil and the shops of industry; strength in morality and virtue."[76] The influence of both Rousseau and Montesquieu in this phase of the American image is obvious.

[72] *Op.cit.*, p. 16.
[73] *Essais historiques et politiques sur les Anglo-Américains* (Brussels, 1781-1782), I, 53.
[74] *Oeuvres*, III, 324-325.  [75] *Op.cit.*, IX, 13.   [76] *Ibid.*, IX, 237-238.

The third element in the picture was that of dynamic prosperity. Franklin's estimate that the population was doubling every twenty-five years had made a great impression, and the Physiocrats had preached American prosperity in order to prove the soundness of a free agricultural economy. Burke's *Account of the European Settlements in North America,* Cluny's *American Traveler,* and other English works, read both in the original and in translation, furnished additional convincing evidence. In substance, of course, these reports were true, for the standard of living of the American farmer was much higher than that of the French peasant, but they were the more readily accepted because the *Philosophes* took for granted that enlightened legislation would produce economic prosperity. Dubuisson, whose *Abrégé de la révolution de l'Amérique anglaise* expressed an unreserved and uncritical admiration for all things American, gave special emphasis to this concept of a dynamic, expanding America. The anonymous *Histoire de la guerre d'Amérique* (1783) presented a vision of America's future growth, wealth, and maritime power. Brizard told of a rich land which repaid a hundredfold the labors of the settlers. Hilliard d'Auberteuil denied some statements which Raynal had made on the lack of fertile lands and the impossibility of a large population, and reasserted the Physiocratic arguments in favor of an agricultural economy. A "Description des colonies anglaises," published in the *Courier de l'Europe,* reported of the Americans, "One has no idea of the abundance in which the least wealthy live, nor of the comforts, and even luxury, with which their houses are furnished."[77] In fact nearly every work on the United States contributed in some degree to this image of a prosperous, energetic, and expanding civilization. Diderot's warnings against excessive wealth and Linguet's against the danger of American economic power were reflections of this common impression. The popular currency of the idea was aptly illustrated by a book of burlesque prophecies entitled *Paul Jones, ou Prophéties sur l'Amérique, l'Angleterre, la*

[77] Sept. 23, 1777.

*France, l'Espagne, la Hollande, etc.*, in which the seer predicted for the United States, "Thou shalt have gold and diamonds and rubies, even as a laden Devil. . . . All the kings shall seek thine alliance; the princes shall be thy nurses, and the princesses, their wives, thy nursemaids. All the peoples shall lick the dust from thy feet. . . . There shall be no end to the growth of thine empire and of thy prosperity. . . . Thy teeth are like the teeth of the elephants. . . . Thy navel is like the dome of the Invalides."[78]

One of the most remarkable things in practically all of the French literature on America of these years was the insistence that was placed on American scientific, artistic, and educational achievements and on the enlightenment of the American mind. This emphasis was simply a necessary consequence of one of the prime articles of philosophic faith of the latter half of the century: man's ability through natural reason and experience to attain material well-being and freedom from oppression and superstition, and hence virtue and happiness. If Americans were prosperous, free, tolerant, and virtuous, they must of necessity be enlightened. The examples of Franklin and Philadelphia were generalized to apply to the whole nation, and the intellectual stature of the American leaders whom the French knew—men like Jefferson, Paine, Dickinson, John Adams, and Washington—made it indeed seem that here at last was realized Plato's republic of philosophers. "The beaux arts and sciences," Dubuisson wrote "more intimately linked with the political destinies of empire than is commonly realized, prepare and produce revolutions. A sufficient enlightenment, when diffused in countries formerly covered with the veil of ignorance, teaches to the inhabitants their inherent power. Knowledge, after having made a people think for themselves, instills in them the courage to act for themselves." This, he believed, was the explanation for the American Revolution and the reason that Philadelphia, which with its college and Philosophical Society was the American city in which the sciences had made

[78] *Paul Jones, ou Prophéties sur l'Amérique* (Basle, 1781), pp. 18-21, 41.

the greatest progress, had become the birthplace of revolution and an asylum of liberty.[79]

There was implicit in this idealization of the American enlightenment a new idea produced by the effort for synthesis which characterized these years of the Age of Reason. When Mandrillon told his European readers to cease regarding America as a savage wilderness and said, "You must realize that civilization there has attained the same degree of perfection as in Europe, and that perhaps it will surpass yours and force from you admiration and wonder," he was in effect saying that the assumption that the arts and sciences could flourish only in an aristocratic and urban society was false and that Rousseau had been right in stating that "the human mind conceives and ferments better in tranquil solitude."[80] The danger that the Americans faced was not ignorance but the luxury and corruption which, as Rousseau had warned, had hitherto seemed the inevitable products of the arts and sciences. It was precisely here, however, that Americans offered the great hope, for they seemed to be giving the lie to Rousseau's First Discourse by proving that enlightenment could be united to simple rustic virtue. "We must hope," Mandrillon wrote, "that the Americans, in general wiser than we, will profit by their knowledge and our examples to avoid the vices of our constitutions, laws, and societies."[81] Like their prototype Franklin, they would succeed in uniting Voltaire's enlightened philosopher and Rousseau's man of virtue.

One of the most interesting interpretations of American culture—also given, as we shall see, by Chastellux and apparently fairly common—was what might be called the Greek-colony concept of America. According to this idea, America was not to be a new and different civilization, a Rome to Europe's Greece, but rather a second Syracuse, a Salente, a colonial transplantation and extension of European culture. This theory was most effectively propounded by the

[79] Paul Ulrich Dubuisson, *Abrégé de la révolution de l'Amérique anglaise* (Paris, 1778), pp. 58-59.
[80] *Lettre à d'Alembert.*                    [81] *Op.cit.*, pp. 34, 66-67.

Abbé Brizard in his *Fragment de Xénophon*. Employing the fiction of a newly discovered Greek manuscript, he described the new American republic under the guise of a Greek colony of ancient times in which had reigned a golden age of liberty, plenty, virtue, and peace, which in its arts and sciences as well as in its population and commerce had become the rival of Greece itself, and which was a sort of sublimation of all the best in Greek civilization. It was with this same idea in mind that Louis Mercier wrote in *De la littérature* (1778). "It is perhaps in America that the human race is to be re-created; that it is to adopt a new and sublime legislation, that it is to perfect the arts and sciences, that it is to recreate the nations of antiquity. America is the asylum of liberty in which Grecian souls, strong and noble souls, will rise up, or to which they will migrate, and this great example granted to the universe will prove what Man can do when he adds to knowledge a courageous heart."[82]

All these examples are so many indications of the prevalence of this faith in the American enlightenment, but as usual it was Raynal who gave the widest currency to the idea. Converted from the theory of American degeneration, he now, as we have seen, staunchly championed the intellectual capacity of Americans, praised their scientific contributions, and asserted his faith in their ability to produce works of artistic merit. America, he said, enlightened by reason and liberated from superstition and intolerance, would be the only nation in the world free from cant and scholasticism.[83]

Thus by 1783 there had emerged three fundamental interpretations of the westward expansion of European civilization into the new frontier environment of America: one, that of De Pauw, that it constituted a moral and cultural degeneration and debilitation; the second, that of Linguet, that it was a cancerous and monstrous outgrowth threatening the life of the European mother-body; and the third, temporarily raised to dominance by the war and the libertarian

[82] Louis Sébastien Mercier, *De la littérature et des littérateurs* (Yverdon, 1778), p. 19.
[83] *Op.cit.*, IX, 26.

movement, that this western expansion was the most vigorous and advanced manifestation of western man's accelerating drive to an enlightened and just social order.

The oversimplification of all these interpretations produced a gross distortion of the image. In spite of the greatly increased flow of information on America into France, the supply of facts was by far inadequate to give a balanced picture or to support the top-heavy superstructures of hypothesis. Moreover, the reporting of the facts was inaccurate because of the carelessness, inexperience, and ignorance of the reporters.

The main cause of distortion, however, was that the image was a reflection not of reality but of domestic preoccupations. The basic problem in France in the 1770's and 1780's was the urgent need for the reorganization of an antiquated and inefficient social and political order. The impression, which both fate and Franklin fostered, that America had achieved a social revolution along the very same lines that the French liberal reformers were advocating for France quite naturally produced an irresistible urge to magnify and misinterpret the success of the American Revolution. America was for the French "the hope of the human race" because she furnished the chance to prove for all time the idea of progress: that man, once granted the free use of his enlightened reason, could not fail to create a golden age of prosperity, justice, and happiness.

# CHAPTER III

## FRENCHMEN IN AMERICA,
### 1776-1783

WHEN the Marquis de Lafayette stepped ashore early in June 1777 near Charleston, South Carolina, his arrival symbolized the opening of a new and very different chapter in French-American relations. For the first time Frenchmen in significant numbers were able to observe American life at first hand. Out of this experience was to come an image necessarily different from the philosophic construction being elaborated in Paris. To drop from Voltaire's Golden Age, from Beaurieu's Arcadia, from the utopia of liberty and enlightenment to the sufferings of Valley Forge, to the headaches and heartaches of fighting a war with inferior forces, inferior equipment, and no money—this was a descent from one planet to another.

The image came to be backed by the substance of experience, and at the same time it lost its facile homogeneity. Public opinion based on hearsay tends to develop in broadly accepted patterns, and the Americanists in Paris were all repeating pretty much the same set of ideas. On the other hand, eyewitnesses seldom agree, and the testimonies of these first French visitors to America were various and individual, depending on the circumstances of the visit and the personality of the observer. No doubt these men influenced each other's reactions to some extent, but what we find in their writings is not a true group opinion, but simply a heterogeneous collection of private impressions.

A certain distinction, however, can be made. The French visitor could assume either one of two positions in observing American life—that of a philosopher or that of a Frenchman. The two were not identical. Nearly all the French officers were to a degree conscious of the ideas of their time—of such notions as Physiocracy, Rousseauist egalitarianism, and Voltairian liberty and toleration. A handful, in fact, were professional *Philosophes*. But even the least intellectual would occasionally interpret American life philosophically, holding the observed reality up against ideal patterns. Economic conditions were discussed in Physiocratic terms, New England equality in Rousseauan terms, and Philadelphian toleration in Voltairian terms. Like the intellectual Marxists a century and a half later journeying to Moscow, these men came to Boston and Philadelphia to compare fact with theory and to render judgment. Approval or disapproval depended on how well the Americans lived up to the French preconceptions.

At the same time, few of these young officers were true intellectuals, and even those who were did not always react intellectually. They were first of all Frenchmen, and they were apt to behave as men brought up in a special and unique milieu would be expected to behave when suddenly thrust into an alien environment. Their instinct was to judge American life by the same standards they were used to applying at home, and they were most acutely conscious of those American customs which most differed from the French. Consequently, American society was evaluated both absolutely against philosophic doctrines and relatively against French practices. When a Rhode Island farmer caught the Baron de Vioménil hunting on his land and threatened to hit him over the head with a stick, the incident could be interpreted either as a proof of a truly egalitarian society or it could be resented, as it was by one peevish young aristocrat, the Viscount de Tressan, as an unspeakable outrage.

Contemporary observers say that in Paris enthusiasm for the American cause was strongest among the young men of the aristocracy and the army. Barbeu Dubourg and Beaumarchais recruited some officers even before the coming of the American envoys, and soon after Silas Deane's arrival in June 1776 the younger officers rushed to volunteer for service in the American army. There is no evidence that they were motivated to any great extent by a disinterested or idealistic devotion to the cause of liberty. As young men they cared more about mistresses than metaphysics; the ideas of the *Philosophes* had in most cases made only a superficial impression on them. As professional soldiers bored with garrison duty, they eagerly grasped at the chance for a real fight and some easy glory. Adventurers all, they were lovers of action, not of ideas. They had only the vaguest of notions of what they would find in America. Individual motives varied, but in general they were impelled by the spirit of adventure, the desire for glory and rank in the American army, the chance for advancement in their careers, the prospect of an active campaign, and the opportunity for revenge against England. Lafayette himself was perhaps at the first not wholly prompted by the love of liberty.[1] No doubt Stephen Du Ponceau, Von Steuben's aide-de-camp, was typical. Years later he confessed: "I shall not set up the vain pretension of having come to this country for the sake of freedom, or of a republican government. I was, it is true, a friend of liberty and hated despotism, but that was not my predominate passion at the time. My most anxious desire was that of traveling . . . and to make the confession complete, I must add that the glitter of military service did not contribute a little to confirm my resolution. . . . All that I knew in fact, on my arrival in this country, respecting the United States, and other parts of this continent, is what is contained in the Abbé Raynal's history of the European Colonies, which I read with Baron Steuben on board the ship which brought us from Marseilles."[2]

A few of the volunteers joined the Americans in 1776, but the majority arrived the following year. The famous group on the *Victoire*, led by Lafayette and including De Kalb, Dubuysson, Du Rousseau, and others, landed in Charleston and painfully made their way north on horseback and afoot to Philadelphia, where they arrived on July 27. Early that

[1] See L. Gottschalk, *Lafayette Comes to America* (Chicago, 1935), Appendix ix; and, "The Attitude of European Officers in the Revolutionary Army toward George Washington," *Journal, Illinois State Hist. Soc.*, xxxii (1939), 20-50.

[2] "Autobiography," *Penna. Mag. of Hist. and Biog.*, lxiii (1939), 446-449.

spring a considerable number had arrived in Portsmouth on board Beaumarchais' ships the *Amphitrite* and the *Mercure*. A smaller but important group were Gouvion, La Radière, Laumoy, and Duportail, the engineering officers engaged by Franklin. Others, like Du Coudray, traveled separately. All of these men converged on the Congress in Philadelphia in the summer of 1777, expecting to be welcomed as saviors and insisting on commissions as senior officers. They had been deceived by Beaumarchais' enthusiasm, Deane's facile promises, Franklin's reluctant recommendations, and their own overweening ambitions. There simply were not commissions available, especially at the ranks they expected, for such a number; besides, many of them spoke English imperfectly or not at all, and a number, as it turned out, were temperamentally unsuited to duty under the conditions existing in the American army. The harassed delegates to Congress, their tempers worn thin by the seemingly endless stream of would-be generals, were much less cordial than the French had expected. Many of the volunteers had to return home ignominiously without commissions and without, they claimed, proper appreciation and compensation. Others, however, like Lafayette, obtained what they had expected and made valuable contributions in leadership and technical advice.

So the volunteers were divided into two groups: the accepted and the rejected. Naturally the latter were mostly embittered and their comments were often critical and even hostile. The reports they made after returning to France could have been prejudicial to the efforts of Franklin, and Washington later said that one of Lafayette's greatest contributions was his neutralization of the influence of these disappointed men. What really neutralized them, however, was, as we have seen, the torrent of pro-American sentiment in Paris; there is no evidence that their scattered voices of disillusion had much effect on current popular opinion.

It would be unfair, however, to ascribe their bitterness only to frustrated ambition, for the accepted volunteers were often equally critical at first. Only gradually did the months of common hardships and common achievements produce sympathy, the acceptance of American values, and a devotion to the cause of liberty.

To understand fully the volunteers' reactions to America we must remember the prejudices they encountered. Until 1763 the French and their Indian allies had been, throughout a succession of cruel and bitter wars, the enemies of the American colonists; so deep-rooted a hostility could not disappear overnight. When Du Ponceau arrived in Boston he was introduced to Samuel Adams, to whom he promptly expressed his devotion to republican principles.

"Where did you learn all that?" Adams asked him.

"In France," replied Du Ponceau.

"In France!" snorted Adams. "That's impossible." Then, after a moment's consideration, he added, "Well, because a man was born in a stable, it is no reason why he should be a horse."[3]

Du Ponceau soon learned "that an Englishman could beat three Frenchmen; that the French were a poor, meager, puny, little, dark-colored and almost dwarfish nation; that they fed on *soupe maigre* and frogs; that they wore wooden shoes and ruffles without shirts, to which popery and slavery being added the French nation was represented as sufficiently contemptible. . . . I was often complimented," he said, "with the observation that I did not look like a Frenchman."[4] Even in 1779, as one Frenchman observed, the French were "more liked than esteemed."[5]

Most of the French complaints and censures were directed against the welcome received, the Americans' political and military ineptitude, and the popular apathy toward the war. Du Rousseau, one of the bitterest of the rejected volunteers, complained that Congress' reception had been as discourteous as it could possibly be. All the Americans, he said, were most unobliging, and he and his companions had been able to

[3] *Ibid.*, LXIII, 201.

[4] *Ibid.*, LXIV (1940), 266. See also Charles Albert, Comte de Moré, *Mémoires* (Paris, 1898), p. 68.

[5] J. Durand, *New Materials for the History of the American Revolution* (New York, 1889), p. 18.

get help only by paying for it in hard cash. The situation was the opposite of what he had been told in France, and he saw little chance for an American victory. The people were disunited, the army disorganized and undisciplined, the leaders ignorant, vain, and ambitious. "One thing is certain," he concluded. "I have no desire to fight for their liberty, since all an honest man has to gain here is dishonor or death."[6] In a similar vein Du Portail, one of the officers who organized the American army engineers, wrote Saint Germain, Minister of War, that the Americans were a soft, unenergetic people, used to spending "a large part of their time smoking and drinking tea or spirituous liquors," and that "the sudden change from an effeminate life to that of a warrior, which is hard and painful, made them prefer the yoke of the English to a liberty bought at the expense of life's amenities. . . . There is a hundred times more enthusiasm for this revolution in any café in Paris," he concluded, "than there is in all the United States together."[7] The Baron de Kalb told his wife in disgust, "It is impossible to habituate the people of this country to anything like order or regularity of living, and equally impossible for one who has grown up in the midst of order, discipline and punctuality to accustom himself to the indolence of these people. . . . These annoyances are aggravated by the mortifications growing out of the differences in manners and customs between Americans and Europeans, and the jealousy of the native against the foreign officers. Scarce one of the latter is contented with his position."[8]

One of the returning volunteers wrote a clever poem circulated widely in Paris in which he blamed the Abbé Raynal

[6] Pierre Du Rousseau de Fayolle, "Journal d'une campagne en Amérique," Société des antiquaires de l'ouest. Bulletin et mémoires, série 2, xxv, année 1901 (Poitiers, 1902), pp. 8-10.

[7] Quoted in C. Stedman, The History of the Origin, Progress, and Termination of the American War (Dublin, 1794), I, 432-433.

[8] F. Kapp, Life of John Kalb (New York, 1870), pp. 165-166. See also a letter of Pierre L'Enfant printed in the Royal Gazette, New York, June 3, 1778; also "Letters of Colonel Armand," N.Y. Hist. Soc. Collections, series II, 1879, p. 300.

for the foolish enthusiasm which had misled him to America. Some of the stanzas went

> De ce peuple encore dans l'enfance,
> J'ai vu les asiles divers:
> Son orgueil, son indépendance
> Préparent sourdement ses fers.
>
> Il est sobre par indolence,
> A peine l'on peut l'émouvoir,
> Et la liberté qu'il encense
> N'est que la haine du devoir.
>
> J'ai vu le Quaker pacifique,
> Dont l'orgueil perçait le manteau,
> J'ai vu l'insolence cynique
> Qui fixe son vaste chapeau.[9]

These young officers were often baffled and even disgusted by American manners. One of them complained, "Here a woman will kiss you all day; will do a thousand foolish things with you—crush your foot, make your arm black and blue by dint of pinching you while walking with you, and will give you a couple of slaps. . . . You are often no further advanced with them for all that." At Easton he attended a dance where he learned that "the polite usage of the country is to take the lady's handkerchief to wipe your face and return it to her." His attentions to the colonel's lady, he complained, were thwarted by a rival, a great hulk of a man who sang through his nose like a grenadier and danced barefoot in a pair of greasy leathern breeches.[10] To many of these young aristocrats, Americans seemed a nation of ignoble shopkeepers and one reported from Boston, "Republicans

---

[9] "I have seen the various abodes of this infant people; their pride and their independence are secretly forging their fetters. They are temperate only through apathy; scarcely anything can stir them. The liberty they adore is nothing but their hatred of their duty. I have seen the pacific Quaker, whose pride shines through his cloak, and I have witnessed the cynical insolence of his broad hat." Louis de Bachaumont, *Mémoires secrets* (London, 1777-1788), XIV, 302.

[10] "Letters of a French Officer, Written at Easton, Pennsylvania, in 1777-1778," *Penna. Mag. of Hist. and Biog.*, XXXV (1911), 95-97.

here, like the Carthaginians, know to a penny the value of life and liberty."[11]

Aristide du Petit-Thouars, a naval officer who spent some time in Virginia after France had entered the war, reported that the volunteers (of whom he said nine out of ten had come to the United States solely in search of money and advancement) generally did not like the Americans, accused them of being a pack of Tories, and rebelled at fighting by the side of tradesmen and mechanics. He said these volunteers ridiculed whatever manners and customs they found different from their own and that they were always trying to seduce American wives and daughters. "These ambitious men," he concluded, "showed not the slightest moderation in their pretensions, and their excessive conceit revolted every one."[12]

Whatever were the faults of the volunteers, probably the basic cause of the difficulties was the differences between the American and the European mind. Baron von Steuben wrote to a friend, "The genius of this nation is not in the least to be compared with that of the Prussians, Austrians, or French. You say to your soldier, 'Do this,' and he does it; but I am obliged to say, 'This is the reason why you ought to do that'; and then he does it."[13] Lafayette himself was well aware of the incompatibilities. He once wrote to D'Estaing that this was "a country where they do not laugh so much as in our own," and he warned Vergennes, apropos of Rochambeau's army, "We must have officers who know how to endure boredom, live on little, permit themselves no airs, and especially no quick, cutting ways of speaking, be able for a year to go without the pleasures, the women and the letters of Paris; then we must take very few colonels and gentlemen of the Court, whose ways are not at all American."[14]

The unfavorable reactions, however, were counteracted, even from the first moment, by a disposition on the part

[11] Durand, op.cit., pp. 18, 20-21.
[12] Mémoires et voyages (Paris, 1822), I, 261, 264-265.
[13] Steuben MSS, New York Historical Society.
[14] Brand Whitlock, Lafayette (New York, 1929), p. 196.

of many officers to like and admire Americans. One young man, who came without intention of volunteering and who may have been sent as an observer by the French government, wrote a lengthy account of his impressions. He complained about the American sabbath, when "No one, high or low, may laugh or dance or sing or play any game, even after the divine service," though this did not keep the good citizens from flocking to the taverns outside the city to get sedately and gravely drunk. Moreover, like many of his compatriots, he was disillusioned by the Quakers, even though he had been, as he said, "a warmer partisan of Quakerism than any other Frenchman. . . . They are (I shall not say all, but most of them at the present time) the hardest, the deafest, the most ungrateful people, once it is a matter of anything but the good of their own sect." His total impression, however, was most favorable. He was struck by the beauty and fertility of the land, the prosperity of the citizens, and the handsome appearance of Charleston and Philadelphia. Americans were "generous, brusque, sincere, frugal, energetic, and whatever anybody may say, a very likeable people to anyone who looks at them without French prejudices, or who can lay aside his own prejudices in order not to offend theirs." Their interest in trade "does not prevent there being among them excellent men of letters, learned chemists, great mathematicians, etc., though in less numbers than in France, but still enough so that one can say that this country is not, in proportion, inferior either in wealth or worth or learning to either France or England." Moreover Americans were the only persons who understood and practiced true patriotism, putting devotion to the public interest above private gain. For the military qualities of the American soldiers and their leaders he had great respect and he was confident of American victory.[15]

[15] Anonymous ms, *Un Voyage en Amérique au temps de la guerre de l'indépendance*, dated April 1778, Bibliothèque Nationale, Paris, F.F. 14695. The first pages of this account were published in the *Revue du dix-huitième siècle*, année V (1918), 52-73. It appears to have been written by the author of the military report entitled "Quelques observations sur l'ensemble des Etats-Unis de l'Amérique," also dated April 1778, Archives de la Guerre, no.

The case of Lafayette is too well known to require more than passing comment. He arrived prepared to admire everything he saw, and immediately after he landed he wrote his wife, "The manners of these people are simple, virtuous and in every way worthy of the country where all things echo to the beautiful name of liberty."[16] Four days later he wrote from Charleston a long, rhapsodical letter celebrating the "sweet equality" of this land where all men were brothers, where there were no poor and all enjoyed equal rights, where love of country and love of liberty reigned, and where he had been received with a simplicity and courtesy which delighted him.[17]

Lafayette's case was paralleled by others. De Lisle, another young volunteer, had a high respect for both the American troops and the American officers. It was true, he admitted, that the latter seemed less men of the world and had been reproached (presumably by the French) with being tradesmen. But being a tradesman, he explained, was a very different thing in America from what it was in France. Many of these officers were from the best families in America and nearly all were from well-to-do homes. A number had been trained in the learned professions. He had been charmed, he said, "to find many of them whose manners were liberal—and whose minds were enlarged with a considerable acquaintance with politics and history. . . . I have the pleasure of knowing some of them who would not pass unnoticed in the politest court in Europe." But what he admired most was their bravery and patriotism, for they fought neither under compulsion nor in hope of gain, with "no other wish but to establish the liberties and independence of their country."[18]

Armand de la Roüerie, who came to enjoy a popularity

---

1681, published by A. Lasseray, *Les Français sous les treize étoiles* (Paris, 1935), II, 541-552.

16 *Mémoires, correspondance et manuscrits* (Paris, 1837-1838), I, 91.

17 *Ibid.*, I, 93-94.

18 "A Frenchman's Comments on the Discipline of the American and British Armies in 1777," *Penna. Mag. of Hist. and Biog.*, XXXV (1911), 367.

in America second only to Lafayette's, wrote Washington after the war begging to be allowed to retain his commission in the army and saying, "At this period in the affairs of America it could have been expected that my warmest wishes would be to return to France and enjoy there the fruits of my conduct here and a family happiness—but motives of attachment to Your Excellency, to the form of a republican government and to the great quality of this people as soldiers create in me wishes stronger than those which I may gratify at home."[19]

The explanation of such contradictory reactions seems to lie in the personalities of the individuals. Peter Stephen Du Ponceau, for instance, had taught himself English as a child, was more familiar with English than French literature, at sixteen had become a Protestant in rebellion against his mother's efforts to make him a priest, and had been, as he said, "a stern republican from the first moment I began to reflect." So it was natural that when he landed at Portsmouth in 1777 "he felt at home from the first moment" and in a consciously symbolic gesture rushed to kiss the first American girl he saw. In fact, he never returned to France but remained to become a citizen of Pennsylvania even before the war was over, to marry an American girl, and to be Second Under-Secretary of State, a very successful Philadelphia lawyer, and president of the American Philosophical Society.[20]

Individual predispositions would not have been enough, however, without something in America which caught the hearts and minds of some of these Frenchmen. If we are to judge by what they themselves said, this something was not the abstract principles of liberty and republicanism, however devoted they might be to these ideals, but rather the personalities of individual Americans they came to know and the way of life these Americans embodied. It is for this reason that Washington was so powerful a force in winning these

19 "Letters of Colonel Armand," N.Y. Hist. Soc. Collections, series II, 1879, p. 359.

20 "Autobiographical Letters" and "Autobiography," Penna. Mag. of Hist. and Biog., XL (1916), 172-186; LXIII (1939), 189-227, 311-343, 432-461; LXIV (1940), 97-120, 243-269.

young aristocrats to the American cause. They were unanimous in their admiration. Lafayette's filial affection for his leader is well known. The Count de Moré, who as an old man still remembered his admiration for American fortitude at Valley Forge, spoke of his former commander-in-chief as "one of those noble products of nature who at first sight impose a confidence and respect."[21]

The reactions of the French diplomats accredited to the new republic were particularly interesting, for these men had the best opportunity to gain an intimate acquaintance with American life. Conrad Gérard, the first minister, arrived in Philadelphia on July 12, 1778; he was replaced the following year by Anne César de La Luzerne, who brought with him an attaché and private secretary, Louis Guillaume Otto, and as first secretary, François Marbois.

Living in Philadelphia in the handsome and spacious house surrounded by walks and gardens on Chestnut Street which Gérard had purchased as the legation and being entertained by Philadelphia society was a very different thing from spending the winter at Valley Forge. These diplomats were welcomed into the intellectual and social life of the capital, and their stay must have been a reasonably pleasant one. Gérard was elected to the American Philosophical Society in 1779, La Luzerne and Marbois in 1781, and Otto some years later. On the social side there were many pleasant intimate contacts, and the French diplomats were favorite guests at tea parties and dinners in Philadelphia. One of the major social events of the war years was the great ball given in 1782 by La Luzerne in honor of the birth of the Dauphin, witnessed by 10,000 spectators and attended by 700 guests, among whom were the officers of the French army, Washington and the other American leaders, all the beauties of Philadelphia, and even a few Indian chiefs.[22]

Marbois, who landed in Boston thoroughly indoctrinated with the philosophic image of America, started by seeing all

21 Moré, op.cit., p. 59.
22 Benjamin Rush, Letters, ed. L. H. Butterfield (Princeton, 1951), I, 278-284.

that he had expected to see. He was delighted by the prosperity, equality, and simple virtue he found everywhere. One day soon after his arrival he came upon two pretty girls in snow-white dresses and straw hats decorated with wild flowers, sitting under an oak tree beside a babbling brook, weaving willow baskets. "On the grass near them," he wrote in his diary, "we saw milk, bread and fruit, and our imaginations were transported into the vales of Arcady. It was the image of innocence and peace, and if I have ever believed in happiness I did so then."[23] This was the land of liberty and equality—no restriction on the press or on travel, no seignorial rights, no salt taxes, no monopolies. In visits to Harvard and Yale Colleges he found it to be likewise the land of enlightenment, but an enlightenment rightly devoted to "useful and general knowledge rather than the sublime productions of genius."[24] What if there were no American Titians or Raphaels? Here was freedom and equality, "united to the real advantages which the older societies of Europe enjoy, without any of the maladies which afflict some of those exhausted and decrepit social structures."[25]

Marbois soon, however, ceased parroting the idealized image he had learned in Paris, and without losing his admiration for America he began to react more like a Frenchman and less like a *Philosophe*. He could not help being shocked to see Governor Trumbull blow his nose with his fingers, and he soon began to long for that "lovely climate of France, and the society which we have left and which can be found nowhere else." This was "a coldly beautiful land . . . where a stranger is still a stranger at the end of six months," a land where the people care nothing for elegance or taste and "have thought only of utility."[26]

The ministers themselves were never much blinded by philosophy. In spite of the ceremonious welcome he received, Gérard felt himself obliged to warn Rochambeau that "the

---

[23] *Our Revolutionary Forefathers*, tr. E. P. Chase (New York, 1929), p. 92.
[24] *Ibid.*, pp. 78-79. See also Ezra Stiles, *Literary Diary* (New York, 1901), II. 370-371.
[25] Marbois, *op.cit.*, pp. 85-89.
[26] *Ibid.*, pp. 133, 137.

inhabitants are not used to living with French people, for whom they cannot have any very decided inclination."[27] He was especially unfavorably impressed by the American attitude toward money, and he wrote Vergennes, "I am sorry to be obliged to add, Your Excellency, that personal disinterestedness and pecuniary probity do not honor the birth of the American Republic with their presence. . . . The spirit of mercantile cupidity forms perhaps one of the most distinctive traits of Americans, particularly of those of the North, and this character will no doubt exert an essential influence over the future destinies of the American Republic."[28] La Luzerne had the same sort of trouble. Once he wrote peevishly to Rochambeau, excusing an unwise bargain he had made with some gentlemen from Virginia, that it was "not among the requisites of a Minister of His Most Christian Majesty to be a horsetrader."[29]

Yet, as was likewise true of the volunteers who remained to the end of the war, years of intimacy wrought a change. Otto had a romantic love affair with Nancy Shippen, daughter of Dr. William Shippen. Her family opposed the match, and he later married Elizabeth Livingston and after her death took as his second wife America-Frances, daughter of Saint John de Crèvecoeur.[30] Marbois too married an American girl, Elizabeth Moore, daughter of the president of the executive council of Pennsylvania. These marriages were only part of the process of Americanization of these two men, who were to remain firm friends of the United States. Years later, in the darkest moment of the undeclared war between France and the United States in the late 1790's, Otto dared to champion the United States against his own government.[31] In 1803, Marbois, who had become the Marquis de

---

[27] Rochambeau Papers, Library of Congress, quoted by J. Jusserand, En Amérique jadis et maintenant (Paris, 1918), pp. 35-36.

[28] Dispatches and Instructions of Conrad Alexandre Gérard (1778-1780) (Baltimore, 1939), p. 212.

[29] La Luzerne Correspondence, Archives Nationales, Paris, Marine B4 183.

[30] See Ethel Armes, Nancy Shippen. Her Journal Book (Philadelphia, 1935).

[31] Considérations sur la conduite du gouvernement américain envers la France, depuis le commencement de la Révolution jusqu'en 1797, ed. G. Chinard (Princeton, 1945).

Barbé-Marbois, did much to facilitate the Louisiana Purchase and to the end of his life he remained an eloquent apologist of the United States.[32] Better than any other single figure, Marbois illustrated the three dominant reactions of the French visitors to America during the Revolution: first, the prejudiced philosophic idealization; then the Gallic aversion to American materialism and utilitarianism; and, finally, the sympathetic identification with American values, interests, and viewpoints.

These same three reactions reappeared in the officers of Rochambeau's army. Of all the French to visit America before 1789, this group, both because of its size and the prominence of many of its members, was to have the greatest influence on French attitudes toward the United States. When later, after the French Revolution, royalists railed against the *jeunes philosophes à talons rouges* who had returned from America poisoned by the subversive doctrines of liberty, equality, and republicanism, it was these officers that they meant.

Like the volunteers before them, they had not left France impelled to any degree by devotion to liberty or to any other ideal, and only a very few were really *Philosophes*. True, they pulled all the wires they could to be transferred to one of the lucky regiments going to America, but this was only in hopes of taking part in what promised to be the most active and interesting campaign of the war. Nevertheless, it was quite true that many did return home enthusiastic converts to the liberal and equalitarian principles of American society.

The French fleet dropped anchor in Newport Harbor the evening of June 11, 1780. The initial reception was not auspicious, for when General Rochambeau went ashore he found no one to greet him and he had to put up at an inn. By the next morning, however, the town fathers had got over their suspicion and General Heath had arrived to extend an official welcome. Rochambeau was received courteously and that night the town was illuminated in celebration.

[32] Marbois, *Complot d'Arnold* (Paris, 1816) and *Histoire de la Louisiane* (Paris, 1829).

The troops were established in a camp outside the town while the officers were quartered in the homes of various citizens. Here they remained until the following June, their inactivity interrupted only by fears of a British attack, by a delegation of nineteen Iroquois chiefs, and by Washington's visit and inspection of the troops. The officers were bored, and they complained of having come all the way to America to do nothing but drill their troops. But they spent the winter comfortably in what had been until the Revolution one of the largest and most prosperous American cities. Rochambeau built for them an officers' "pavilion" and there were many pleasant social events. The officers met a number of unusually attractive girls in Newport, especially one named Polly Lawton, and personal relationships were on a most cordial basis. The policy of placing the officers in American families had the happy result of creating real and close friendships between the French and their American hosts. That gay lover and adventurer, the Duke de Lauzun, stayed with a Mrs. Deborah Hunter, a widow of thirty-six, and her "two charming daughters," living on the corner of Thames and Mary Streets. "Mrs. Hunter took a great liking to me," he wrote, "and I was soon one of the family. I spent all my time there. I was rather ill, and she took me into her house and did everything she could for me. I was never in love with the Hunter girls, but if they had been my sisters I could not have been more fond of them, especially the elder, who is one of the most lovable persons I have ever known." In 1782 when he was left in charge of the few remaining French troops in the United States, Lauzun found the "tumult of Philadelphia" so insupportable that he fled to Newport "to visit once more that charming family which loved me so tenderly."[33] The young Baron de Montesquieu, the philosopher's grandson, who traveled widely through the United States with General Chastellux, wrote home, "You cannot have any idea how happy I am in the life I am leading here."[34]

[33] *Mémoires du duc de Lauzun et du comte de Tilly* (Paris, 1862), pp. 190, 215.
[34] "Quelques lettres du baron de Montesquieu," *Franco-American Review*, II (1938), 201.

"All the army had a delightful winter in Newport," Berthier, Rochambeau's official historiographer, recorded, and when they left "there was one universal feeling of regret. Everyone was so changed in his feelings that every officer had become one of the family in his host's home, and the most rabid Tories were now friends of the French."[35] Nor were the officers the only ones to establish close relations; when the army left the city, ten lovesick soldiers had to be forcibly separated from their American sweethearts.

One of the reasons for this good feeling was the excellent discipline of the French troops and the respect for civilian property which Rochambeau rigorously enforced. American chickens and pigs wandered untouched between the French tents, and a cornfield growing in the midst of the camp had not a leaf damaged. Such good behavior, supplemented by the large amount of solid cash the French army brought to the city, could not fail to render the Americans cordial. On the other hand, the French, though occasionally bored, had a pleasant enough time, and they felt at home among the green Rhode Island meadows and in the mild climate. Besides, a good many were making money selling *pacotille* and wrote home for more clothes and trinkets to sell to the Rhode Islanders.[36] There were, of course, inevitably some points of friction. Blanchard, Rochambeau's supply officer, had his troubles in dealing with Rhode Island farmers for supplies and firewood. There was the unfortunate incident of the farmer who threatened to hit the Baron de Vioménil over the head with a stick, and Paris received occasional letters of complaint like that of the Viscount de Tressan, who said, "We are here with a people who in the name of liberty

[35] Alexandre Berthier, "Journal de la campagne d'Amérique," *Bulletin de l'Institut Français de Washington*, nouvelle série, no. 1, 1951, p. 102. See also Francis W. Dawson, "Un Garde suisse de Louis XVI au service de l'Amérique," *Le Correspondant*, vol. 324 (1931), 333; "Deux Français aux Etats-Unis et dans la Nouvelle Espagne en 1782. Journal de voyage du prince de Broglie et lettres du comte de Ségur," *Mélanges publiés par la Société des bibliophiles français* (Paris, 1903), pp. 65-69; A. F. Downing and V. J. Scully, Jr., *The Architectural Heritage of Newport, Rhode Island, 1640-1915* (Cambridge, 1952), pp. 86-93; Robertnier Diary, Rhode Island Historical Society.

[36] Vicomte de Tressan Correspondence, Bibliothèque Nationale, Paris, N.A.F. 21510.

vex and ruin us and whom the sham title of friend and ally forces us to tolerate."[37] But even though a certain number did not like Americans and were discontented, relations were on the whole remarkably good.

In June 1781 the troops finally broke camp and marched through Connecticut to join Washington's forces near Dobbs Ferry. From there the combined armies marched south through New Jersey, Philadelphia, and Maryland to join De Grasse's fleet and the regiments under Saint Simon before Yorktown. Dressed in their colorful uniforms with flags streaming in the wind and bands sounding, the French troops made an impressive sight to the gaping Americans. The march was a triumphal procession. Curious countryfolk flocked to the camps, impromptu dances were organized, and, as the good Abbé Robin said, it was "a festival of equality." "Whatever may be the success of this army," he wrote enthusiastically, "it will always have had the glory of having made in this country an everlasting impression and of having rendered precious forever the name of Frenchmen."[38] In New Jersey the girls put on their best ribbons and silks to sell fruit and eggs to the passing soldiers. When the armies entered Philadelphia they paraded through the city and the French regiments were reviewed by the President of Congress. At Yorktown the Americans, badly equipped, ill fed, and often unpaid as they were, nevertheless impressed the French by their gallant conduct under fire. Moreover, the presence of Lafayette and other Frenchmen in American uniforms further strengthened the fraternal sentiment. A defeat could have led to recriminations, but a victory produced mutual congratulations and esteem.

After the battle it was decided that the French army would remain on the York peninsula. The second winter was no less pleasant than the first, especially for the officers, who enjoyed the dinners and hunt breakfasts given them at the nearby plantations. Rochambeau and his aide Von Closen

[37] *Ibid.*

[38] Charles César Robin, *Nouveau voyage dans l'Amérique Septentrionale* (Paris, 1782), p. 38.

did a lot of fox-hunting. "We have forced more than thirty foxes," the latter said. "The pack of hounds of the local gentlemen is perfect."[39] Finally, in June, Rochambeau started slowly north, pausing in Philadelphia for more parties, including La Luzerne's famous ball in honor of the Dauphin. In September his forces rejoined Washington's army near Crampound in New York, where they were much impressed by the smart appearance of the American forces, at last well-uniformed and well-supplied. From here they proceeded to Providence and finally to Boston, where the army embarked for the West Indies.

So pleasant and successful a campaign naturally produced favorable impressions, but reactions varied greatly. As one officer said, "The opinions of those who have seen the United States are more contrary than the winds which dispute the turbulent obedience of the waves."[40] On the one hand were those like the Count de Fersen, the man who later was gallantly to attempt to rescue Marie Antoinette from the Parisian Revolutionists, who said, "M. de Rochambeau was the only man capable of commanding us here, and of maintaining that perfect harmony which reigned between two nations so different in their customs and languages and which, in their hearts, do not like each other. There were never any disputes between the two armies during the time that they were together, but there were often just causes for complaint on our part. Our allies did not always treat us well, and the time we have spent with them has taught us neither to love them nor esteem them."[41] On the other hand were those like the Count de Ségur, who wrote his wife on the eve of his departure: "I am going to sail tomorrow, or the day after, and I shall leave with infinite regret a land where men are what they ought to be—sincere, straightforward, honest, free. I wish I could live here with you; we should be very

[39] S. Bonsal, *When the French Were Here* (New York, 1945), p. 184.
[40] Mathieu, Comte Dumas, *Souvenirs* (Paris, 1839), I, 112.
[41] *Le Comte de Fersen et la cour de France*, ed. Baron R. M. de Klinekowström (Paris, 1877), I, 69-70. See also Dumas, *op.cit.*, and for the reactions of officers participating in the attack on Savannah, Comte Félix de Romain, *Souvenirs d'un officier royaliste* (Paris, 1824), I, 50.

happy. . . . I have been treated like a brother by all America; I have seen nothing but public confidence, hospitality, cordiality. . . . Indeed, my heart aches as I quit this land."[42]

Other opinions lay scattered between these two extremes. Nevertheless, the evidence of the many surviving letters and diaries is that a substantial majority of the officers departed on the whole well pleased with what they had seen. (What the common soldiers thought no one bothered to record.) This sentiment, however, had neither the unanimity of the enthusiasm reigning in France nor the same political and ideological motivations. It was, of course, in part a continuation of the pro-Americanism in Paris, but it was also the product of the success of the campaign, the pleasant life led in Newport and Virginia, Rochambeau's wise discipline, the excellent liaison work of Lafayette, and Washington's phenomenal popularity, from the very first, with the French officers. After Rochambeau's staff's first conference with the American commander-in-chief, "they all returned," one officer said, "delighted with General Washington. They conceived for him an unbelievable enthusiasm."[43] Significantly, the causes of ill will which did exist were not the political or ideological differences but rather the frictions and misunderstandings which always arise between allied soldiers with different traditions, customs, and values.

A *Philosophe* like the Abbé de Sepvigny, one of Rochambeau's chaplains, would be expected to write President Stiles of Yale of his joy in being in a land where men were free to think and speak as their hearts and judgments dictated,[44] but the young nobles showed little interest in American political liberty. Even when Rochambeau was arrested by a country sheriff in execution of a farmer's claim for an unpaid bill for firewood, they found the incident more curious than significant. What did strike them was the success of religious

[42] "Extraits des lettres écrites d'Amérique par le comte de Ségur," *Mélanges publiés par la Société des bibliophiles français* (Paris, 1903), pp. 182-184.

[43] Comte de Charlus Correspondence, Archives Nationales, Paris, Marine B4 183. See my "The Iroquois Visit Rochambeau at Newport in 1780," *Rhode Island History*, II (1952), 80.

[44] Stiles, *op.cit.*, II, 517.

toleration and social equality. Voltaire, they saw, had been right in saying that toleration created peace and concord, not civil strife. Of Philadelphia the Count de Ségur wrote, "The whole city is itself a temple raised to Tolerance, for one sees there in large numbers Catholics, Presbyterians, Calvinists, Methodists and Quakers, who all practice their religion in complete liberty and who live together in perfect harmony."[45]

How little respect was left in France for the principle of aristocratic privilege and power is revealed by these officers' contrary reactions to the egalitarian Yankees and the Southern plantation owners. Of the former, Blanchard wrote, "Their education is very nearly the same; so that a worker is often elected to their assemblies, where there is no distinction, no separate order. . . . The country farmers all own their own land. They plow their fields themselves and drive their own oxen. This way of living, this sweet equality has charms for thinking men. This life would suit me pretty well."[46] It was the social freedom and simplicity of this classless society that many envied wistfully. "Here a man thinks and says and does what he pleases," Ségur said. "He is in no way forced to be a rich man or a poor man, a liar or a fool, a courtier or a soldier; he can be commonplace or extraordinary, hard working or lazy, a traveler or a stay-at-home, a politician, a writer or a merchant—nobody cares. Here by following a few simple laws and respecting customs one can lead a happy and peaceful life. In Paris it is only by flouting them that one is fashionable."[47] But for the Virginian aristocracy they felt the same contempt as for their own society. "They have negro slaves," one officer wrote, "like our colonials in the islands, and they lead an idle life, caring about nothing but food and drink. In general they are not the equals of the Northerners in morals or honesty, and one might say that they are really two different peoples."[48]

Not all, however, admired American equalitarianism. The

---

[45] *Mémoires, souvenirs et anecdotes* (Paris, 1859), I, 199.
[46] Claude Blanchard, *Guerre d'Amérique, 1780-1783* (Paris, 1881), pp. 58-59.
[47] "Extraits des lettres," p. 183.
[48] Blanchard, *op.cit.*, p. 109.

Count de Fersen gave an economic interpretation of the Revolution which was not uncommon and which sounds not unlike that of some modern historians: "The Whigs . . . are all for liberty and independence and are made up of the people of the lower classes who own no property at all; most of the inhabitants of the rural areas belong to this party. The Tories are for the English, or rather, they are for peace, without caring much whether they are independent or not. These are people of more distinguished breeding, and they are the only ones who have any property. . . . When the Whigs have the upper hand, they rob the Tories unmercifully."[49]

Buffon's and De Pauw's polemics on America as a human habitat and on the physical and intellectual degeneration of man in the New World seem to have made little impression on these officers. They found the health of their soldiers better than in France,[50] and they frequently remarked on the tall and vigorous appearance of the Americans.[51] Used to the depressed condition of the French peasants, they were surprised by the prosperous, fertile countryside through which they passed and the well-dressed American farmers living in attractive houses furnished with fine china and glassware, handsome wall papers, and carpets "even upon the stairs."[52]

They neither assumed that Americans were intellectually or artistically inferior by nature to Europeans nor did they exaggerate American achievements. It was naturally their typical comment that "the arts here are in their infancy,"[53] but they had no interest in proving that this was a permanent defect due to climate, or economic, social, or political causes, and they were ready to praise every achievement. Boston and Philadelphia were both judged handsome, well-designed cities, for the wide and regular streets struck them as a pleasing contrast to eighteenth-century Paris. Though they thought Independence Hall in Philadelphia badly pro-

[49] Fersen, *op.cit.*, p. 41.
[50] Blanchard, *op. cit.*, p. 74
[51] Broglie, *op.cit.*, p. 49.
[52] Blanchard, *op. cit.*, p. 58
[53] Charles Louis de Montesquieu, "Un Petit-fils de Montesquieu en Amérique," *Revue philomatique de Bordeaux et du Sud-Ouest*, année 5, no. 12, 1902, p. 544.

portioned, they admired the churches, the hospital, and the prison. Some of the larger mansions in the South, particularly Mount Vernon and Monticello, impressed them by their charm and good taste.

Although American college life had been badly disrupted by the war, the French found, in their visits to Cambridge, Princeton, Philadelphia, and Williamsburg that American education was equal to that of Europe. An officer named Cromot du Bourg described Harvard as a charming college in which he found 150 scholars studying Latin and Greek, a fine large library, a well-equipped "museum of physics," and a still incompleted natural history museum already containing many interesting exhibits. "I left Cambridge," he said, "delighted with what I had seen in a country still barbarous in its manners and slight cultivations."[54] The Baron de Montesquieu found Princeton to be "a very handsome college" which offered, he said, an education equivalent to that furnished by European colleges.

French acceptance of Americans as intellectual equals was best revealed in the comments on American leaders. Washington was a special case. The unrestrained and universal admiration he received was unquestionably sincere. No journal was complete without its eulogy, and Berthier's was typical of many: "The nobility of his bearing and of his countenance, imprinted with every virtue, inspired in all of us the affection and respect owed to his character, thus augmenting, if that were possible, the high opinion we held of his rare merit."[55] They described him as a man of imposing appearance, gracious and affable, possessing all the social graces and capable of dancing a minuet as well as any courtier, a modern Fabius, unmoved in defeat and restrained in victory, a sound tactician and strategist, honest, sincere, modest, and worshipped by all. Perhaps the key to this unqualified French admiration of Washington was that to these members of a demoralized aristocracy Washington appeared to

[54] Marie François, Baron Cromot du Bourg, "Diary of a French Officer, 1781," *Mag. of Amer. Hist.*, IV (1880), 214.
[55] Berthier, *op.cit.*, p. 93.

be the ideal aristocrat—polished, capable, patriotic, virtuous, and universally popular. Even the royalists who later condemned the example of the American Revolution most violently for its influence in France were to remain united in this unanimous adulation.

No other American received this sort of hero worship, but many were highly respected. The French visitors to Monticello in 1781 and 1782 were inevitably impressed by Jefferson's encyclopedic learning and his large and well-chosen library. "Before I had spent two hours with him," wrote the Chevalier de Chastellux, "I felt I had known him all my life. Walks taken together, hours spent in his library, and especially the interesting talks we enjoyed on an endless variety of subjects, together with that deep satisfaction which two men feel who in exchanging opinions and ideas constantly find themselves in agreement and understand each other almost without need of words—all these things made my four days at Monticello pass like four minutes."[56] They recited Ossian to each other, inspected Jefferson's herd of deer, discussed politics, the arts, and meteorology. Chastellux greatly admired Monticello and made the classic remark that "Mr. Jefferson is the first American who consulted the beaux arts to learn how to shelter himself from the weather."[57] Indeed, the magnificent site Jefferson had chosen seemed to symbolize his unique and universal genius. "From his youth Jefferson set his spirit, like his abode, on a lofty eminence, whence he could contemplate the whole universe."[58]

During the two years there were many opportunities to meet a variety of American politicians and intellectuals—Dr. Samuel Cooper of Boston, an eloquent Francophile whose eloquence, intellect, and acquaintance with French authors, particularly Voltaire and Rousseau, impressed many; Thomas Paine, Samuel Adams, James Wilson, David Rittenhouse, Professor Madison at William and Mary and Professor Wil-

[56] François Jean, Marquis de Chastellux, *Voyages dans l'Amérique Septentrionale* (Paris, 1786), II, 35-36.
[57] *Ibid.*, II, 34.
[58] *Ibid.*, II, 34-37. See also Bonsal, *op.cit.*, p. 185, and Aristide Aubert du Petit-Thouars, *Mémoires et voyages* (Paris, 1822), p. 267.

lard at Harvard, Robert Morris, whom Chastellux called an "epicurean philosopher," John Hancock, James Bowdoin, Alexander Hamilton, and many more.[59] The Count de Ségur wrote his wife, "I have been enchanted with my stay in Boston. I have met here men of letters and of genius who have become my friends and with whom I intend to correspond. I am leaving Boston with real regret."[60]

The many invitations to dinners and dances in Newport, Providence, Virginia, Philadelphia, and Boston opened up the most cultivated social circles to the officers, and the comments on American woman are particularly enlightening. In Boston, Chastellux found many who spoke French fluently and he was particularly charmed by a Mrs. Tudor who possessed, he said, "not only wit but also grace and delicacy both of mind and manner."[61] In Philadelphia he met a Mrs. Meredith, "very attractive and very well informed," with whom he talked for an hour on literature, poetry, novels, and especially French history. "The comparisons between Francis I and Henry IV, between Turenne and Condé, and between Richelieu and Mazarin seemed familiar to her and she made them with much grace, wit, and naturalness."[62]

Inevitably there were many love affairs, some, naturally, not very serious. The Duke de Lauzun and Lafayette once stopped at the house of a farmer who had two pretty daughters. When Lauzun tried out his talents on the elder, she said reproachfully, "Your words surprise me, My Lord, for I have heard that you are married and have a wife back in France."

"Married! Oh, yes," replied Lauzun, "but just a little bit, such a very, very little bit that it's not worth mentioning. Just ask Lafayette."[63]

But others were more sentimental. Von Closen filled his diaries with silhouettes cut in "memory of a few pretty persons, more or less kind-hearted and interesting, either because

[59] Broglie, op.cit., pp. 73-74; Jean E. Weelen, Rochambeau, Father and Son (New York, 1936), pp. 277-278; Blanchard, op.cit., p. 42.
[60] "Extraits des lettres," p. 184.     [61] Chastellux, op.cit., II, 198.
[62] Ibid., I, 257-258.     [63] Lauzun, op.cit., p. 3.

of their good breeding, education, or talents."[64] Another young officer, De Galvin, was so smitten by a Philadelphia coquette, Sally Shippen, that he killed himself when she refused his proposal, in hopes, as he said in his suicide note, that he would "succeed better in outflanking love than I did in outflanking the British."[65]

It is obvious that even though much of American life was still uncouth, the French officers accepted as a matter of course Americans of the upper economic and political levels as their social and intellectual equals. The European disposition, which was soon to appear, to condemn American society as vulgar and the American intellect as inferior was not apparent.

They could not help noticing, of course, that Americans took financial transactions very seriously and that some were unwilling to let patriotism, ideals, friendship, or anything else come between them and an honest shilling. As Blanchard said, "Americans love money, and *hard* money."[66] Rochambeau complained that he was at the mercy of a small group of bankers who controlled the money market. "The cupidity of the speculators here," he declared indignantly, "is without equal. Their troops, stark naked, cannot extract a penny from the pocket of the most patriotic businessman except at an exorbitant rate of interest."[67] Even the Quakers, suspected of war profiteering, did not escape. They were, said the young Montesquieu, "just as selfish, hypocritical, and vicious as the rest of humanity."[68] But this shopkeeper materialism, though it was condemned on moral grounds,

[64] C. W. Bowen, "A French Officer with Washington and Rochambeau," *Century Magazine*, LXXIII (1907), 536. See also Bonsal, *op.cit.*, p. 218.

[65] Bowen, *op.cit.*, p. 537. For other examples of French-American love affairs, see Du Petit-Thouars, *op.cit.*, I, 243ff., and the story of Lapommeraie, the officer who (it is said) ravished a young Quakeress but atoned by marrying her and becoming a Quaker himself, *Mercure de France*, June 28 and July 19, 1817.

[66] Blanchard, *op.cit.*, p. 54.

[67] Amblard Raymond, Vicomte de Noailles, *Marins et soldats français en Amérique pendant la Guerre de l'Indépendance* (Paris, 1903), p. 232. See also *Extrait du journal d'un officier de la marine de l'escadre de M. le comte d'Estaing* (Paris, 1782), pp. 39-40.

[68] "Quelques lettres du baron de Montesquieu," II, 198.

did not appear to those French as a danger to the progress of the arts and sciences in America. It was part of the *moeurs* of the land and as much English as it was American.

It was quite possible for these men of the eighteenth century to respect American political practices and the cultivation of the American mind and still regard with a mixture of amusement, wonder, and condescension the pattern of American morals, traditions, and customs.

For instance, the rules governing the behavior of women were the opposite of those in France. Unmarried girls, instead of being strictly chaperoned, were not only allowed great freedom but even were permitted to engage in an astounding custom known as "bundling." "It is customary," Berthier reported in amazement, "for two lovers . . . to spend several hours alone together lying on a bed and talking of their future happiness. I have frequently entered rooms where I found young people doing this, and they never bothered to move but kept right on exchanging all the suitable expressions of their mutual affection." Yet for all this, "nothing happened which was not perfectly proper."[69] On the other hand, married women, instead of enjoying the sexual freedom granted in France, were models of chastity and domesticity. The odd Americans "did not believe that a man is ever free to try to seduce a girl,"[70] and women could travel alone anywhere without fear of being molested.

The strict observance of the Sabbath led to many misunderstandings. An officer playing a flute in Boston one Sunday almost caused a riot.[71] Another time a group of officers were playing cards when their scandalized landlady burst in and tried to snatch the cards from the table. They had to send for their chaplain, an Irish Catholic, to explain to her that "it was not contrary to the principles of their religion to play cards on Sunday."[72]

Naturally there were obvious differences in social customs and courtesies. The women of Philadelphia, despite their

69 Berthier, *op.cit.*, pp. 102-103.
70 Berthier MSS, Princeton Univ. Library.
71 Robin, *op.cit.*, p. 11.
72 Blanchard, *op.cit.*, p. 121.

magnificent dresses, seemed to curtsey awkwardly and dance badly.[73] Americans were generous and considerate, but the politeness of an American gentleman seemed more a formula and a ceremony than a personal compliment. "Politeness here is like religion in Italy," Chastellux said, "all in the practice and nothing in the principle."[74]

Two things the French particularly objected to in American inns: dirty sheets and strange bedfellows. The Prince de Broglie said he always found it a good idea to flatter the innkeeper and kiss his wife (if she were pretty) in order to be given the best room. "I also got," he explained, "what is even rarer, the privilege of having on my bed sheets that had not already served some other gentleman, and I gave evidence of so much aversion to sleeping in company (unless it were with my hostess) that they also permitted me not to be awakened during the night by some new arrival."[75]

These random comments recorded in journals and letters were spontaneous reactions without any ideological bias. The two books produced by the campaign, the Abbé Robin's *Nouveau voyage dans l'Amérique Septentrionale* and the Chevalier de Chastellux's *Voyages dans l'Amérique Septentrionale* gave a quite different picture because they interpreted the United States in reference to the social theories under discussion in France. Moreover these works were popular successes in France and therefore represented not merely samples of opinion, but also books which did much to shape French opinion of America in the 1780's.[76]

The Abbé Charles César Robin was a typical minor *Philosophe*, moderately liberal in his views. As a member of the Lodge of the Nine Sisters and a friend of Franklin he was

[73] Broglie, *op.cit.*, p. 46.
[74] Chastellux, *op.cit.*, I, 150.
[75] Broglie, *op.cit.*, p. 50.
[76] Robin's *Nouveau Voyage* was published in four French editions in 1782 and 1783, two American editions in 1783 and 1784, and in Dutch and German translations in 1782 and 1783. Chastellux's *Voyages* first appeared in part in a private edition published in 1781 by the press of the French fleet in Newport, subsequently in several pirated and incomplete publications in Europe, and in complete authorized editions in Paris in 1786 and 1788-1791. Three editions of the English translation were published in 1787 and three of a German version in 1785 and 1786.

a confirmed Americanist even before his departure from France. Later he was to take an active part in the Revolution. He arrived in Boston in June 1781 as the army was leaving Newport, made the march to Yorktown, and apparently returned to France not long after. His impressions were necessarily hasty and superficial and often erroneous. Not speaking English, he did not meet, it appears, many Americans, and he often had to make his investigations in rather bizarre ways. For instance, he gathered his vital statistics by inspecting tombstones and he studied American reading habits by poking about in the ashes of Yorktown for abandoned books.

In part his interpretation was pessimistic. His tombstone researches convinced him that De Pauw had been right in saying Americans aged early and died young. Moreover, like Diderot, he was worried by the problem of excess wealth and economic inequality. The sumptuously furnished mansions and the elegant carriages driven by richly liveried slaves which he saw in Philadelphia and Annapolis persuaded him that moral decay had already set in, and this, he predicted, would lead to the breakdown of religious toleration. Pennsylvania, which had been "the most virtuous colony that history has ever known . . . will soon be only a brilliant meteor which shone for an instant before the eyes of the universe."[77]

Nevertheless, America by its material progress offered man a clean, fresh start. "While our cities," he wrote, "for the most part, in their gloomy, unhealthful sites, girded by crenelated walls and formidable towers, with crowded, unventilated buildings and tortuous, muddy streets, still recall the ignorance and barbarism of our ancestors, all the cities of America already rise proudly on pleasant, healthful situations, bathed by pure waters, surrounded by fertile fields, pierced by wide, regular streets, and ornamented with clean, comfortable, regular buildings."[78] Here man at last was to achieve equal justice under the law and the abolition of aristocratic privilege. "The accused in his chains will dare to raise his voice and call upon his defenders; and the law, slow to order the shedding of blood, will not pass judgment until the accused

[77] Robin, *op.cit.*, pp. 94, 104.     [78] *Ibid.*, pp. 180-181.

*107*

has had his say. . . . Legions of birds and animals will not devastate with impunity the field of the farmer, and like any lord he will cast his nets for the fish in the rivers winding through his own meadows."[79] This was pure Voltaire.

Robin's most interesting comments were on the American Enlightenment, which he saw at the College of William and Mary and particularly at Harvard, where he attended plays acted by students—one of which probably was Hugh H. Brackenridge's popular *Battle of Bunker Hill*. He drew the conclusion that a new naturalistic and national drama was arising in the United States. "The subject is always national, such as the burning of Charleston, the capture of Burgoyne, or the treason of Arnold. You may presume that these plays of a new nation must be far removed from the perfection of our own. Yet they are much more effective than ours for the very reason that they depict the manners and customs of the land in which they are acted, and because they recall events of immediate interest. Here is the stage restored to its ancient origins."[80] Robin foresaw in the United States the development of a nationalistic and "naturalistic" drama of the sort proposed by Diderot, and he gave as a parallel to the new American plays Greuze's reaction against neo-classicism in painting. He hoped that America, free from the restraints of the classical tradition, would take the lead in creating new and more authentic art forms.

He was also struck, however, like Marbois, by the American lack of aesthetic interest: "Americans appear to be guided by reason rather than by sentiment. They prefer to meditate rather than to feel, and they care more about the useful than the beautiful. Therefore legislation, politics, physics, and mechanics progress in America, while the agreeable arts remain unknown, and poetry, which in all other nations preceded science, fails here to utter her sublime and moving harmonies. The cities, towns, and houses may offer comfort, health, and good order, but they present nothing to interest or delight the imagination: no lines of trees meeting in bowers of delightful shade; no gardens whose fanciful plots, agreeable symmetry, and lovely harmony of blossoms intoxicate the senses and enchant the soul; no dances, no public fetes to express the happiness and joy of the people."[81]

Yet it is a curious index to the French eighteenth-century mind that American utilitarianism and lack of interest in the cultivation of beauty and graceful living did not greatly disturb these observers. It could not yet occur to them to attribute these defects to a libertarian and egalitarian social system, and such shortcomings seemed of far less consequence than the material and political progress being achieved.

This was indicated by the comments on Robin's book in the French press. "Every eye," Joseph Garat wrote in 1783, "today is fixed upon North America; it is there that the greatest interests of the Universe are at stake. It is there that all the hopes and fears of the two worlds are joined. . . . The philosophers of all Europe see in the new constitutions . . . the noblest, and perhaps the last, hope of the human race." Consequently he attacked Robin sharply for his pessimism about the growth of American population and his predictions of the decline of American morals and toleration.[82]

Chastellux's analysis of American society was both more searching and more influential. A member of the French Academy, one of the founders of the social sciences, and major general on Rochambeau's staff, he was easily the foremost intellectual in the French forces in America. In an earlier work, *De la Félicité* (1772), he had sought to determine whether "society is susceptible, if not of perfection, at least of amelioration," that is, of an increase in human felicity.[83] The solution to man's predicament lay, not, he said, in Rousseau's return to nature, nor in Christianity, nor in metaphysical philosophy, nor, finally, in the cultivation of the agreeable arts—painting, sculpture, and architecture—or of "the frivolous talents like poetry and music." These belonged to the infancy of mankind and the example of the Greeks proved that artistic perfection could be accompanied by the

81 *Ibid.*, pp. 205-206.
82 *Mercure de France*, Mar. 8, 1783. See also *ibid.*, Mar. 29, 1783.
83 *De la Félicité* (Amsterdam, 1772) , I, vii.

worst sort of moral corruption and political tyranny.[84] The only possible answer was in social reform. The function of government, he posited, was to achieve "the greatest happiness of the greatest number."[85] Man must create through the free and enlightened use of his reason a liberal government midway between the extremes of pure democracy and pure absolutism, based upon a true understanding of economic principles (Physiocracy), which would guarantee a high standard of living, adequate leisure, and the right to private property.

In this earlier work Chastellux had cited America as an example of man's ability to progress through liberty, reason, equality, and agriculturalism. He arrived in the New World, consequently, with the most favorable prejudices, and he left with his optimism undiminished. The prosperity of the independent American farmer confirmed his faith in a free agricultural economy. On the matter of American morals, he disagreed with Robin's forebodings. This was a simple and virtuous society where sin was so rare that an unmarried mother, he reported from Connecticut, was pitied rather than punished. *Luxe*, luxurious living, was not a serious danger, for it was not a vice of a mercantile and agricultural people like the Americans. If anything, he would have liked to see a little less moral rigidity, and more gaiety and sociability on the Sabbath. He even ridiculed, though not unkindly, the Quakers.

In politics Chastellux was a liberal but not a democrat or a revolutionary, and his instincts were thoroughly aristocratic. Though he approved of religious liberty and representative government, he warned of the dangers of unlimited franchise, and recommended to his American friends honors and titles as legitimate awards for public service. Absolute equality, either economic or political, he believed an impossibility, and he predicted that the United States would develop into a union of liberal and moderate semi-aristocratic republics. He saw clearly that, in spite of the similarities of

[84] *Ibid.*, I, 31.                    [85] *Ibid.*, II, 55.

the state constitutions, some of the states had very dissimilar origins and traditions.

The interesting thing was that Chastellux said much less about the American political system than the progress of the arts and sciences in the new republics. He had the usual impression that Americans were insensitive to beauty and to the pleasures of cultured society. Once caught by a two-day rain at Governor Nelson's home in Virginia, he grew bored and regretted that "music, drawing, reading aloud and lady's fancy needlework are resources unknown in America." "But," he added politely, "we must hope that America will not be long in acquiring them."[86] In Philadelphia he had tea one afternoon at the Shippens'. "This was the first time," he said, "since my arrival in America that I saw music insinuate itself into a social gathering and mingle with the other amusements." Nancy sang, accompanied on the harp by her sweetheart Louis Otto, and the Viscount de Noailles played the violin and the young people danced. "If music and the beaux arts prosper in Philadelphia," Chastellux later wrote in describing the evening, "if society becomes easy and gay, and if people can learn to accept pleasures as they come without being formally organized, then Americans will enjoy all the advantages to be derived both from agreeable manners and good government, and they will have nothing left to envy of Europe."[87]

This optimism he supported by the publication of a long letter on the future of the arts and sciences in the United States, addressed to President Madison of William and Mary, who had awarded him an honorary degree. He had been much impressed by the American Philosophical Society and the American Academy of Arts and Sciences in Boston, both of which elected him to membership. His visits to American colleges had convinced him that American education was not inferior to European standards. The Latin and English orations he had heard at a commencement exercise in Philadelphia were equal, he said, to those at Oxford and Cambridge. After inspecting Harvard, he wrote, "If one compares our

[86] *Voyages*, II, 18.          [87] *Ibid.*, I, 246-247.

universities, and our education in general, with what is to be found in America, it would scarcely be to our interest to try to decide which of the two nations deserves to be called an infant people."[88] In his wide travels throughout the states he met many of the American leaders. He shared the universal admiration for Washington, and in a passage frequently quoted in France he described eloquently the perfect harmony, proportion, and moderation of his friend's character and gave unqualified praise to his military skill. In addition, Chastellux had, as we have seen, great respect for Jefferson, and he spoke highly of Thomas Paine, Samuel Adams, and many others. It was therefore no wonder that he wrote Madison, "Must we not foresee scientific progress in a country already famous for its academies, its universities equal to those of Europe, and its scientists—or better said, its distinguished genuises—whose names will stand as monuments in the history of human thought? Have no doubts, Sir. America will be just as famous for its science as for its arms and its government."[89]

On the future of the arts in America, Chastellux had less evidence of achievement, but he was equally optimistic. He believed they would flourish under the patronage of the American aristocracy and would center, not in the too mercantile and cosmopolitan coastal ports, but in inland state capitals with adjoining state universities, in a truly national and rural atmosphere. Here was to be nurtured a colonial extension of the European Enlightenment. Transplantation, however, by no means implied inferiority. America was not to be a new Rome, but a Syracuse to Europe's Athens. In a passage which probably inspired Brizard's *Fragment de Xénophon*, he wrote, "Let America not fear the fate of the Romans, to whom she has the apparent vanity but the real humility to compare herself. The Roman, fierce, unjust, grasping by nature and ostentatious by vanity, could buy masterpieces but he could not purchase good taste. The Americans, most of whom have come from the most civilized

[88] *Ibid.*, I, 216.   [89] *Ibid.*, II, 293-294.

112

states of Europe, have no such barbarism to outgrow. It is rather the Greek colonies that they are to resemble; and certainly Syracuse, Marseilles, Crotona, and Agrigentum had nothing to envy the motherland."[90]

This was the "Greek colony concept." It did not mean that American art was to be a pale copy of European models. Like the Abbé Robin and many others, Chastellux hoped that the Americans, drawing directly and freely from their new environment, would find inspiration for fresh, authentic art forms and would lead the revolt against neo-classicism. Chastellux wrote, "Your citizens live, and will long continue to live close to nature. Nature is for them always close at hand; she is always grand and beautiful. If they study and consult her, they will never go astray. Warn them only to trust no more the pedantic legislations of the Universities of Cambridge, Oxford, and Edinburgh, which have for so long ruled tyrannically over the empire of men's minds and have promulgated a vast 'classic' code which is fit only to hold men in classes, as though they were children in school."[91]

Chastellux found evidence that his prophecies were already being fulfilled. At Washington's headquarters at New Windsor, New York, he met Colonel David Humphreys, one of the Hartford Wits, and he was greatly impressed by his rhetorical poem, *An Address to the Armies of the United States*, published in 1780.[92] When Humphreys came to Paris in 1784 as secretary to the legation, Chastellux published an edition with the English original and his own prose translation on opposite pages. In the notes he called particular attention to American painters and particularly to West, Copley, and Trumbull, all then living in London.[93]

Chastellux professed no doubts. "The beaux arts belong in America," he wrote Madison. "They have already made considerable progress; they will make still more in the years ahead. No obstacle, no objection can bar their way."[94]

Chastellux's only worry was that the progress of the arts

---

[90] *Ibid.*, II, 285.    [91] *Ibid.*, II, 286.    [92] *Ibid.*, I, 288.
[93] David Humphreys, *Discours en vers adressé aux officiers et aux soldats des différentes armées américaines* (Paris, 1786), p. 63.
[94] *Voyages*, II, 291.

might, as Rousseau had said, bring moral corruption. "It would be far better," he said, "to postpone for a long time the development of the arts than to corrupt in the slightest degree the morals of the people."[95] But he thought this unlikely, especially as long as the love of art was allied to a rural, domestic existence, the bulwark of American virtue. Another objection he foresaw was that the arts might distract Americans from "more useful though less pleasant tasks."[96] He dismissed this by saying, "There is not a single American who does not enjoy twice as much leisure in his day as does his European counterpart."[97]

Chastellux was perhaps less than a prophet. He erred in seeing in Monticello the pattern of the future of America. He was not alone, however, in his optimism concerning the cultivation and enlightenment of the American mind, an optimism which contrasted oddly with the pessimism which was soon to become far more common with European commentators. The reason was that these men were not thinking of culture in the modern sense of the word, but of the liberation of men's minds from ignorance and prejudice—the Enlightenment. This enlightenment was for them only part of greater light that was breaking upon the world—and nowhere brighter than in the West—the hope of the human race, the hope for a new city of men free from want, injustice, and oppression.

Yet it was clearly an injustice on the part of posterity to make these officer veterans of the American war responsible for the extremism of the French Revolution. A considerable number, it must be remembered, were conservative monarchists and more or less anti-American; and there is no available evidence that any of the pro-American majority returned home as revolutionists. None were Brissots or Robespierres. They were curiously little interested in the mechanics of democratic government, or even in American guarantees of political liberty. They were at the most moderate equalitarian reformers, concerned with the establishment of civil liberties,

[95] *Loc.cit.*        [96] *Ibid.*, ii, 286.        [97] *Ibid.*, ii, 287.

particularly religious toleration, equality under the law, freedom of thought, and the right of private property, and far more intent on moral regeneration and economic progress than on political radicalism. Americanism was indeed to become a radical political force in the hands of men like Brissot; but the ideological and political effect of the American example as transmitted through these officers was to be to reinforce the position of the moderate constitutional liberals under the leadership of men like Lafayette.

If any revolutionary or radical virus was picked up by the French in America it was not the aristocratic officers but the peasant soldiers who were infected. From 1780 to 1782 the common soldiers—to the number of about 8,000—were in daily contact with the free, prosperous American farmers, who owned their land without restrictions and who had never heard of the multitude of seignorial rights which burdened the French peasant. There is some evidence—as yet inconclusive—that these conscripts later became leaders in the peasant revolts against economic feudalism which occurred in 1789 even before the news of the fall of the Bastille had reached the provinces. It is at least true that the centers of agrarian radicalism, where the rebellions against feudal rights broke out first and were most violent and where there was the greatest evidence of clear intent to destroy the very foundations of feudalism, were invariably those areas which contained the largest number of peasant veterans of the American war.[98]

[98] F. McDonald, "The Relationship of the French Peasant Veterans of the American Revolution to the Fall of Feudalism in France, 1789-1792," *Agricultural History*, XXV (1951), 151-161.

## CHAPTER IV

# THE AMERICAN DREAM,
## 1784-1794

THE period from the signature of the Treaty of Paris to the Revolutionary Convention, though it included the last uncertain years of the *ancien régime* and the worst violence of the Terror, constituted in French-American relations a single episode. Between these two dates French good will toward America, after having been engendered by the *Philosophes* before 1776 and after having been infused with the heat of popular enthusiasm and the strength of fraternal cooperation during the war years, now reached its fullest expression. The American Dream was the first of those great moments of secular mysticism which modern man has been experiencing for the last two hundred years. In its purest form, it was an act of faith, as was so much of eighteenth-century thought, in man's power to create an earthly heaven, and a vision of the realization of this faith. Yet, like all things human, however simple it may appear in retrospect, it was in actuality a most complex phenomenon, opposed by contrary forces, containing within itself divergencies and contradictions, and showing, even in the short space of a decade, a succession of different phases.

One of the most important results of the Treaty of Paris was that it for the first time permitted unrestricted communication between the United States and the non-British world. The flow of information from America to France, which had been hitherto a trickle, most of it coming indirectly through London, now became a comparative flood pouring directly across the Atlantic. English books and especially English newspapers were still important sources,[1] but they were now

[1] E.g., T. Anburey, *Voyages dans les parties intérieures de l'Amérique Sep-*

secondary to the direct channels—the packet-boat service to American ports started in 1783, the unrestricted movement of merchant ships and the development of French-American trade, the establishment of correspondents for French papers in American cities, and of course the greatly increased transatlantic travel. With the return of the veterans it was easier to find in Paris a man who had been in Philadelphia than one who had visited Lisbon or St. Petersburg. Even before the fall of the Bastille, curiosity and the unsettled conditions in France impelled an increasing number of Frenchmen to cross the Atlantic as travelers or emigrants. Lafayette's triumphal return in 1784 and Brissot de Warville's philosophic pilgrimage in 1788 were only two of many.[2] The various French consuls and diplomats in the United States—men like G. J. A. Ducher, Saint John de Crèvecoeur, and De Moustier, the French minister in 1787—were particularly active as interpreters of the American scene.[3]

---

*tentrionale* (Paris, 1790); J. F. D. Smyth, *Voyage dans les Etats-Unis* (Paris, 1791); J. B. Holroyd, Earl of Sheffield, *Observations sur le commerce des Etats-Unis d'Amérique* (London, 1789 and Rouen, 1789). All the French periodicals continued to rely heavily on English papers for American news.

[2] The new citizens included, besides earlier arrivals like Albert Gallatin, Stephen Du Ponceau, Pierre L'Enfant, and Quesnay de Beaurepaire (see his *Mémoire et prospectus, concernant l'académie des sciences et beaux arts des Etats-Unis de l'Amérique,* Paris, 1788), post-war arrivals like Stephen Louis Le Couteulx de Caumont, of the international banking family (see M. Murray, "Memoir of Stephen Louis Le Couteulx de Caumont," *Buffalo Hist. Soc. Publications,* IX [1906], 433-483); Peter Sailly, later a U.S. Congressman (see G. J. Bixby, *Peter Sailly, 1754-1826, with Extracts from his Diary and Letters,* Bulletin 680 [History Bulletin 12], Univ. of State of N.Y., Albany, 1919, pp. 58-70); Lucas Despeintreaux, befriender of the Scioto colonists (see *Calendar of the Papers of Benjamin Franklin* [Philadelphia, 1908,], III, 157, 377; *Considérations sur les fonds publics* [Paris, 1793], p. 34; Claude F. A. de Lezay-Marnésia, *Lettres écrites des rives de l'Ohio* [Paris, an XI], pp. 113ff.); and Joseph Nancrède, professor of French at Harvard (see A. Schintz, "Un 'Rousseauiste' en Amérique," *Modern Language Notes,* XXXV [1920], 10-18; F. Baldensperger, "Le premier 'instructeur' de français à Harvard College: Joseph Nancrède," *Harvard Advocate,* XCVI [1913], 76-79). Among the travelers were André Michaux, the botanist (1785); James Donatien le Ray de Chaumont, son of Franklin's old friend (1785); Cadet de Vaux, the chemist (1787); the Marquis de Chartier de Lotbinière (1787); and the Marquis de Chappe de Laisne (1787). Brissot reported many French in Philadelphia in 1788.

[3] Others were Marbois, Otto, Philippe Létombe, and Victor Du Pont. For their published comments see Crèvecoeur's *Lettres d'un cultivateur américain* (Paris, 1787); Ducher's *Nouvelle alliance à proposer entre les républiques française et américaine* (1792), *Analyse des loix commerciales dans les treize*

It was during these years that that famous species, the American in Paris, came into existence. American business-men, tourists, diplomats, artists, writers, adventurers, land promoters, and political agitators became familiar figures in the streets and salons and political meetings of Paris, and they were to be seen in the seaports as well as in the capital. A number attempted to establish themselves in various French cities as importers, exporters, or speculators. Many went bankrupt, but some succeeded. In Dunkirk, William and Benjamin Rotch headed from 1787 to 1793 a large colony of Nantucket whalers.[4] The speculator Colonel James Swan obtained, with the help of Lafayette, lucrative government contracts for naval stores and salt meat.[5] Often they became involved in French politics: John Skey Eustace, a soldier of fortune, wrote political pamphlets and served as *maréchal de camp* in the Revolutionary army;[6] the adventurer Gilbert Imlay and Mark Leavenworth, a Yale graduate, were in-volved in schemes for the French seizure of Louisiana.[7]

There were famous names among these Americans. John

*Etats-Unis de l'Amérique* [1790], *De la dette publique en France, en Angleterre et dans les Etats-Unis de l'Amérique* (Paris, 1791), and *Les Deux hémisphères* (Paris, 1793); and Eléonore François, Marquis de Moustier, *Observations sur les différents rapports de la liberté ou de la prohibition de la culture du tabac, suivies d'une lettre à M. Necker* (Paris, 1790). See H. C. Rice, "French Consular Agents in the United States, 1778-1791," *Franco-American Review*, I (1936), 368-370.

[4] See *Memorandum Written by William Rotch* (Boston, 1916); *Moniteur universel*, Oct. 28, 1793; Rotch Letters, John Carter Brown Library, Providence, R.I.; Edouard A. Stackpole, *The Sea-Hunters* (New York, 1953), pp. 116-120, 159-163, 167-170.

[5] See James Swan, *Causes qui se sont opposées au progrès du commerce entre la France et les Etats-Unis* (Paris, 1790).

[6] J. S. Eustace, *Lettre de M. J. S. Eustace . . . à M. Joseph Fenwick, consul des Etats-Unis de l'Amérique à Bordeaux* (Bordeaux, 1792); *Le Citoyen des Etats-Unis d'Amérique, Jean-Skey Eustace, général . . . à ses frères d'armes* (Paris, 1793); *Lettres sur les crimes du roi Georges III par un officier américain* (Paris [1794]); *Letters on the Crimes of George III* (Paris, an II); *Official and Private Correspondence of Major General J. S. Eustace* (Paris, 1796); *Traité d'amitié, de commerce et de navigation entre Sa Majesté Britannique et les Etats-Unis d'Amérique . . . suivi d'un projet fraternel adressé aux négocians français* (Paris, an IV).

[7] "Observations du Cap. Imlay," *Annual Report of Amer. Hist. Assoc. for 1896*, I, 953-954; "Mémoire sur la Louisiane," *Amer. Hist. Review*, III (1898), 491-494; R. F. Durden, "Joel Barlow in the French Revolution," *William and Mary Quarterly*, 3rd series, VIII (1951), 350-351.

Paul Jones, after his return to Paris in 1784, moved in the best intellectual circles and enjoyed no small reputation as a poet.[8] In 1790 he was back again, after an unhappy experience in the service of Catherine the Great, and in July he appeared before the National Assembly with a group of ten Americans to affirm their solidarity with the leaders of the Revolution.[9] In this same delegation was the poet Joel Barlow, who had arrived in 1788 to promote land sales and who remained to become deeply involved as a Girondist in French politics, taking part in the annexation of Savoy and seeking election, unsuccessfully, as a delegate to the Convention.[10] He meanwhile published a number of his poetic works in Paris. John Trumbull, the painter, was in Paris in 1786 and with the help of Jefferson met French artists like Houdon and David and Mme Vigée-Lebrun, and wealthy amateurs like the Count de Vaudreuil.[11] Jefferson also introduced the American architect Charles Bulfinch to Paris.

When Thomas Paine arrived in Paris in 1787 he was already known and admired for translations of his *Common Sense*, his *Letter Addressed to the Abbé Raynal*, and other works.[12] Upon Franklin's recommendation, Jefferson took him under his wing and he was soon on familiar terms with men like Malesherbes and the Abbé Morellet. Jean Baptiste Le Roy showed him around Paris, took him to call on the aged Buffon, and sat on the committee appointed by the Academy of Sciences to examine his famous design for an iron bridge.[13] He became an associate of the Americanists Condorcet, Brissot, and Mme Roland in the political struggles of the Revolution and was elected to a seat in the Con-

[8] *Mercure de France*, July 31, 1784.
[9] *Moniteur universel*, July 12, 1790; *Archives parlémentaires* (Paris, 1884), 1st series, XVII, 40-41; J. G. Alger, *Paris in 1789-1794* (London, 1902), pp. 71-73.
[10] Durden, *op.cit.*, pp. 327-354; Barlow, *Lettre adressée aux habitants de Piémont* [Grenoble, 1793].
[11] John Trumbull, *Autobiography* (New York, 1841), pp. 95ff.; see also E. Wind, "The Revolution of History Painting," *Journal of the Warburg Institute*, II (1938), 126.
[12] E.g., an essay on the dangers of paper money, in the *Journal politique de Bruxelles*, Aug. 26, 1786.
[13] See Frank Smith, *Thomas Paine, Liberator* (New York, 1938), pp. 119-120.

vention. At least forty-three different French editions of his various works were published, including no less than eleven of his *Rights of Man.*

At the head of this motley collection of energetic individ-ualists were the American Ministers—Franklin, Jefferson, and Gouverneur Morris. The latter, who had originally come to Paris as Robert Morris' agent to negotiate a tobacco con-tract with the Farmers General, was the least influential of the three. He had a wide circle of friends among the aristo-crats, but he made himself so unpopular by his monarchist sympathies that the Revolutionary government had to re-quest his recall as *persona non grata.*[14] Franklin and Jefferson, however, were key factors in the determination of French attitudes toward the United States.

Even after his return to Philadelphia in 1785, Franklin continued to exert a powerful influence. His many friends bade him an affectionate and melancholy farewell, knowing they were seeing him for the last time. "Let us console our regret by this noble thought," said Louis de Lacretelle. "Franklin owed his ashes to America."[15] The Abbés Morellet and De La Roche translated and published the speeches of welcome by which he was greeted in the United States.[16] Back in Philadelphia he was soon receiving a deluge of letters from France, written by great and small, of every sort, from in-quiries on the new American constitution to a request for help in locating a lost son. In his replies he took great pains to counteract the reports of American disunion and anarchy circulating in Europe, and he continued his characteristic methods in congratulating Crèvecoeur and Chastellux on the "handsome likenesses" they had given of his country, in forwarding American publications to his European friends, and in furnishing prominent American travelers to France with letters of introduction.[17]

14 On Gouverneur Morris as well as other Americans in Paris, see his *Diary of the French Revolution, 1789-1793,* ed. B. C. Davenport (Boston, 1939).

15 *Oeuvres* (Paris, 1824), V, 140.

16 *Extraits des gazettes américaines* (Paris, 1786); see *Writings of Benjamin Franklin,* ed. Smyth (New York, 1905), IX, 505, 579.

17 See *Calendar of the Papers of Benjamin Franklin.*

The American Philosophical Society continued to enjoy an undiminished reputation in France, if we may judge by the requests for election, the French contributions, and the comments on the second volume of the *Transactions* published in 1786, which Franklin sent to his friends abroad.[18] No doubt largely at Franklin's recommendation, no less than thirty-one Frenchmen were elected to the society between 1784 and 1793, and they included such figures as Brissot de Warville, George Cabanis, Condorcet, Crèvecoeur, La Rochefoucauld d'Anville, and Vergennes, the minister of foreign affairs.[19] The American Academy of Arts and Sciences in Boston (the plan for which had been conceived by John Adams while on his first visit to Paris) also elected a number of French members, among whom were D'Alembert, Chastellux, De Lalande, Condorcet, and Brissot.

Jefferson's influence as a promoter of Americanism was second only to Franklin's, though his methods differed. He lacked his predecessor's gift for self-dramatization, and during his first years he consciously chose to remain in the background behind his older colleague. It was characteristic that he would occasionally escape the press of affairs by taking refuge in a Carthusian monastery in Paris. His only publications in France during these years were the anonymous limited first edition of his *Notes on Virginia* and Morellet's translation of it, modestly signed "Par M. J***." His authorship of this work and of the Virginia Bill for Establishing Religious Freedom and of the Declaration of Independence

18 *Journal encyclopédique*, April, 1788, pp. 3-28.
19 The others were the Count d'Angiviller, Louis XVI's *directeur général des bâtiments*; Charles Arthaud, of Santo Domingo; Cadet-Gassincourt and Antoine Cadet de Vaux, both chemists; Jacques-Alexandre-César Charles, the aeronaut; M. Coupigny, of Santo Domingo; Stephen Du Ponceau, the veteran volunteer, later to be elected president of the society; Feutry, the poet; René Georges Gastelier; Hubert de Gerbier; the Count de Granchain; Guillaume Grivel; Admiral Guichen; Antoine de La Forest, French consul in Philadelphia; Pierre Le Gaux; Julien David Le Roy; Le Veillard, with whom Franklin had left the manuscript of his *Autobiography;* Moreau de Saint Méry, then in Santo Domingo; Dr. David Nassy, then practicing in Philadelphia; Dr. Noel, who had been a surgeon general in the American army during the war; Louis Otto, secretary of the Legation; Palisot de Beauvois, the botanist; the Abbé de Soulavie, another of Franklin's intimates; Ternant, French minister to the United States; and Dr. Louis Valentin, of Santo Domingo.

were known to the French public, but he did little to publicize his contributions to the American Revolution. Consequently, in the political debates which so frequently cited American examples Jefferson was seldom mentioned. Much more of a nationalist than the cosmopolitan Franklin, he was reserved in his acceptance of French ways, and his friendships in Paris, though they were many, were discriminating. He could never become a public hero like Franklin; he was never represented on the French stage or celebrated in a popular song.[20]

Jefferson's circle of acquaintances, nevertheless, was wide and influential. Franklin had introduced him to Mme Hélvetius' salon at Auteuil, where he had met the Abbé Morellet, Cabanis, Destutt de Tracy, and Volney, and he became intimate with many other old friends of Franklin's like La Rochefoucauld, Mme d'Houdetot, and Du Pont de Nemours.[21] Lafayette, whom he had met first in Virginia, became his close collaborator in negotiations with the French government.[22] Other friends were Condorcet, Marmontel, Chastellux, Lavoisier, Buffon, and De Moustier, for whose appointment as Minister to the United States he was probably largely responsible. Jefferson's chief source of pleasure in France was his enjoyment of architecture, painting, sculpture, and music, so it was natural that he made many friends among the artists in Paris: Houdon, whom he commissioned to go to Mount Vernon to do a statue of Washington; the architects Legrand, Molinos, and Clérisseau; the English painters Richard and Maria Cosway; the sculptor Ceracchi, and the Count d'Angiviller, the *directeur général des bâtiments du roi*.[23]

Whereas Franklin's efforts had been mainly directed toward creating in the French mind a favorable picture of

[20] See Jefferson's letter to Charles Bettini, Sept. 30, 1785, *The Papers of Thomas Jefferson*, ed. J. P. Boyd (Princeton, 1950ff.), VIII, 568-570. *The Papers of Thomas Jefferson* will hereafter be cited as *Jefferson Papers, op.cit.*

[21] See G. Chinard, *Les Amitiés américaines de Madame d'Houdetot* (Paris, 1924) and *Trois amitiés françaises de Jefferson* (Paris, 1927).

[22] See G. Chinard, *Letters of Lafayette and Jefferson* (Baltimore, 1929).

[23] See M. Kimball, "Jefferson in Paris," *North American Review*, CCXLVIII (1939), 73-86.

America, Jefferson's were directed toward creating an accurate one. He was much disturbed by the reports of political chaos in the United States being spread in Europe by the English press, and he attempted to refute them by articles planted in Etienne Luzac's pro-American *Gazette de Leyde* and other European newspapers.[24] He was also worried by the theory of American degeneration. The most important section of his *Notes on Virginia* (written at the request of François Marbois and intended primarily for European readers) was devoted to refuting Buffon, De Pauw, Raynal, and their English imitator Robertson.[25] John Adams had called French misconceptions of America an "Augean Stables,"[26] and Jefferson attempted the herculean task of correction. "If the histories of D'Auberteuil and of Longchamps, and the travels of the Abbé Robin, "he wrote in a letter to the *Journal de Paris,*" can be published in the face of the world, and can be read and believed by those cotemporary with the events they pretend to relate, how may we expect that future ages shall be any better informed?"[27] When Jean Démeunier consulted him in January 1786 on the article on the United States he was commissioned to write for the *Encyclopédie méthodique*, Jefferson jumped at the chance. He gave Démeunier at least three interviews and wrote for him four careful and detailed memoranda, ranging in length from twelve to thirty-seven pages. The resulting article was the most accurate French description of the United States up to this time and included, besides the Declaration of Independence and the Articles of Confederation, the first French translation of the important Virginia Bill for Establishing Religious Freedom, the text of which was supplied by Jefferson.[28]

24 See *Nouvelles extraordinaires de divers endroits* (*Gazette de Leyde*), Dec. 7 and 10, 1784; *Jefferson Papers, op.cit.*, VII, 539-545; also IX, 256-258 (Mazzei's letter to Jefferson, Feb. 6, 1786); VIII, 679 (Mazzei to J. Adams, Jan. 23, 1786); IX, 4-7 (Jefferson's account of the Stanhope Affair); IX, 47-49 (Jefferson to Abigail Adams, Nov. 20, 1785).
25 See also Jefferson's letter to Chastellux, June 7, 1785, *Jefferson Papers, op.cit.*, VIII, 184-186.
26 J. Adams to Mazzei, Dec. 15, 1785, cited *ibid.*, VIII, 678. 27 Aug. 29, 1787.
28 See *Jefferson Papers, op.cit.*, IX, 155-156, 192-193, 382-383; X, 3-65. The

Jefferson likewise helped Filippo Mazzei, an excitable Italian who had been his neighbor in Albemarle County, in writing his *Recherches historiques et politiques sur les Etats-Unis* (1788), a refutation of both Raynal and the Abbé Mably's recently published *Observations sur le gouvernement et les lois des Etats-Unis*. The original suggestion for the book had come from William Short, Jefferson's secretary, but Jefferson approved the idea, lent Mazzei copies of the notes he had prepared for Démeunier, and wrote for his use a long memorandum on American law.[29]

One of the most important accomplishments of these Americans in Paris, and of their French friends, was to make available to the French public the best products of American thought and to provide for the first time a valid documentation for the French image of America. Naturally most of these writings were political. In addition to the continued publications, by Démeunier and others, of the state constitutions, the Declaration of Independence, and the Articles of Confederation, and in addition to the frequent publications after 1787 of the new federal Constitution, the French could read translations of such important expositions of American political theory as *The Federalist* (1792), the many works of Paine, John Adams' *Defence of the Constitutions of the United States* (1792), John Stevens' *Observations on Government* (1789), and Barlow's *Advice to the Privileged Orders* (1794). A picture of American geography and natural history was provided by Jefferson's *Notes on Virginia* (1786) Filson's *Kentucke* (1785), Carver's *Travels* (1784), and Hum-

---

article "Etats-Unis" appeared in the *Encyclopédie méthodique*, section *Economie politique et diplomatique*, II (1786), 345-433, and was republished separately as *Essai sur les Etats-Unis* (Paris, 1786) and later, together with the *Encyclopédie* articles on the individual states, in four volumes as *L'Amérique indépendante* (Ghent, 1790-1791). On Jefferson's similar, but less successful, aid to François Soulès, see *Jefferson Papers*, *op.cit.*, X, 364-383.

29 Jefferson to Mazzei, Nov. 1785, *Jefferson Papers*, *op.cit.*, IX, 67-72. On Jefferson's aid to Mazzei, see *Memoirs of the Life and Peregrinations of the Florentine Philip Mazzei, 1730-1816*, tr. H. R. Marraro (New York, 1942), pp. 293-299; also Jefferson to Démeunier, Feb. 15, 1788, Jefferson Papers, Library of Congress. For a similar effort by Jefferson to aid French writers to gather accurate information, see Jefferson to D'Auberteuil, Feb. 20, 1786, *Jefferson Papers*, *op.cit.*, IX, 290-291.

phrey Marshall's *American Grove* (1788), a catalogue of American trees and shrubs translated by Lézermes, who was in charge of the experimental garden established at Rambouillet to grow American plants sent by the botanist André Michaux.[30] American history was represented by David Ramsay's *History of the American Revolution* (1787), and American literature by Franklin's *Autobiography* (published in French translation in 1791 before it had appeared in English), by various lesser works of Franklin, and by the poetry of Humphreys and Barlow.[31] The significant fact is not that these works were published but that they were widely and attentively read. Many appeared in two or more editions, the most important were given long and careful reviews in the periodicals, particularly in the *Journal encyclopédique* and the *Mercure*, and they were frequently cited by contemporary French writers.[32]

The activity of American diplomats and of French collaborators like Lafayette in disseminating pro-American propaganda was stimulated by the fact that from 1783 on there appeared in France an important current of anti-Americanism. It is true that the government, both royal and Revolutionary, remained officially friendly, that a large majority of the intellectuals and liberal politicians were strongly pro-American, and that the people had not lost the fraternal affection aroused by Franklin and the war. Nevertheless there was a considerable minority who, without being aggressively hostile, were pessimistic about the success of the new nation, took pleasure in debunking the American Dream, and received news of American difficulties and failures with something approaching satisfaction. The division of opinion was not philosophic, as it had been before the war, nor a matter of personal reactions, as it had been in the French army in America, but instead a conflict of political and economic in-

30 See François André Michaux, *Mémoire sur la naturalisation des arbres forestiers de l'Amérique Septentrionale* (Paris, 1805).
31 Dates given are those of the first French versions.
32 E.g., the poet André Chénier planned a poem based on Filson's *Kentucke* and was an attentive reader of Paine, whom he quoted in a letter to Raynal in 1791. *Oeuvres poétiques* (Paris, 1878), II, 124-125; *Oeuvres en prose* (Paris, 1879), p. 83.

terests on which the United States had a very real bearing. As one observer remarked in 1786, "Since the revolution which assured the sovereignty of the United States, European observers have painted of conditions there pictures which are sometimes enthusiastic and sometimes lamentable. The different colors under which the United States has been represented are the product of a great diversity of opinions, and we may affirm without fear of contradiction that party spirit, prejudice, and politics have invented three-quarters of the descriptions."[33]

The principal source of unfavorable news on the United States was the English press, which, quite understandably, was eager in many cases to report and exaggerate every indication of failure among the rebellious colonists. From these sources French papers copied verbatim reports that the population of the United States had decreased by a million during the war, that the importation of slaves had increased, that indentured servants were actually "white slaves," and that Americans were failing to meet their obligations to British creditors. Particularly telling was a letter allegedly written by Dr. Richard Price, printed by the English papers and copied in France, in which that old champion of American freedom admitted that the reports he was receiving from his American correspondents made him fear that he had made himself ridiculous by the importance he had attributed to the American Revolution and that his hopes for the future of the United States had been chimerical.[34]

French publications of these reports were not necessarily prompted by ill will, for as Mazzei wrote Adams, editors frequently were forced to print them for lack of any other sources of American news.[35] It was also true that reports forwarded from American correspondents were often scarcely more encouraging. They told of popular opposition to the Society of the Cincinnati, of squabbles between Congress and the states over the public debt, of Vermont's armed resistance to New York's claims, of "disunion in our councils and lack

[33] *Journal politique de Bruxelles*, Aug. 12, 1786.
[34] *Ibid.*, Dec. 1785, p. 164.       [35] *Jefferson Papers, op.cit.*, VIII, 679.

of power and energy in our executive departments," of bank failures, of Shays' Rebellion, of the impotence of Congress, of separatist movements within the states, of restrictions placed on the freedom of the press, of disorders and riots caused by popular demands for paper money, and of widespread hostility to the proposed federal Constitution. There was, consequently, perhaps some injustice in the total blame that Jefferson, Adams, Mazzei, Lafayette, and French journalists placed on the English press.[36] The *Journal politique de Bruxelles* once footnoted an item of American news with the notice: "We wish to advise the public, and especially those enthusiasts who write us insulting letters whenever the news from America contradicts their reveries, that this news is not taken from English papers, as they say, but is literally translated from American papers."[37]

Whatever the sources of these reports, they were welcomed by conservatives and royalists who, reacting against the idealization of America as the triumph of liberalism, democracy, and republicanism, were anxious to find evidence of the failure of these principles. Lafayette found such sentiments prevalent in European courts, and he wrote Washington and Jefferson that the reports of American weakness and disorder under the Confederation, spread by European papers and English ambassadors, were causing a decline in America's reputation, "which delights her enemies, harms her interests even with her friends, and provides the opponents of liberty with anti-republican arguments."[38]

The danger to the United States was diplomatic, for Jefferson discovered that refusal of the state legislatures to cooperate with Congress was a severe handicap in his negotiations with Vergennes on French-American trade problems.[39]

[36] E.g., Lafayette to Jefferson, Sept. 4, 1785, *ibid.*, VIII, 478-479; *ibid.*, VII, 540-543; John Adams to President of Congress, Sept. 8, 1783, *The Revolutionary Diplomatic Correspondence of the United States*, ed. F. Wharton, VI, 682; *Mercure de France*, Mar. 1, 1788.

[37] Aug. 19, 1786.

[38] *Mémoires, correspondance et manuscrits* (Paris, 1837-1838), II, 135, 203; Lafayette to Jefferson, Sept. 4, 1785, *Jefferson Papers, op.cit.*, VIII, 478-479.

[39] "Jefferson's Report on Conversations with Vergennes," *Jefferson Papers, op.cit.*, IX, 143.

To the French liberals the danger was even greater, for it threatened to produce an attitude of cynicism and disillusion toward America and the political ideals she represented.

There were ample signs of such an attitude. The Abbé Mably, in his influential *Observations sur le gouvernement et les lois des Etats-Unis* (1784), had expressed serious doubts about the success of the American republics. He had little faith in the political wisdom of the common man, and he warned that democracy, however good it might be in principle, when unmodified as in the United States by aristocratic institutions, was dangerous and impractical. He saw similar dangers in religious liberty and freedom of the press, and he predicted that the development of trade and industry would inevitably corrupt the morals of the American people.

Such ideas were echoed by others, and often in a less friendly tone. François Soulès, in his *Histoire des troubles de l'Amérique anglaise* (1787), derided the writers who had been induced by their enthusiasm and philanthropy to see in the United States a republic of philosophers and a haven of liberty for all thinking men. They had blindly believed all the inhabitants of North America to be virtuous, enlightened men acting on noble principles. "They do not realize that in America the wise are few indeed in comparison with the ignorant, the selfish, and those men who blindly allow themselves to be led—those who in the kingdoms of Europe are known as the people."[40]

To this distrust of American democracy was added a cynical disbelief in the reality of American liberty. Mallet du Pan, an inveterate royalist, reviewing Ramsay's *History of American Revolution*, pointed out that the colonies had been prosperous and contented before the Revolution, that many Americans had opposed the war, and that the states had been forced to draft "idlers and profligates" to fill out the ranks of the army. "It was the dregs of America which fought the dregs of Europe, for the highest and noblest of causes. It was not thus that liberty founded its rule in the

40 IV, 263-264.

mountains of Switzerland or in the marshes of Holland."[41] In the same tone was the following item from the *Mercure de France*: "The friends of justice and humanity will be perhaps astonished to learn that in the United States, in that asylum of peace, happiness and liberty, which has so often re-echoed to those sacred words 'All men are created equal,' there still are today nearly seven hundred thousand slaves."[42]

The danger of such ideas to the liberal cause was well expressed by one writer in 1788: "False reports on the principles of the American government and the effects of the Revolution have been spread and are still being spread every day, and some of these lies could have tragic results. By giving to mercenary declaimers the right boldly to calumniate Liberty, such misinformation may inspire in men indifference, or even hesitation, about the exercise of their natural rights, and thus render legitimate or at least excusable all the attacks of political perversity."[43]

Clearly, as Brissot said, "it was important to refute all these lies," particularly because "many Frenchmen, unfamiliar with republican constitutions and deceived by the prejudices of their education, regard that form of government as equivalent to a state of perpetual chaos, in which life and property are constantly in the greatest danger."[44] The true nature of conditions in America thus became a political issue, and the efforts of Jefferson and Franklin were strongly supported by Lafayette, who sent articles to various papers,[45] by Mazzei in his *Recherches*, by Otto in his official reports to the government from the United States,[46] by Brissot,[47] and by many others of the Americanist camp.

Unfortunately the American cause suffered from a certain amount of internal feuding. Chastellux ridiculed the Quakers

41 *Mercure de France*, Oct. 6, 1787.
42 Mar. 1, 1788.
43 *Mercure de France*, Feb. 23, 1788.
44 Jacques Pierre Brissot de Warville and Etienne Clavière, *De la France et des Etats-Unis* (London, 1787), pp. 304-305.
45 *Jefferson Papers*, *op.cit.*, VIII, 478, 679.
46 See George Bancroft, *History of the Formation of the Constitution* (New York, 1882), p. 454.
47 Brissot and Clavière, *op.cit.*

in his *Voyages* and Mazzei supported him, adding a scathing attack on William Penn, and both men frankly deplored the existence of slavery in the South. Moreover, Mazzei warned his readers that Crèvecoeur's picture of bucolic felicity given in his *Lettres d'un cultivateur américain* was by no means typical of the United States as a whole. Such criticisms were heresy to a radical Americanist like Brissot, who attacked both men violently and succeeded in stirring up both bitterness and some confusion in the public mind.[48]

Not all anti-Americanism was political in nature. Some arose from economic causes. Vergennes, in making the decision in 1778 to support the United States against England, had argued that American independence would inflict irreparable losses on English trade and would considerably extend that of France. After the conclusion of the peace treaties, the French government and French exporters apparently expected that American enmity toward England and gratitude to France would divert to France the profitable trade England had monopolized before the war. They were encouraged in this hope by the English refusal to negotiate a trade treaty with the United States and by the resentment of the Americans against the English restrictive trade policy. But in such expectations they were badly deceived. By 1789 British exports had risen to pre-war levels and their excess over imports from America was greater even than in 1772.[49] On the other hand, French exports to America, though of course greater than before the war, remained far below those of England. Americans were discouraged from shipping their products to French ports by the tobacco monopoly of the Farmers General, by the strangling mass of red tape which delayed unloadings, by excessive duties on certain items, and by the lack of demand for a number of important American products. In addition, French exporters got off to a bad start right after the war by attempting to dump in the United

[48] J. P. Brissot de Warville, *Examen critique des Voyages de M. le marquis de Chastellux* (London, 1786), and *Réponse à une critique des Lettres d'un cultivateur américain* (Paris, 1788).

[49] See S. Morison and H. S. Commager, *The Growth of the American Republic* (New York, 1942), p. 269.

States shoddy merchandise unsuited to American buying habits, which went unsold or was sold at a loss, thus destroying both American confidence in French manufacturers and French interest in the American market. Americans were used to English goods, and French manufacturers would not modify their products to fit the demands of American consumers. More serious was the fact that the French were unable or unwilling to grant the long terms of credit which the Americans were used to receiving from the English. Moreover in the chaotic and depressed economic conditions following the Revolution, there were many American bankruptcies and a number of French exporters suffered serious losses. Some debts contracted by Americans in France during the war were not honored, many of the American firms established in France went bankrupt, and those American houses, in particular that of Robert Morris, which obtained credit in France often failed to meet their obligations.[50] Lastly, there was the matter of the American public debt. The United States still owed the French volunteer officers a large amount of back pay, plus interest, a neglected obligation which Jefferson warned would "give birth to new imputations, and a relapse of credit." In addition, of course, was the national foreign debt, the repayment of which seemed very uncertain.

These unfortunate circumstances produced two results. First, they created the idea that Americans had a low standard of business ethics and that the economic position of the United States was very shaky. This idea fitted with the picture of political chaos and disunity. Second, they gave rise to the belief that the Americans felt no genuine gratitude for French aid and that at heart they remained attached to England.

An additional source of ill feeling was the trade rivalry in

50 Swan, op.cit.; "Jefferson's Amplification of Subjects Discussed with Vergennes," Jefferson Papers, op.cit., IX, 107-112; "Jefferson's Report on Conversations with Vergennes," ibid., IX, 139-145; Lafayette's "Résumé au Comité du Commerce avec les Etats-Unis," ibid., IX, 338-344; "Letter from American and French Merchants at L'Orient, April 21, 1786," ibid., IX, 390-393; Otto to Vergennes, June 30, 1785, ibid., VIII, 272.

the West Indies. In 1784 the colonial planters persuaded the French government to issue an *arrêt* opening seven West Indian ports into which foreign traders would be permitted to import from the United States and other nations certain products, notably salt beef, salt fish, and wheat, and to export molasses, rum, and goods of French origin. This decree provoked a storm of protests on the part of French shippers, who had hitherto had a monopoly on this trade. A war of pamphlets ensued, with one Dubucq, chief clerk in the Ministry of the Navy, defending the government's position against a volley of anonymous invective. While the immediate objects of attack in these pamphlets were not the foreign (i.e., English and American) traders, the entire source of the bitter feeling was the fear that considerable profits would be transferred from French to American and English pockets.[51] Throughout the decade after the American war, commercial rivalry in the Caribbean remained a point of friction and was one of the chief sources of anti-American feeling among French merchants.

The many Frenchmen and Americans who were anxious to preserve good relations and to promote mutually profitable trade did all they could to counteract such feelings and improve commercial relations. Jefferson attempted to have modified the tobacco monopoly of the Farmers General, which was choking off the main French import from the United States, and to promote trade in other American products. Lafayette, as a member of a government committee on American trade, did all he could to help him. During his visit to the United States in 1784 Lafayette asked James Swan to draw up a memorandum on French-American commerce, which was translated by Létombe, French consul in Boston, and forwarded to the French government. Later, Swan expanded this memorandum into a thorough study of the

[51] *Arrêt du Conseil d'Etat du Roi, concernant le commerce étranger dans les isles françaises de l'Amérique. Du 30 août 1784* (Paris, 1784); Dubucq, *Le Pour et le contre sur un objet de grande discorde et d'importance majeure* (London, 1784); memoirs published in 1784 by merchants of Nantes, Marseilles, Le Havre, Bordeaux, and La Rochelle; *Réplique à l'auteur du Pour et contre* (London, 1785); etc., etc.

problem which he published in Paris in French.[52] Brissot, with his friends Etienne Clavière, Crèvecoeur, and Nicholas Bergasse, a Parisian lawyer, founded in 1787 the Société Gallo-Américaine to promote commercial relations between the two countries and foster mutual understanding and friendship. The same year Brissot and Clavière published *De la France et des Etats-Unis*, a lengthy study of French-American trade which showed how it could be expanded to France's benefit. Mazzei's *Recherches* also had a chapter on this problem. Pointing up the political implications of this commercial tension, he wrote, "It is claimed in Europe that Americans feel as great an inclination toward the English as they have an antipathy for the French, and it is to this predisposition that is attributed the difficulty in establishing a flourishing trade between France and the new republics."[53] In a letter to Necker written in 1789 and published the following year, De Moustier said French merchants had been discouraged by their large losses, but he blamed them for sending inferior goods, for not taking into account the lack of specie in the United States, and for not selecting reliable agents, and he insisted that the economic revival in the United States, which he dated from 1785, offered many fine opportunities to French exporters.[54] The following year Ducher, recently returned from his consulship in the United States, published, as a practical means of promoting trade with the United States, the bill recently passed by Congress regulating foreign trade.[55] All these friendly efforts did bring about some action on the part of the French government, but it is doubtful that they had much effect on the opinions of French businessmen.

This sort of hostile opinion was reinforced by the questionable activities of American land companies in Paris. From about 1788 on, agents of American speculators began to come to Paris to sell frontier lands, either as speculative

[52] *Op.cit.*
[53] *Recherches historiques et politiques sur les Etats-Unis de l'Amérique Septentrionale* (Paris, 1788), IV, 54.
[54] *Op.cit.*        [55] *Analyse des loix commerciales.*

investments or for the purpose of actual settlement. The social chaos of the Revolution boosted their sales greatly. The chance of obtaining large tracts of what was represented as very fertile land at prices which seemed ridiculously low by European standards appealed to nervous Frenchmen looking for a safe foreign investment for their capital, to frightened aristocrats in search of asylum, and to many bourgeois who had lost their livelihood in the general social and economic dislocation. There were a number of such agents in Paris and the usual practice was to set up a dummy French company to handle the sales.

A Colonel Blackden was in Paris in 1789 trying to sell 50,000 acres of Kentucky land.[56] In 1790 a lawyer named Gibé was advertising 300,000 acres in western Virginia.[57] William Constable came to Paris in 1792 to sell a large tract in northern New York known as Macomb's Purchase. He succeeded in interesting Paul Chassanis, who, in association with Le Ray de Chaumont, formed the Compagnie de New York, which raised £25,000 to purchase a tract of 215,000 acres to be resold to French emigrants.[58]

The most famous—or infamous—affair was that of the Scioto Company. This group of American speculators, headed by a financier named William Duer, sent the poet Joel Barlow to Paris as their agent in 1788, where he enlisted the services of an English adventurer, ironically named William Playfair. Together they organized the French Compagnie du Scioto in August 1789, one month after the fall of the Bastille. In that atmosphere of violence, uncertainty, and insecurity the glowing picture these salesmen painted in their prospectuses seemed to many French men and women a miraculous solution to all their fears and problems.[59] A veritable mania

[56] *Plan d'un établissement qu'une compagnie pourrait former à Kentucky* [Paris?, 1789]; *Notice sur Kentucke, contrée de l'Ohio* [Paris?, 1789].
[57] *Moniteur universel,* Aug. 9, 1790.
[58] See T. W. Clarke, *Emigrés in the Wilderness* (New York, 1941).
[59] Manasseh Cutler, *Description du sol, des productions, &c., sur cette portion des Etats-Unis située entre la Pensylvanie, les rivières de l'Ohio et du Scioto, et le lac Erié* (Paris, 1789); *Observations générales et impartiales sur l'affaire du Scioto* (Paris, 1790); *Prospectus pour l'établissement sur les rivières d'Ohio et de Scioto en Amérique* (Paris, 1789-1790).

swept the city; citizens of all classes and professions rushed to buy Scioto lands before they were all sold. During the summer of 1790 about 1,000 emigrants bound for the Scioto sailed on a number of different ships. On arrival they learned to their dismay that the company could not give clear title to the lands it had sold since it held only a preemption on the tract from the Ohio Company; that the lands, located in southern Ohio, were a long, hard journey from the coast; that an Indian war made travel down .the Ohio unsafe; that no provision (which the prospectus had specifically guaranteed) had been made either for their transportation or their shelter during the approaching winter; and that the company was on the verge of bankruptcy, for the misnamed Playfair had absconded with most of the Paris funds. About 500 persons appear to have eventually reached the site of the proposed town, patriotically christened Gallipolis, and spent the first winter there. However, the site was unhealth‧ ful, and the settlers were totally unprepared both by temperament and experience for the rigors of frontier life. Though some persistent individuals stayed on, the French gradually dispersed and the town was finally taken over by native Americans. Many scattered to various American towns and cities, but a large number returned to France, some immediately after their arrival.[60]

This tragic affair received a great deal of attention and occasioned many pamphlets and newspaper articles. Among both the revolutionary and royalist parties the reaction, which began in the spring of 1790, was political. The leaders of this emigration were conservative aristocrats horrified by the violence of the Revolution, and their flight to a transatlantic asylum was interpreted by the democrats as glaring lack of faith in the new order and hence as an unpatriotic act, and by the royalists as a further proof of the tragic state into which France had fallen.[61] The line taken by the demo-

[60] See T. T. Belote, *The Scioto Speculation and the French Settlement at Gallipolis* (Cincinnati, 1907); J. R. McGovern, "The Gallipolis Colony," *Amer. Cath. Hist. Soc.*, XXXVII (1926); H. Carré, *Les Emigrés français en Amérique, 1789-1793* (Paris, 1898); etc.

[61] E.g., *Le Fouet national*, Feb. 9, 1790.

crats was that there was no longer need for Frenchmen to go to America in search of liberty, and that if these people wished so strongly to become farmers they should patriotically remain at home and develop French lands.[62] These politicians greeted the failure of the venture with satisfaction, but they felt no ill will toward the Americans for contributing to the discomfort of the recalcitrant aristocrats. But in their efforts to dissuade bourgeois from following the pernicious example set by the nobles, they willfully painted life in the United States in the darkest colors. One pamphlet, *Le Nouveau Mississippi, ou les Dangers d'habiter les bords du Scioto* (1790), revived all the old slogans of De Pauw's theory of American degeneration—that the land was not fertile, that the climate was cold and harsh, that Americans died young, that their women were barren at thirty, and that they were a lazy, apathetic people, eating coarse food and indifferent to the arts and comforts of life.

The unhappy emigrants who straggled back to Paris had, understandably, little good to say of the United States. They felt, with some justification, that they had been swindled, and their resentment was transmuted and generalized into extreme anti-Americanism. One of them described the United States thus: "The inhabitant bears on his brow the mark of poverty and dishonor; religion and marriage are unknown; bad food and bad drink; the only thing that is good and common is the wood. Winter lasts six months there, and it is very cold; the heat too is excessive, and the days are very short in all seasons."[63]

Besides giving rise to such pictures of life in America, the Scioto episode was also considered a prime example of American unscrupulousness. De Moustier sent a letter to the National Assembly, denouncing the scheme as a fraud and a deceit and urging the passage of a law forbidding such emigrations.[64]

[62] *Moniteur universel*, Mar. 6, 1790; *Le Nouveau Mississippi, ou les Dangers d'habiter les bords du Scioto* (Paris, 1790); *Chronique de Paris*, Aug. 5, 1790; *Songe d'un habitant du Scioto* (Paris, 1790); etc.

[63] D'Allemagne, *Nouvelles du Scioto* (Paris, 1790).

[64] *Lettre à l'Assemblée Nationale. Séance du 2 août 1790* [Paris, 1790].

There were not a few French travelers and residents in America before the Emigration who shared these unfavorable views of American society. When Brissot visited the United States in 1788, he found among the French consuls and travelers a violent prejudice against democratic and republican government. The Frenchmen all told him that the American government was on the verge of chaos, the constitution was ludicrous, the finances were unsound, the public debt would never be paid, and that there was no good faith or justice or respect for law to be found in America. According to his account, the French were insolent to Americans, ridiculed them, and continually complained that Philadelphia lacked the amenities of Paris.[65]

Perhaps Brissot's report of French prejudices was exaggerated, but it certainly was not without truth. French businessmen who had attempted to establish themselves in the United States often left America "sick of its Liberty, its manners and its laws."[66] G. J. A. Ducher, when he was consul in Portsmouth, New Hampshire, and Wilmington, North Carolina, was miserable in the United States and made himself thoroughly disliked by Americans.[67] Victor Du Pont in his letters home complained of the dullness of American dances and the awkward manners of American girls, their eager pursuit of husbands, and the heavy drinking by the men after dinner.[68] De Moustier, the French minister, was irked by the Americans' inflated concept of their own importance in world politics and he reported to his king that the government of the United States was hopelessly disorganized and that this "phantom of democracy" would inevitably degenerate into despotism.[69] His sister-in-law, Madame de Bréhan, had had fantastic illusions of the bucolic simplicity of the society to which she was going, and she was most bitterly

<hr />

[65] *Nouveau voyage dans les Etats-Unis* (Paris, 1791).

[66] Gilles de Lavallée to G. Washington, Mar. 13, 1787, *Jefferson Papers, op.cit.*, VIII, 379.

[67] See F. L. Nussbaum, *Commercial Policy in the French Revolution: A Study of the Career of G. J. A. Ducher* (Washington, 1923).

[68] *Life of Eleuthère Irénée Du Pont* (Newark, 1923-1927), I, 101.

[69] "Correspondence of the Comte de Moustier with the Comte Montmorin, 1787-1789," *Amer. Hist. Review*, VIII (1903), 733; IX (1903), 86.

disappointed. She wrote Jefferson querulously, "I miss most sincerely your presence here. Everybody in the United States does not think like you; in general Americans are not fond of candor, simplicity and goodness. I had but these virtues to offer them; they were not enough. You thought that I should be loved by your countrymen. . . . How badly you were deceived!"[70]

This strong anti-democratic and anti-republican bias of the diplomatic agents merely reflected the attitude of the Ministry of Foreign Affairs. In August 1787 Otto, then Chargé d'Affaires, received from his government the following advice: "It appears, sir, that in all the American provinces there is more or less tendency toward democracy; that in many this extreme form of government will finally prevail. The result will be that the confederation will have little stability, and that by degrees the different states will subsist in perfect independence of each other. This revolution will not be regretted by us. We have never pretended to make of America a useful ally; we have had no other object than to deprive Great Britain of that vast continent. Therefore we can regard with indifference both the movements which agitate certain provinces and the fermentation which prevails in Congress."[71]

In addition to these political and diplomatic sources of unfriendly opinions, there also existed, apparently, a wide popular acceptance of the theory of American degeneration. Curiously, its existence is attested principally by the frequent refutations. Having been retracted by Raynal and Buffon, the theory was no longer intellectually respectable, and apparently no writer of any standing championed it during these years. But the earlier works of Buffon, De Pauw, and Raynal were still on the library shelves and were still being read. The belief that the American environment condemned Americans to physical and intellectual inferiority had taken deep root in men's minds and had become a perma-

[70] Chinard, *Trois amitiés françaises de Jefferson*, p. 46.
[71] Quoted in Bancroft, *op.cit.*, p. 438. See also "Correspondence of De Moustier and Montmorin," VIII, 713.

nent part of the mythology of America. If it had not been so widely believed, it would not have been so frequently and vigorously attacked. Jefferson's refutation in the *Notes on Virginia* was perhaps the most convincing and the most frequently quoted. When Morellet's translation of the book was reviewed in the *Mercure,* Jefferson's arguments on this point were cited in detail and the reviewer concluded approvingly, "It is indeed a very powerful argument against that alleged degeneration to name George Washington, Benjamin Franklin, Rittenhouse, the Adamses, Hancock, Benezet, Gates, Stark, Greene, Laurens, and the author himself."[72]

But Jefferson was by no means alone in combatting the idea. Joseph Mandrillon, Démeunier, Mazzei, and Brissot all felt it necessary to emphasize that the climate had no harmful effects on American intelligence, longevity, or fertility.[73] The most important refutation of the theory was contained in an anonymous article published in the *Mercure* on August 5, 1786, "Observations sur une opinion de M. de Paw." The author said that several of De Pauw's errors had been corrected, "but there is a principal one . . . which has not, it seems to us, been challenged and which deserves to be. We feel all the more justified in denouncing it, because many people still accept it." This error was precisely the theory that the American environment enfeebled the human species, and that "the descendants of Europeans are so affected by the influence of this climate that we must not expect from them anything great in the arts, in science, in war, or in letters." De Pauw had, the author emphasized, especially singled out the English colonies as an example of his thesis, and the article was devoted to refuting De Pauw by extolling American genius.

It is against this minority current of anti-Americanism that the American Dream appears in its true perspective. It

[72] June 2, 1787. See also Chastellux's letter to Jefferson on this subject, June 2, 1785, *Jefferson Papers, op.cit.,* VIII, 174-175, and Jefferson's reply, June 7, 1785, *ibid.,* VIII, 184-186.
[73] Joseph Mandrillon, *Le Spectateur américain* (Amsterdam, 1785), p. 128; *Encyclopédie méthodique, Economie politique et diplomatique,* II (1786), 396; Mazzei, *Recherches,* III, 91-93; Brissot, *Nouveau voyage,* II, 139-160.

was the defense as well as the affirmation of a certain ideological and political position. As such, it constituted an important element in the current of ideas flowing toward the
French Revolution.[74] It was essentially the belief that certain
key doctrines of the century were achieving their first realization in the United States. The greater the faith in these
doctrines, the greater was the tendency to exaggerate their
success in America, and thus to fashion an idealized image
of American life. It was a projection of French aspirations
upon a scene which was both accommodating and distant
enough to blur the inconsistencies and contradictions.

It is, of course, impossible to say with any precision in what
sections of French society this mirage or dream was accepted.
In general it seems to have been, on the one hand, the belief
of the majority of the liberal intellectuals, among whom
were a good percentage of aristocrats, and on the other hand
it appears to have been accepted in diluted and sentimentalized version by the bourgeoisie and lower classes.

Public opinion is difficult to evaluate at a distance. After
1783 there were fewer manifestations of popular Americanism, and the intense enthusiasm of the war years never returned. Nevertheless the general sentiment appears to have
remained unaffected. Franklin continued to hold a high
reputation among the people, and his death in 1790 occasioned a city-wide expression of grief. In 1793 the citizens
of the Pont Neuf section petitioned to have a street renamed
Rue Franklin,[75] and the same year at a popular festival in
Versailles Franklin's bust was carried at the head of the
parade.[76] The hero worship of John Paul Jones was a parallel
manifestation. The Scioto mania of 1790, which infected all
classes, was in itself a revelation of the broad basis of this
idealized picture of life in America.

It does not appear that the anti-Americanism of the businessman, certain aristocrats, and conservative politicians and

[74] See D. Mornet, *Les Origines intellectuelles de la Révolution Française*
(Paris, 1933), pp. 389ff.
[75] *Annales de la République Française*, Feb. 9, 1793.
[76] *Journal universel*, Aug. 29, 1793.

intellectuals had much influence on the average Frenchman. On the other hand, the popular concept of life in America was neither specific nor intellectualized. What existed was a general sympathy towards the Americans as recent allies against England and later, during the French Revolution's early stages, the belief that the Americans were the only friends of a France surrounded by reactionary enemies. In addition there was the general but somewhat vague impression that the Americans were simple, virtuous farmers who had bravely defended the cause of liberty and who were grateful admirers of the French.

The best available index to this opinion is found in the popular plays, novels, poetry, and prints of the time which treated American themes. Local color was rare in these, and there was little political or ideological content. The main interest was in the pathos of the incidents, in idealized portraits of Franklin, Washington, Lafayette, and other American heroes, and in the theme of French-American fraternity.

A favorite subject was the story of Captain Charles Asgill, an English officer who had been held hostage in retaliation for a British atrocity and who had been saved from execution, it was believed, by a last-minute plea from Marie Antoinette to Washington. De Mayer's novel *Asgill* (1784) and the several dramatic versions of the episode, of which the best was Marsollier's play produced in 1793, all offered opportunities for tributes to Washington and affecting tableaux of French-American brotherhood.[77]

Love stories involving French officers and American girls permitted the sentimentalizing of the French-American theme, as in Gorgy's play *Les Torts apparents, ou la famille américaine* (1787), Artaud's story "Le préjugé détruit" (1789),[78] and Nougaret's novel *Honorine Clarens* (1792). Certain incidents from the war also lent themselves to the popular sentimental taste. The anonymous "Histoire du

[77] R——— de M., *Asgill* [1784?]; Le Barbier, *Asgill* (London, 1785); Billardon de Sauvigny, *Abdir* (Paris, 1785); Marsollier de Vivetières, *Asgill* (Paris, 1793).
[78] *Mercure de France*, Nov. 27, 1784.

Major André" added to the tragic story of the English spy an unhappy love affair,[79] and D'Auberteuil's *Miss MacRae* (1784) was a typical eighteenth-century sentimental novel involving seductions, death scenes, and the usual bathetic paraphernalia. Ducray-Duminil's long novel, *Lolotte et Fanfan* (1788), was laid in part in the United States and painted an idealized picture of American life culled from a variety of second-hand sources.

Poetic treatment of the American theme was also fairly frequent, and here too was the same tendency to present an idealized but undefined picture of American life. For instance, L. G. Bourdon, who is said to have visited the United States, in his very long and very bad poem *Voyage d'Amérique* (1786), described the Americans as a "wise, free and happy people," living according to the dictates of reason and the laws of nature, who combined the blessings of tolerance and equality, the joys of a simple virtuous existence, and the cultivation of the arts and sciences. Sometimes American subjects were mere pretexts for light and sentimental verse, as in Castéra's "A une jeune Quakeresse";[80] sometimes they formed the theme of patriotic poems, as in Le Normand de l'Osier's *Ode sur la conquête de l'Amérique* (1786), which lauded Washington and Franklin. These two heroes occasioned a host of minor pieces of poetry and doggerel, such as Nogent's "Inscription pour le buste du general Washington"[81] and the Baroness de Bourdic's "Impromptu pour le portrait de M. Franklin, fait au crayon, par Mademoiselle de Givonne, âgée de douze ans."[82] Exotic themes inspired by the Indians and the primitive forest were still rare, though they were present in *Honorine Clarens* and in Dumaniant's comedy, *Le Français en Huronie* (1787).

Numerous prints were published of famous scenes from the war and of American and French heroes, of which the most popular were published by Godefroy and Ponce.[83] In

[79] *Ibid.*, Feb. 28, 1789.  [80] *Almanach des muses*, 1786, p. 117.
[81] *Ibid.*, 1788, p. 64, and *Mercure de France*, May 12, 1787.
[82] *Almanach des muses*, 1784, p. 70. See G. Chinard, "Benjamin Franklin et la muse provinciale," *Proc. Amer. Philos. Soc.*, XCVII (1953), 493-510.
[83] François Godefroy and Nicolas Ponce, *Collection d'estampes représentant*

these engravings American street scenes were, in the costumes of the figures and the architecture of the buildings, indistinguishable from European settings.

After the Bastille, the American became a familiar character on the French stage.[84] Franklin was a favorite,[85] and after his death he was deified as one of the demi-gods of the Revolution. In Dejaure's *L'Ombre de Mirabeau* (1791) he was represented in the Elysian Fields in company with Cicero, Demosthenes, Jean Jacques Rousseau, Voltaire, and Brutus welcoming the shade of Mirabeau. Washington was the hero of Billardon de Sauvigny's famous *Vashington ou la liberté du nouveau monde* (1791), and was of course the central figure in the several Asgill plays.

As opposition to the Revolution by the hostile European coalition developed, the emphasis returned to the theme of America the ally of France. In *La Prise de Toulon* (1794) an American declaimed

> Tyrans, tyrans, vous m'êtes en horreur,
> Craignez ma haine et ma fureur.
> Vous avez sauvé ma patrie
> O vous! Français, nos bons amis,
> Je ne servirai point parmi vos ennemis.[86]

In *Le Dîner des peuples* (1794), an allegorical play by the popular and prolific playwright Alexandre Duval, the goddess of Nature announces a tableau in which "the people of America, friends of republicans for they are the friends of Liberty, which they, like us, have won by their courage

---

les événements de la guerre pour la liberté de l'Amérique Septentrionale (Paris [1784]).

[84] See K. N. McKee, "The Popularity of the 'American' on the French Stage during the Revolution," *Proc. Amer. Philos. Soc.*, LXXXIII (1940), 479-491.

[85] Rude, *Le Journaliste des ombres* (1790); Chaussard, *La France régénérée* (Paris, 1791); Dejaure, *L'Ombre de Mirabeau* (Paris, 1791); Des Fontaines, *L'Imprimeur ou la Fête de Franklin* (1791); Sauvigny, *Vashington* (Paris, 1791).

[86] "Tyrants, tyrants, I behold you with horror. Fear my hatred and my fury. You, O French, our good friends, you saved my land, and I shall not serve in the ranks of your enemies." L. B. Picard, *La Prise de Toulon* (Paris, an II), p. 4.

*143*

and perseverance, meet and embrace their allies, the people of France."[87]

Undoubtedly, public opinion—that is, the opinion of the non-intellectual majority, on all social levels—was to a great extent shaped by the writings of the various Americanists, both directly and indirectly. Raynal's *Histoire philosophique* was one of the most widely read books of the time, and works like Crèvecoeur's *Lettres d'un cultivateur américain* could appeal to a broad audience. An example of the process by which ideas were diffused is Madame Renelle's *Nouvelle géographie*, a widely used schoolbook first published in 1786. It repeated all of Buffon's and De Pauw's theories on the degenerative effect of American climate on animals and Indians, but at the same time it described the United States with all the clichés of the Americanist *Philosophes* as a land of prosperity, liberty, equality, religious freedom, virtue, and enlightenment.[88]

The Americanism of the intellectuals and politicians was of a quite different order from this imprecise popular sympathy. Such upper-strata Americanism of course found a ready audience in a pro-American public and was supported by popular opinion, but it differed in that it had definite ideological and political purposes and in that it was the product of a relatively small but influential group of thinkers. These men and women included a large share of the intellectual, artistic, and scientific leaders of France, among whom were many of the figures who were to dominate the National Assembly. The most active and influential Americanists were Lafayette, Brissot de Warville, Crèvecoeur, Madame d'Houdetot, Madame Helvétius, Condorcet, Madame Roland, La Rochefoucauld d'Anville, Du Pont de Nemours, Chastellux, Delacroix, Démeunier, the Abbés Morellet and De La Roche, Hilliard d'Auberteuil, Lacretelle, and Madame de Tessé, and in Holland Joseph Mandrillon, and C. G. F. Dumas. Moving in the same circles, sympathetic and occasionally contributing,

[87] McKee, *op.cit.*, p. 489.
[88] L. E. B. Renelle, *Nouvelle géographie à l'usage des instituts et des gouvernantes françaises* (Berlin, 1786-1789), III, 7-10, 49-75.

*144*

were men such as Cabanis, Buffon, Guillotin, Sieyès, Bailly, Chamfort, Barbeu Dubourg, Mirabeau, Houdon, Court de Gébelin, Rabaut Saint Etienne, André and Marie Joseph Chénier, Billardon de Sauvigny, Moreau de Saint Méry, Liancourt, Parny, Cadet de Vaux, Volney, Ginguené, the Prince de Beauvau, Lalande, Roederer, Gallois, Fauchet, Target, Saint Lambert, De Moustier, Marmontel, and Malesherbes. Practically all of these men and women were friends of Franklin and Jefferson and they welcomed cordially such new arrivals from America as Paine, Crèvecoeur, Gouverneur Morris, and Mazzei.

In no sense could these persons be said to form a party; this Americanism was too diffuse for that. But there were certain *foyers* of Americanism such as Mme Helvétius' salon at Auteuil, Mme d'Houdetot's circle, the Lodge of the Nine Sisters, the revolutionary Société de 1789 which met at the Palais Royal, Brissot's Société Gallo-Américaine, and the Musée. All these groups were interlocked by common members and together formed a closely knit body in which Americanism was one of the governing ideas. Out of this elite, Americanism, both as a philosophical and political doctrine, radiated and influenced a host of minor intellectuals, both in Paris and in the provinces.

Among such intelligent and vigorous thinkers there naturally arose differences of interest and opinion, and occasionally open quarrels, such as those occasioned by Brissot's attack on Chastellux and Mazzei, and Mazzei's on Crèvecoeur. But on the whole the group constituted a strong and coherent force of opinion that was occasionally close to fanaticism in its refusal to compromise. The attitude was very similar to that of present-day intellectual communists toward Russia. These thinkers were the apostles of a political and ideological credo of which the United States was the symbol and model.

The image produced by such heated enthusiasm was inevitably a distorted one. This distortion was due not only to factual errors, though these were frequent enough (one much-read publication, the *Almanach américain*, reported that Rhode Island was north of Massachusetts and that the

*145*

principal products of New Hampshire were cocoa, cotton, and coffee), but also to the exaggeration of American virtues in an effort to demonstrate the validity of French principles. The Americans, as much shocked by French overpraise as they were by English decrial, attempted vainly to bring the image into focus with reality—Franklin in his *Advice to Such as Would Remove to America*, Paine in his *A Letter Addressed to the Abbé Raynal*, Jefferson in his *Notes on Virginia*, and particularly Mazzei in his *Recherches*. The latter criticized for their too rosy pictures Hilliard d'Auberteuil, Démeunier, the Abbé Longchamps (whose *Histoire impartiale de la dernière guerre* appeared in 1785), and especially Crèvecoeur, of whom he wrote, "I ought to warn the readers of the *Lettres d'un cultivateur américain* to be careful not to imagine that the manners and customs described in that book are general in America. . . . I have been very much surprised to learn that many people have conceived the most chimerical notions from the reading of this book. . . . My intention is not to discourage Europeans who would like to become American citizens, but only to save them from regretting too late that they have done so."[89] The reviews of Mazzei's book showed some realization of the problem, and the *Mercure* agreed that superficial and uninformed writers were creating a false picture of America. "Some," the article said, "carried away by their uncontrolled imaginings, which they mistake for moral courage, or dominated by a restless humor which they mistake for wisdom, have seen in their subject only what already existed in their own minds, have exaggerated the motives of their own fears and hopes, and have mixed with false or imaginary events both unreasonable praise and unfair criticism. Others, guided by absurd political principles or by their own self-interest (which they understand far better), have intentionally distorted all the facts to create a certain impression corresponding to their own notions or desires."[90]

[89] *Recherches*, IV, 98-100. See also Mazzei's article on Longchamps, *Mercure de France*, Mar. 11, 1786.
[90] Feb. 23, 1788. See also *Journal encyclopédique*, April, 1788, p. 215.

Such sensible warnings had, however, little effect. The image of America presented by the liberal intellectuals continued to be a mirage. The mirage was not, however, a single, consistent, and unchanging image. It had several phases, and showed a marked evolution between 1784 and 1794. In 1784, and for several subsequent years, the image was still "philosophic"; that is, it tended to represent the Americans as the exponents of the doctrines of the *Philosophes*—the liberty, toleration, and humanitarianism of the Voltairians, the enlightenment of the Progressionists, the equality and virtue of the Rousseauists, and the ruralism and agrarianism of the Physiocrats, though the influence of the last group was disappearing. In this first part of the decade, two distinct concepts of America took shape. The first, Rousseauan, was that America had succeeded in uniting the simplicity, virtue, equality, and liberty of a young people with the enlightenment of a mature nation. The second concept, progressionist, was that America stood as the torchbearer of man's march toward perfection. With the summoning of the States General, however, political realities began to displace philosophic abstractions, and interest shifted to the specific reforms that America could suggest, particularly to the American constitutions and bills of rights. Thus America evolved from a philosophic symbol to a political slogan. Simultaneously, to those persons whose lives were being disrupted or threatened by all the violence, change, and disorder, America for the first time since the Huguenot emigration became for the French an asylum, and many began to dream of peace, happiness, and security on the banks of the Ohio or the Susquehanna.

Saint John de Crèvecoeur was the key figure in the idea of America as the union of virtue and enlightenment. After having lived for a number of years as a farmer in Orange County, New York, he returned to his native France in 1781 with an account of his experiences in America, written in English. Part of his manuscript was published in London in 1782 under the title *Letters from an American Farmer*. Mme d'Houdetot, under whose influence he came, encouraged

*147*

him to translate his book into French. She and several of her friends—Saint Lambert, Louis de Lacretelle, the Prince and Princess de Beauvau, and Jean Baptiste Target—advised Crèvecoeur both in the translation and in the complete revision which they felt was necessary. Their influence, which substituted a "literary," rhetorical, and sentimental style for the graphic terseness of the English original and which eliminated the more realistic and earthy letters and added new ones more suitable to French taste, succeeded in so transforming the character of the book that it ended by reflecting exactly that French mirage peculiar to the milieu in which it suffered its transformation. The image of America presented by the *Lettres d'un cultivateur américain* was the image in which Mme d'Houdetot, Lacretelle, and the others of their circle believed.[91]

Crèvecoeur's book projected all the aspirations of a troubled Europe: the agricultural economy of the Physiocrats; the simplicity, virtue, equality, and return to nature of Rousseau; the tolerance, liberty, and humanitarianism of Voltaire; the political reform and enlightenment of Condorcet and the other progressionists; and the promise of unlimited opportunity and new hope for the weary citizens of Europe. There were two editions, the first in two volumes published in Paris in 1784 and the second, considerably augmented, in three volumes in 1787.

The message which Crèvecoeur proclaimed was that in America man had been able to make a new start and had succeeded in combining the simplicity and moral innocence of a young rural society with the political sophistication, the enlightenment, and the arts and sciences of a modern nation. Most of the letters were tableaux of rustic felicity, but they were balanced by others which championed with earnest sincerity and occasionally with eloquence the freedom and vigor of the new American spirit. America, Crèvecoeur said, was "a new birth," a "second creation" of man under a new sun and in a new world free from the errors, the prejudices,

91 See H. C. Rice, *Le Cultivateur américain* (Paris, 1933), pp. 75ff.

and the ignorance of the Old World. The new nation had been founded in "an age of enlightenment" by courageous and enlightened men fleeing the fanaticism and catastrophes of Europe. Here the energy of men's minds, long confined by poverty, ignorance, and oppression, could at last exert itself and find fulfillment. As American civilization developed, the American mind was growing in both knowledge and power. Everything was contributing to this growth— the colleges, the academies, the libraries, the free press, the circulation of books, the stimulus provided by political debate. Crèvecoeur proudly listed all the achievements of American genius, and he could foresee only an unlimited progress of the human mind in America. "Thus it is very probable," he predicted, "in view of the state of human society among us, that this continent will become one day the theater on which the liberated forces of the human mind will acquire all the energy of which they are susceptible— the theater on which human nature, so long confined, so long reduced to the measure of pygmies, will achieve perhaps its final and greatest honors in all the arts, in all the sciences, as well as in the art of government and the art of war."[92] All this was promised of a new society in which any man could enjoy a life of plenty, in which all men lived in liberty and equality, and in which the simple antique virtue of the Golden Age was at last renewed.

Louis de Lacretelle, an influential man of letters and editor of the *Mercure*, zealously publicized Crèvecoeur's book in a series of articles in which he heavily underlined the idea that America demonstrated the possibility of modern man's moral regeneration without loss of intellectual and political progress.[93] A series of fortunate circumstances, he said, had created in the United States a free, egalitarian society liberated from the vices and prejudices of the Old World yet one which could inherit and profit by the wisdom and experiences of Europe. "In a state of society in which everything shines

[92] *Lettres d'un cultivateur américain* (Paris, 1784), I, 31-32.
[93] *Mercure de France*, Jan. 4, 1783; Jan. 24, 1784; Jan. 22 and 29, 1785. These articles were republished in the two editions of the *Lettres*.

with the freshness of youth, Americans possess already the maturity of older nations."[94]

This image of America was repeated by many lesser writers —by Démeunier, who incorporated verbatim long passages from Lacretelle in his contributions to the *Encyclopédie méthodique*,[95] by Joseph Mandrillon in his *Spectateur américain*,[96] and by the Abbé Longchamps in his *Histoire impartiale*.[97] The Americans, one contributor to the *Mercure* wrote, "unite goodness, equanimity and kindness to the genius and boldness necessary in important undertakings and high enterprises. Gentleness, moderation and tranquility of soul are the distinctive characteristics of this people. With such qualities, when they are accompanied, as they are in Americans, by firmness, courage, constancy and exquisite judgment, one is very close to a perfect character."[98] The Chevalier Deslandes, in an essay written in competition for a prize offered by the Académie des Jeux Floraux of Toulouse on the importance of the American Revolution, wrote, "The Senate of Rome seemed to Cineas an assembly of kings; the Senate of Philadelphia will appear to the philosopher an assembly of sages. . . . May America have her artists and her philosophers and still preserve her virtues! Philadelphia has already given the example. Since her foundation she has cultivated the arts and sciences, and yet is no less the city of Penn, the city of virtue."[99] The anonymous author of the *Dissertation sur les suites de la découverte de l'Amérique* (1787), written in competition for a prize offered by the Academy of Lyons and subscribed by the Abbé Raynal, said, "America has recreated in her rural areas the age of the patriarchs and at the same time has preserved all the advantages of our present century. The cities have brought together citizens of all nations; all the arts of Europe are

[94] *Lettres d'un cultivateur américain* (Paris, 1787), I, xvii.
[95] *Economie politique et diplomatique*, II, 398ff.
[96] *Op.cit.*, p. 153.
[97] Pierre de Longchamps, *Histoire impartiale des événements militaires et politiques de la dernière guerre* (Paris, 1785), p. 8.
[98] Aug. 5, 1786.
[99] *Discours sur la grandeur et l'importance de la révolution qui vient de s'opérer dans l'Amérique Septentrionale* (Frankfort, 1785), pp. 35, 38, 149.

cultivated, all the sciences have found devotees, and a simple and kindly urbanity has embellished by its touch all their virtue."[100] The Abbé Genty, in another essay submitted for Raynal's prize, *L'Influence de la découverte de l'Amérique sur le bonheur du genre humain* (1788), wrote, "In the bosom of America are three million men, happy, free, strong, and virtuous. Their hearts have still their native purity, and they know neither the cold pleasures of vanity nor the seductions of the corrupting arts. They have among them magnanimous warriors, statesmen, legislators, philosophers."[101] Brissot was one of the most fervent defenders of this image of America. His attack on Chastellux was chiefly for the latter's failure to esteem highly enough the moral qualities of Americans, and his defense of Crèvecoeur against Mazzei was intended to preserve unsullied the former's image of America. He concentrated on arguments proving the moral superiority of Americans and their scientific genius.[102]

The tremendous appeal of this idealization of American society to the French at this particular moment is a curious thing. The century was torn by two aspirations. The first, born of the scientific movement, was toward an ever-expanding progress of knowledge and material well-being. The other, of which Rousseau was the chief exponent but of which Marie Antoinette's *Hameau* at Versailles was as good an example, was a yearning for a lost simplicity, virtue, and tranquility of spirit. Rousseau's life work was an attempt to solve the problem of man's moral regeneration, not by a return to nature (as he was often misunderstood), but in the society and in the historic moment of the present. The magic appeal of America was that this new nation seemed to demonstrate a solution to the dilemma, to show that man could in fact find his moral salvation without sacrificing the material and political comforts of the Enlightenment. This is why Brissot wrote of Crèvecoeur's book, "These letters will inspire or reawaken perhaps in blasé souls of Europeans

[100] P. 51.  [101] P. 192.
[102] *Examen critique des Voyages de Chastellux* and *Réponse à une critique des Lettres d'un cultivateur américain.*

the taste for virtue and for the simple life. . . . Energetic souls will find in them something more. They will see here a country, a government, where the desires of their hearts have been realized, a land which speaks to them in their own language. The happiness for which they have sighed finally does in truth exist."[103] This was why Lacretelle said to America, "The whole world watches you. In fifty years it will know, by your example, whether modern peoples still can maintain republican constitutions, whether high moral principles are compatible with the grand progress of civilization, and whether America is to make better or worse the fate of humanity."[104]

This thesis that America demonstrated the possibility of the marriage of virtue and enlightenment was basically conservative, in that it looked backward, not forward. It aspired to the re-creation of Rousseau's natural man and to the preservation of the achievements of the present, but not the creation of a new social order. This was its fundamental difference from the idea of progress, which operated in the new time sense, oriented toward the future, not toward the past or present, and which discussed man in terms of what he was to become, not of what he eternally was.

As it was applied to the United States, the idea of progress stated that human happiness results from three factors: first, liberty and equality; second, the enlightenment and liberation of men's minds; third, material prosperity. It was believed that these three conditions not only separately contribute to human felicity, but that they also support and strengthen one another. To be free and prosperous, man must be enlightened, and to be enlightened and prosperous he must be free. Progress was therefore a process to be set in motion by the liberation and enlightenment of mankind. The United States was the demonstration of this truth.

The chief apostle of this gospel was the Marquis de Condorcet, the mathematician, economist, and philosopher, and perhaps the most brilliant of all the Americanists, who later

103 *Réponse à une critique*, pp. 2-3.
104 *Lettres d'un cultivateur américain* (Paris, 1787) , I, xxiii.

was to give the doctrine of progress its definitive expression in his *Esquisse d'un tableau historique des progrès de l'esprit humain.* In 1786 he published a remarkable essay entitled *L'Influence de la révolution de l'Amérique sur l'Europe,* later republished by Mazzei in his *Recherches.* Condorcet assumed that the supreme purpose of society is to achieve the happiness of its members. This, he stated, can be achieved by two means: the free enjoyment by men of their natural rights and the maximum satisfaction of their material needs. Man's natural rights he reduced to four essentials: the safety of his person, the guaranty and free use of his property, equality before the law, and a voice in the government of society. But to employ these means, man must first be enlightened. "After having long meditated," Condorcet wrote, "on the ways to ameliorate the lot of mankind, I have been forced to the conclusion that there is really only one way, and that is to accelerate the progress of the Enlightenment."[105] Only after prejudice and ignorance had been destroyed could man exercise his rights. On the economic plane, the happiness and welfare of the people could be achieved only by an equal distribution of wealth, which was a corollary of political equality.

The great contribution of America to Europe, Condorcet stated, had been to give to the world a living proof of these universal truths. "It is not enough that the rights of man be written in the books of philosophers and inscribed in the hearts of virtuous men; the weak and ignorant must be able to read them in the example of a great nation. America has given us this example."[106] Moreover, "despite the differences of climate, tradition and constitution, the spectacle of a great nation where the rights of man are respected demonstrates that these rights are universal to all peoples." The success of the American experiment proved "the influence which the enjoyment of these rights has upon the general welfare, by

---

105 *L'Influence de la révolution de l'Amérique sur les opinions et le législation de l'Europe* [Paris, 1786], p. 34. Reprinted in F. Mazzei, *Recherches historiques et politiques sur les Etats-Unis de l'Amérique Septentrionale* (Paris, 1788), IV, 237-283.
106 *Ibid.,* p. 13.

showing that the man who has never feared outrage against his person acquires a nobler and finer soul; that he whose property is always safeguarded finds probity easy; that the citizen who is subject only to law has truer patriotism and greater courage."[107] The protection of the rights of the individual "offers to industry the most appealing hopes" and thus promotes prosperity and proves that "the happiness of mankind organized in society depends almost wholly on good laws."[108] Finally, the United States provided the salutary example of freedom of the press and religious liberty.

In addition to offering this object lesson to Europe, America was making its own important contribution to the Enlightenment and to progress. Condorcet wrote: "America is a country of vast extent where dwell several million men preserved by their surroundings from prejudice and disposed toward study and reflection. There exist no social distinctions, no beckoning ambition which can draw these men away from their natural inclinations to perfect their minds, to devote themselves to useful studies and to seek that glory which is the reward of great ventures and discoveries. Nothing there holds down a part of the human race in that abject state which condemns mankind to ignorance and poverty. There is therefore reason to hope that in a few generations America, by producing almost as many men engaged in the task of adding to the mass of human knowledge as there will be in all of Europe, will thus at least double the progress of mankind and will make this progress at least twice as rapid. This progress will include both the useful arts and the speculative sciences."[109]

Condorcet's function was to crystallize and to systematize these dynamic ideas, which had been implicit in the thinking of many of the Americanists and which, as the Revolution approached, tended to supplant the virtue-enlightenment thesis.

In the augmented 1787 edition of his *Lettres,* Crèvecoeur added two letters which indicated that he too was shifting to this progressionist line. He claimed that political and intel-

107 *Ibid.,* p. 15.     108 *Ibid.,* pp. 23-24.     109 *Ibid.,* pp. 32-33.

lectual freedom allowed the American to make a maximum contribution to the material well-being of the community, and at the same time permitted him to develop fully his natural talents and to add to the store of useful knowledge, to the enlightenment of mankind, and to the general progress of civilization.[110]

Mazzei also served to document and support his friend Condorcet by his defense of the principles of democracy and equality, and by his explanations of the practical applications in America of the principles of liberty, popular sovereignty, representative government, the separation of powers, freedom of the press, religious liberty, and the rights of man. Like Crèvecoeur, Mazzei emphasized the encouragement given to education and science by the state governments and saw here proof that liberal democratic government inevitably acted to free and broaden men's minds. He strongly supported Condorcet on the doctrine of progress, and indeed his whole apology was based on his conviction that "in our time philosophy has made considerable progress and the inhabitants of the civilized world are on the whole much happier than they have been in any century known to history."[111]

Though not always so explicitly formulated, this same idea was implicit in many other books and articles which praised all the liberal and egalitarian features of the American governments while at the same time exaggerating every evidence of the progress of the Enlightenment in America. Mandrillon stressed religious liberty, equality, popular sovereignty, the division of powers, the rights of man, the right to property, and state support of education and science. In emphasizing the progress of the arts and sciences in America, he quoted a provision of the Massachusetts Constitution which stated that the preservation of liberty and the rights of man rests upon an educated and enlightened citizenry.[112] Longchamps declared that the American Revolution would "create happiness under the auspices of liberty, . . . liberate talents and wisdom hitherto stifled by European despotisms, and show to an astonished universe all the arts of Europe

[110] II, 441ff. and 495ff.  [111] *Recherches*, II, 144.  [112] *Op.cit.*, p. 372.

*155*

hurrying to reign in a new continent, to make for themselves a second home, to shine there on a vaster theater, and thus to divide their blessings between two worlds."[113] Deslandes united a eulogy of the great men of America of the present and future with his praise of democracy, representative government, separation of powers, equality, religious liberty, and freedom of thought, speech and press. "O Liberty!" he exclaimed, "What will your Americans not be able to achieve?"[114] Charles Joseph de Mayer, a writer on political subjects as well as the author of an Asgill play, comparing the United States to earlier federations, said the new nation, founded in an age of enlightenment by wise and learned men, enjoyed a freedom made possible only by the liberation of men's reason. He gave special emphasis to the achievement of true democracy in the United States and the guaranties of religious liberty and freedom of thought and press.[115] Mailhe, a Toulouse lawyer who won the prize offered by the Académie des Jeux Floraux, wrote on the theme of American liberty, "Happy is the century in which we live. It has made more progress toward the perfection of humanity than all the others together. . . . Philosophy, encouraged by the spectacle of America, will be no longer frustrated in her progress and will gradually realize that sublime idea which hitherto has been thought visionary and impracticable."[116] Roland de La Platière, the husband of Madame Roland of Revolutionary fame, predicted in a paper read before the Academy of Lyons in 1789 that the universal language of the future would be English. This would come, he said, not through the predominance of England, but through the influence of the Americans, who by their political, intellectual and commercial leadership and by their spirit of cosmopolitan tolerance and fraternity would someday range many peoples "under their consoling religion."[117]

[113] Op.cit., p. 3.          [114] Op.cit., p. 151.
[115] Les Ligues achéenne, suisse et hollandaise, et la révolution des Etats-Unis de l'Amérique (Geneva, 1787).
[116] Discours qui a remporté le prix de l'Académie des Jeux Floraux en 1784 (Toulouse, 1784), pp. 32, 38.
[117] F. Baldensperger, "Une Prédiction inédite sur l'avenir de la langue des

Many more similar statements could be cited, often documented with specific evidence of the progress of the Enlightenment in the United States. For instance in 1784 the *Journal politique de Bruxelles* cited Copley and West as proof of American aptitude for the arts.[118]

Brissot de Warville's opinions were particularly interesting. In his earlier works he subscribed wholly to Condorcet's ideas. He said, in his *Examen critique* addressed to Chastellux, that the dignity of man consists in the perfect development of his moral and intellectual faculties and that these in turn are the product of liberty and equality. "I believe," he wrote, "that the nature of the government determines three-quarters of man's nature. I believe that he progresses as he has more liberty and that he degenerates as he has less. I believe that an ignorant barbaric slave born on the banks of the Bosphorus would be an enlightened republican were he born in Philadelphia."[119] In *De la France et des Etats-Unis* Brissot asserted that the achievement of liberty in America was producing a moral and physical regeneration of the human race and that by freeing men's minds it was permitting a full development of the faculties which could lead only to the perfecting of the arts and sciences. Like Condorcet he saw America's example as a powerful influence toward the reform of European governments.[120]

But when Brissot visited the United States he made an important modification of his ideas. The main purpose of his trip, only a few months long, was to investigate on behalf of a syndicate the possibilities of investment in American government securities. But he also wished "to study men who had just acquired their liberty" and "be taught by them the secret of preserving it."[121] His Americanism certainly suffered no diminution. He left these shores with undiminished enthusiasm for American democracy, liberty, and equality, for the humanitarian institutions, for the high moral standards,

---

Etats-Unis (Roland de La Platière, 1789)," *Modern Philology*, xv (1917), 474-476.

[118] Sept. 11, 1784.        [119] *Examen critique*, p. 104.
[120] Pp. xxviii-xxxi.        [121] *Nouveau voyage*, I, viii.

for the prosperity and happiness of the people, the fertility of the land, the Quakers, the rapid expansion of the settlements, and the bright future of the nation. Nor did he modify his basic belief in the progress of man through liberty. "The man of liberty," he wrote, "is by nature the man of reason." He was impressed by the enlightened, intelligent, and well-informed American minds which he encountered. He praised Harvard College for its learned professors and its excellent laboratory and library. "The heart of a Frenchman beats faster," he wrote, "on finding Racine, Montesquieu, and the Encyclopedia in a place where one hundred and fifty years ago the savage still puffed his calumet."[122] He reported that the American Academy of Arts and Sciences, to which he was elected, was "composed of worthy scholars, of men who cultivate all the sciences."[123]

Nevertheless Brissot was forced to the conclusion that the arts and sciences were not cultivated with the same interest as in France. Scientists and historians could not find subscribers to finance the publication of their works, and poets and artists found still less encouragement. He met a Boston watchmaker named Pope who had spent ten years constructing an orrery but had been unable to raise a subscription to support his undertaking. "This country is too poor," he told Brissot. "It cannot encourage the arts."[124]

This statement prompted Brissot to a long reflection on the position of the arts and sciences in an equalitarian society. America, he said, was far richer than Europe if one considered only the standard of living of the average citizen. But the equal distribution of wealth meant that there were no rich with surplus income out of which to patronize "the agreeable and frivolous arts." Europe was richer in being able to support the arts; American was richer in having prosperous and happy citizens. Brissot left it to the reader to judge which was true wealth.

The conclusion which he drew was that "the ability to encourage the agreeable arts is a symbol of national calamity." "Let us not blame the Bostonians," he continued. "They

122 *Ibid.*, I, 133.     123 *Loc.cit.*     124 *Ibid.*, I, 139.

think of the useful before the agreeable. They have no fine monuments; but they have handsome and comfortable churches and good homes, they possess superb bridges and excellent ships and their streets are lighted at night while there are many ancient cities of Europe where men have not yet thought of eliminating the harmful effects of darkness."[125]

This passage was perhaps the first expression in France of the idea that the egalitarian American society tended to direct its energies to producing what was socially useful to the neglect of the aesthetic and intellectual. The other Americanists had been assuming that a free America would develop the arts and sciences on the same pattern that had hitherto obtained in European monarchies. But with the French Revolution came the new idea that although liberty would produce enlightenment in America, it would be an enlightenment directed toward illuminating the useful rather than the beautiful. To Brissot and the other Revolutionists, still firm in the utilitarianism of their century, there was no question of hesitating between the two alternatives—liberty and street lighting on one hand, and despotism and "the frivolous and agreeable arts" on the other. A year after the publication of Brissot's book, Jacques Vincent Delacroix wrote, "It must be confessed, the arts rarely flourish under a popular regime; it is the luxury of courts and the magnificence of kings which foster such talents. . . . Yet if we must choose between liberty and the arts, we cannot hesitate."[126] Here was already an important modification to the idea of progress.

The choice could also be presented in other terms, for instance, between the education of a privileged few and the enlightenment of the whole people. The concept of political and economic equality also implied intellectual equality, or at least equality of intellectual opportunity. For if liberty enlightened, liberty must enlighten all men. "In a free country," Brissot wrote, "reason extends her empire over all

125 *Ibid.*, I, 139-141.
126 John Adams, *Défense des constitutions américaines*, ed. Jacques V. Delacroix (Paris, 1792), I, 541.

classes of men."[127] Both Crèvecoeur and Mazzei had stressed the development of public education in the United States, and the latter had cited Jefferson's Bill for the More General Diffusion of Knowledge. With the Revolution the point became doubly important. Brissot wrote in his *Patriote français*, "The first building the Americans build is for the minister, the second is for the school, and the third is for a printing press."[128] "There is perhaps not a single American," Necker, Louis XVI's minister, said, "even in the lowest classes of society, who does not know how to read, write, cipher, and who has not had the time to learn and retain the first principles of morality."[129]

But the supreme proof of the equality of intellectual opportunity under the American system was Franklin himself, for his example proved that in a free nation any man, no matter what his origin, could reach the top, and therefore that society could draw its leaders from all classes. Jean Baptiste Le Roy, Franklin's lifelong friend and admirer, wrote in 1790: "M. Malesherbes made the excellent remark, when I introduced Franklin to him, that my illustrious friend was the first scientist who had developed a marked talent for public affairs. Now, that was an advantage which Franklin derived from the government under which he lived, which allowed his mind to direct itself toward those important objects which affect the happiness and well-being of an entire people. In Paris, that great man, under the *ancien régime*, would have remained in obscurity; for how could one have put to use the son of a candlemaker? Or even if his scientific genius could have broken down the barriers erected by his inferior social position, he would have remained at most a member of some academy. Will it never be understood that inasmuch as the most important thing for a nation is to have talented men, we can never have too large a number of aspirants, and that the probability of finding men competent to fill the various posts in a government

[127] *Nouveau voyage*, I, 173.        [128] Feb. 16, 1790.
[129] Jacques Necker, *Du pouvoir exécutif dans les grands états* (1792), II, 10-11.

always increases in proportion to the number of those who are permitted to aspire or claim to fill them."[130]

Chamfort, in writing on Franklin's *Autobiography*, made the same point. Comparing the newly published masterpiece to Rousseau's *Confessions*, he said that both these great philosophers were representative of the rise during the eighteenth century of the *petite bourgeoisie* to positions of intellectual leadership, and he declared this social revolution in both France and America was the product of one and the same movement toward equality of intellectual opportunity.[131]

Obviously such ideas as these of Condorcet, Crèvecoeur, Brissot, and Le Roy had great political significance, for they implied—and were intended to imply—that the political example offered by America should be followed in France. The Americanists had been holding up this example ever since 1769, but for the five or six years immediately preceding the French Revolution they insisted with increasing emphasis on the United States as a practical demonstration of democracy (a word which was becoming politically respectable only in these years), guaranties of person and property, representative government, separation of powers, popular sovereignty, legal and political equality, religious liberty, and freedom of speech and press—in short, the rights of man.

At first such examples remained, as far as France was concerned, political theories rather than political programs. But with the meeting of the States General in 1789 these theories suddenly became immediately applicable, and by this fact the America of the philosophic example was overnight transformed into the America of the political model.

The model consisted of the state constitutions and bills of rights, which had been circulating since 1777, plus such miscellaneous documents as Jefferson's Bill for Establishing

---

[130] In Claude Fauchet, *Eloge civique de Benjamin Franklin* (Paris, 1790; first edition), p. 45.

[131] *Oeuvres complètes* (Paris, 1824), III, 317-318.

Religious Freedom. To these now were added the new federal Constitution and Bill of Rights.

These last two documents had a powerful impact in France. The friends of America, distressed by the weakness of the Confederation, followed with anxiety the deliberations of the Constitutional Convention. Lafayette wrote Washington, "Upon the success of this convention depends perhaps the very existence of the United States. . . . Good Lord! The American people, so enlightened, so wise, so noble, after having so successfully scaled the steep cliffs, now stumble on the easy path."[132]

The first publication of a translation of the proposed text of the Constitution was probably that in the *Journal politique de Bruxelles* on November 17 and 24, 1787, just two months after the document had been signed. The text was also included in Mazzei's *Recherches* early in 1788, together with the Virginia Bill of Rights and the Declaration of Independence, and in Mandrillon's *Fragments de politique et de littérature* of the same year. Other translations soon became current.

The new Constitution was read with great interest. In February Lafayette again wrote Washington, "We are awaiting with anxiety the results of the state conventions. The new constitution has been carefully studied and much admired by the philosophers of Europe."[133] The papers carried frequent reports on the progress of the debates over ratification, and their comments generally reflected approval of the document. It was called a "monument of political legislation" and "the product of all the study which ancient and modern republics, the English, Montesquieu and Rousseau have given to this prime concern of public welfare."[134]

The Constitution was not, however, universally approved, for it was regarded as undemocratic by some of the constitutionalists; Condorcet was opposed to its bicameral system, and the *Mercure* remarked, "The praise which the partisans

[132] *Mémoires*, II, 203.
[133] *Ibid.*, II, 222.
[134] *Journal politique de Bruxelles*, Feb. 2, 1788.

of aristocracy in Europe continue to give to this proposed constitution is sufficient to let the Americans know what they may expect from this form of government now proposed to them."[135] The editor of a new edition in 1792 of La Roche-foucauld and Franklin's collection of American Constitutions wrote, "If the reader compares this [new federal] constitution with the various state constitutions, he will perhaps find reason to bewail the truth that there is no republic, no matter how democratic it may be, that does not soon lead to aristocratic rule."[136] In general, however, the news of the ratification, received in the summer of 1788, was welcomed with enthusiasm. Mme d'Houdetot wrote Franklin, "I could not learn, my dear and venerable doctor, of the happy event which gives a constitution to your country without experiencing the sweetest sentiment of which the human heart is susceptible, namely, that of seeing the happiness of one part of the globe assured by the progress of reason and the success of the Enlightenment."[137]

American influence on the French constitutions was considerable, though of course less than that of the English Constitution and than that of the political theories of Montesquieu and Rousseau. The imitation of American models is clear and definite only in the *Déclaration des droits de l'homme et du citoyen* of August 26, 1789.[138] In relation to the French image of American society, however, the important point is not the precise extent of this influence but rather the degree to which the United States was regarded as a source of political inspiration. Active interest in the American constitutions lasted to 1792—that is, until the formation of the Convention—but was most intense during the years 1789 and 1790.

135 Mar. 1, 1788.
136 *Constitutions des treize Etats-Unis de l'Amérique. Nouvelle édition* (Paris, 1792), II, 270.
137 Chinard, *Les Amitiés américaines de Madame d'Houdetot*, pp. 43-44.
138 See G. Jellinek, *Die Erklärung der Menschen- und Bürgerrechte* (Leipzig, 1895), translated by M. Farrand as *The Declaration of Man and of Citizens* (New York, 1901); G. Lefebvre, *The Coming of the French Revolution*, tr. R. R. Palmer (Princeton, 1947); S. Kent, "The Declaration of the Rights of Man and Citizen," in *Great Expressions of Human Rights*, ed. R. M. MacIver (New York, 1950).

*163*

The new American federal Constitution and Bill of Rights were studied, discussed, and cited. In 1789 Fabre d'Eglantine, Du Pont de Nemours, Condorcet, Gallois, and Mazzei published a translation of John Stevens' *Observations on Government* (a defense of the American Constitution erroneously attributed to William Livingston), to which they added many notes and a translation of the document.[139] In August 1790 Delacroix gave a series of public lectures at the Lycée on the American Constitution, in the course of which he called it "that excellent system of government which has established in one part of the world the rights of humanity and has given to the other part of the world a great example to follow."[140] Delacroix later published these lectures in his *Constitutions des principaux états de l'Europe et des Etats-Unis* (1791). In his analysis he gave high praise to the American Constitution as a "product of the age of enlightenment"[141] and he especially favored the power granted to Congress to override the President's veto, a provision which was particularly pertinent to French constitutional problems and which was the object of prolonged debate in the National Assembly in September 1789.[142] Other aspects of the American Constitution attracted special notice for various reasons. For instance, in 1792 Ducher cited the successful precedent in the United States of the separation of church and state, as guaranteed in the First Amendment, as an argument for the same separation in France.[143] The Federal Bill of Rights and the various state bills of rights were thoroughly examined by the framers of the *Déclaration des droits de l'homme et du citoyen* and the parallels between the French and American documents were analyzed and underlined in a remarkable study published in *L'Ami de la Révolution*, which anticipated the conclusions of modern historians.[144]

139 *Examen du gouvernement d'Angleterre comparé aux constitutions des Etats-Unis de l'Amérique, par un cultivateur de New-Jersey* (Paris, 1789). On authorship of this work, see A. D. Turnbull, *John Stevens* (New York, 1928), pp. 90-91.
140 *Moniteur universel*, Aug. 9, 1790.     141 II, 321.
142 *Journal politique de Bruxelles*, Sept. 12, 1789.
143 *Nouvelle alliance à proposer*, pp. 1-2.
144 *L'Ami de la Révolution*, nos. 10-12, Nov. 1790. Republished under the

The prestige and influence of Franklin and Jefferson contributed a great deal to this interest in American forms of government. A reviewer of Jefferson's *Notes on Virginia* had cited Jefferson in 1787 as an example of wisdom and moderation in constitutional debates, and in 1789 Lafayette sought his advice in drafting the *Déclaration des droits de l'homme et du citoyen*.[145] There was nothing unusual in this, for Americans in Paris frequently were consulted on constitutional problems; Gouverneur Morris and Thomas Paine were likewise asked for suggestions and proposals for the new French constitution.[146] At the same time, back in Philadelphia, Franklin was sending his friends copies of the new Constitution and discussing it in letters to his many correspondents. He was popularly regarded as the founder of both American and French constitutionalism and as a champion of unicameralism, for he was supposed to have been wholly responsible for the radical Pennsylvania constitution of 1776. Upon his death a eulogist in Brest declared, "It is to his genius that we owe the laws of Pennsylvania. This code was the cradle of the rights of man, which have raised the temple of French liberty."[147] The belief that Franklin was the sole author of the Pennsylvania constitution was created by its inclusion in many editions of *La Science du Bonhomme Richard*. An interesting example of Franklin's pervasive influence on the ideology of the French Revolution is the publication in the *Journal de la Societé de 1789* of his essay written in 1784 attacking the Society of the Cincinnati and the principle of aristocracy. This essay (already mentioned in Chapter II), which had been translated by Morellet and which had been used by Mirabeau in his *Considérations sur*

---

title *Déclaration des droits l'homme et du citoyen* (Paris, 1791). See G. Chinard, "Notes on the American Origins of the 'Déclaration des Droits de l'Homme et du Citoyen,'" *Proc. Amer. Philos. Soc.*, XCVIII (1954), 383-396.

[145] See G. Chinard, *La Déclaration des droits de l'homme et du citoyen et ses antécédents américains* (Washington, 1945).

[146] G. Morris, *op.cit.*, I, 161; "Answer to Four Questions on the Legislative and Executive Powers," *Complete Writings of Thomas Paine*, ed. P. S. Foner (New York, 1945), II, 521-534.

[147] Belval, *Oraison funèbre de Benjamin Franklin* (Brest, 1790), p. 2.

*l'Ordre de Cincinnatus,* had remained secret and unpublished but had apparently been circulated surreptitiously in manuscript among the liberals. Now it was published by De Grouvelle, a member of the society, who employed Franklin's ingenious arguments to justify the recent abolition of aristocratic privilege.[148] John Adams too exerted his influence through Delacroix's translation of his *Defence of the Constitutions of Government of the United States.*[149] *The Federalist* was also translated in 1792 and the review in the *Moniteur* emphasized its value as a source of arguments against decentralization of government.[150]

A powerful reinforcement to the example of the American Constitution was its apparent success. Business conditions in the United States had started to improve even before Washington took office. The new government began to function without important difficulties or organized opposition. The nation's finances were placed on a sound basis. All these facts were reported both by diplomatic representatives such as De Moustier, who previously had been so pessimistic,[151] and by the correspondents of French papers. The *Moniteur* reported in November 1789, "The first operations and measures of the government, all crowned by the most complete success, have inspired so high an opinion of the new constitution, and so much respect for the members of the present administration, that satisfaction reigns from one end of the country to the other. Not the slightest complaint is heard, and there does not exist even the shadow of an opposition."[152] The many pamphlets with which speculators interested in selling land and American government securities flooded Paris also contributed to this general impression of American prosperity and political stability.

Expressions of French trust and confidence in the United States as a reliable political mentor were as varied as they were numerous. For instance André Chénier the poet wrote:

[148] *Journal de la Société de 1789,* July 24, 1790.
[149] *Op.cit.*
[150] Nov. 18, 1792.
[151] *Observations sur les différents rapports,* p. 43.
[152] Nov. 20, 1789.

La liberté qui luit aux champs de l'Amérique
Eclaira près de vous, les regards des Français;
Et bientôt des récits fidèles
Vont annoncer à nos modèles
Les fruits de leur exemple et nos heureux succès.[153]

In 1792 Pétion said: "Without attempting to compare Americans to the French, nor Philadelphia to Paris, I may say that there are certain rules of action equally applicable to the two peoples and to the two nations: namely, those which foster the perfection of the human race, its improvement through education, and the universal knowledge and enjoyment of the rights of man."[154] The National Assembly, in an official letter of thanks to the State of Pennsylvania for its message of congratulation, promised in 1791 that it would do its utmost to "transplant and defend in the Old World the inestimable gift of liberty received from the New World. . . . Long live France! Forget not all she owes to your example and to Pennsylvania, in whose bosom the legislators of America first dared to announce to the world the true principles of the social art."[155]

Even more convincing than all these expressions of opinion was the actual influence exerted not only on the framers of the French Bill of Rights, but also on such important leaders as Condorcet, Lafayette, Rabaut-Saint Etienne, Brissot, and Mme Roland, who all turned to American models for guidance in composing the first French constitution. It was this American political tutelage that Brissot was thinking of when he declared, "The American Revolution was the mother of the French Revolution."[156]

Effective international collaboration in the practical reform of a nation was a new thing in history, and it inevitably had important effects on French opinion. One of the most

[153] "Liberty, shining on American shores, kindled a fire in fraternal French eyes. And soon shall faithful accounts announce to our models the fruits of their example and our glorious achievements." *Le Patriote français*, Sept. 3, 1789.
[154] *Chronique de Paris*, July 12, 1792.
[155] *Ibid.*, June 9, 1791.
[156] F. V. A. Aulard, *La Société des Jacobins* (Paris, 1887-1897), II, 622.

important was to strengthen the idea of cosmopolitan fraternity and to create for the first time the concept of an international political movement, an International. America was hailed as the first member of that union of free peoples which was to become one of the great ideals of the French Revolution. The editors of Stevens' *Examen du gouvernement* (Observations on Government) wrote in 1789, "There is in the universe a great republic, in which all thoughtful and honorable men have the right of citizenship. It is the natural ally of all other republics and of all the empires in which men sincerely labor for the common welfare of mankind. It is the natural enemy of all arbitrary and oppressive governments. It has this remarkable quality, that its members, by pledging their allegiance, become by so doing still better citizens of their own countries."[157]

The active participation of Paine, Barlow, and John Paul Jones in the French Revolution dramatized American solidarity. When the Société de 1789 was organized in May 1790 the 124 members, among whom were Sieyès, Roederer, Tallyrand, Bailly, and Lafayette, drank thirteen toasts, beginning with "Our Revolution" and ending with "The United States of America."[158] Washington and Franklin were elected honorary charter members. On July 14, 1790 a delegation of Americans took part in the famous Fête de la Fédération held on the Champ de Mars in Paris.[159] The newspapers reported in detail all the demonstrations of Gallomania which swept the United States, all the extravagant celebrations in honor of the French Revolution and French military victories which were held in Boston, Philadelphia, Baltimore, Charleston, Savannah, and elsewhere. It was widely rumored in 1791 that the United States were planning to send an army of 16,000 men to help defend France against the armies of tyranny.[160] In 1792 Ducher stressed the idea that two nations in which the people rule as sovereign have, necessarily, identical interests and should stand united to defend their common

157 P. vii.  158 *Chronique de Paris*, May 15, 1790.
159 *Moniteur universel*, July 12, 1790.  160 *Ibid.*, Sept. 2, 1791.

cause against the forces of absolutism.[161] When Louis XVI was deposed on August 10, 1792 a delegate named Gaudet was charged by the Convention with the task of announcing the news to President Washington. He wrote, "Amidst the storms which agitate our new born liberty, the French Republic is happy to be able to communicate with republics founded on the same principles as its own. . . . The immense distance which separates us from you prevents you from playing in this glorious regeneration of Europe the role for which your principles and your victories have fitted you. Alone against the coalition of kings, we have shown ourselves worthy of calling ourselves your brothers, and the ignominious retreats of the enemy armies—Jemmapes, Spire, Savoy, Flanders—all these victories must recall to you Saratoga, Trenton, and Yorktown."[162] The next year a letter from Colonel Swan on some misconceptions which Americans had formed about the French Revolution was read before the Société Populaire des Amis de l'Egalité, and the society voted to have printed an answering address by Citizen A. Didot, written to explain and justify to their American allies the course of the Revolution, the execution of Louis XVI, and the persecution of Lafayette.[163] To his last days, Condorcet preserved his faith in the United States as France's partner in the liberation of mankind and the march of human progress. In his *Esquisse*, written on the eve of his death, he asked, "Shall all the nations of the earth some day achieve that stage of civilization to which have arrived the freest and most enlightened peoples, the French and the Americans?"[164] In November 1793 Robespierre presented to the Convention a decree reaffirming French friendship and treaties with the United States, for the increasing friction between the United States and England, which was coming close to the point of war, led the French to believe that soon once more Americans

161 *Nouvelle alliance à proposer*, p. 3.
162 *Moniteur universel*, Dec. 23, 1792.
163 A. Didot, *Précis sur la Révolution et le caractère français, adressé aux citoyens des Etats-Unis d'Amérique* [Paris, 1793].
164 *Oeuvres* (Paris, 1847), VI, 237.

would be their brothers in arms.[165] When James Monroe arrived as the new American minister in 1794, he was greeted in the Convention by speeches of fraternal friendship and hearty Gallic embraces, and he presented the French nation with an American flag to be hung beside the Tricolor in the hall in which the Convention sat.

This sentiment of French-American brotherhood and comradeship in arms against the forces of tyranny was a very real emotion, felt by Frenchmen of all classes. It was powerful and popular in direct proportion to revolutionary France's sense of insecurity and fear in the midst of unsympathetic and hostile European forces.

The intensity of this ephemeral sense of fraternity was revealed in 1790 by the popular reaction to the death of Franklin. In Paris all classes of the city joined in rendering honor to this saint of the Revolution. The tragic news was received on June 10, and the following day Mirabeau rose in the National Assembly to move the decree of a three-day period of mourning: "Gentlemen, Franklin is dead. . . . He has returned to the bosom of Divinity, that genius who liberated America and flooded Europe with light."[166] The motion was seconded by Franklin's old friends Lafayette and La Rochefoucauld and carried by acclamation. The Commune of Paris held ceremonies throughout the city. A society of printers held a funeral service in the Couvent des Cordeliers. Franklin's bust, wearing a civic crown, stood in the middle of the hall, and beneath the bust was a press. As one printer pronounced the eulogy, others printed it, and the oration was distributed to the spectators at the end of the ceremony.[167] The Amis de la Révolution et de l'Humanité hung over the entrance to the famous Café Procope a sign reading *Franklin Est Mort* and held there, in a room draped in black and containing a bust of Franklin crowned with

[165] *Moniteur universel*, Nov. 18, 1793. Decree of 27 brumaire, an II.

[166] Mirabeau, *Oeuvres* (Paris, 1912), II, 221. For a study of the entire episode, see G. Chinard, "The Apotheosis of Benjamin Franklin, Paris, 1790-1791," *Proc. Amer. Philos. Soc.*, XCIX, (1955), 440-473.

[167] Jeanne Louise Campan, *Mémoires sur la vie privée de Marie Antoinette* (Paris, 1822), I, 233.

oak leaves and bearing the single word *Vir*, a memorial
ceremony. The criers who announced this tribute refused out
of respect and patriotism to take any pay for their services.
The next day a distribution of bread to the poor of Paris
was made in Franklin's memory.[168] The Lodge of the Nine
Sisters printed eulogies in Franklin's honor, and Morellet
published in the *Moniteur* anecdotes drawn from his memo-
ries of his old friend.[169] On June 13 La Rochefoucauld delivered to the Société de 1789 a eulogy of Franklin, and
Liancourt, his cousin, moved that Franklin's bust be placed
in the assembly hall of the society.[170] On July 21 Fauchet
delivered a eulogy at the Rotonde to the members of the Assembly and the representatives of the Commune of Paris;[171]
on November 13 Condorcet delivered another before the
Academy of Sciences;[172] and on March 14 of the following
year Vicq d'Azyr, the noted physician, eulogized Franklin before the Royal Society of Medicine.[173] These official eulogies,
incidentally, were well documented, for La Rochefoucauld,
Condorcet, and Vicq d'Azyr all drew their biographical facts
from the manuscript of Franklin's still unpublished *Autobiography*, then in the possession of Franklin's friend Le
Veillard. There was much of significance in these tributes.
For one thing, they showed how the image of Franklin had
evolved from that of the diplomat and scientist to that of the
moral philosopher, the torchbearer of the Enlightenment to
the New World, and the founder of constitutionalism—particularly of unicameralism, as both La Rochefoucauld and
Condorcet stressed. They also revealed that the militant center
of Americanism was among the moderate constitutionalists,
for the royalists and extreme democrats were both noticeably
cooler in their tributes.[174]

[168] *Chronique de Paris*, June 17 and 19, 1790.   [169] July 15, 1790.
[170] *Journal de la Société de 1789*, June 19, 1790.
[171] C. Fauchet, *op.cit.*
[172] *Eloge de M. Franklin* (Paris, 1790).
[173] Félix Vicq d'Azyr, "Eloge de Franklin," *Revue rétrospective*, série II, II (1835), 375-404.
[174] E.g., *L'Ami du Roi*, July 23, 1790; *Révolutions de Paris*, July 24 and 31, 1790. See David J. Hill, "A Missing Chapter in Franco-American History," *Amer. Hist. Review*, XXI (1916), 709-719.

This does not mean, of course, that the anti-Americanism of the European Left can be said to have originated this early. But there is here the indication that by this date the extreme Democrats and egalitarians had reached a position to the left of American republicanism and had ceased to look across the Atlantic for inspiration and justification. Babeuf, in his *Défense* in 1797, was to cite, not Washington or Franklin as his teachers, but Rousseau and the communist Morelly.

Underlying all this Revolutionary idealism there was another kind of image of America, America the refuge from social disorganization. Even before the fall of the Bastille the atmosphere of tension and unrest was beginning to create an urge to escape. In 1787 Dr. Guillotin, soon to be immortalized by his efficient contrivance, wrote his friend Benjamin Franklin a letter expressing a fear and revulsion shared by many: "We are all of us enemies of tumult, of the disorder, the intrigue and extravagance now consuming our cities. We are revolted by the unreasonableness of our laws and that contradiction with tradition and custom which often places a man in the cruel dilemma between appearing ridiculous and committing a crime. We are distressed by the sad and discouraging spectacle of vice everywhere shameless, feted and honored, and of timid virtue crippled and despised. Above all, we are frightened by the horrors spawned by despotism and superstition. Hence have we resolved to flee this poisoned land where a man can find only trouble, disgust, worry, disappointment, and danger. We have formed a plan of establishing a settlement in the United States, and particularly in the Ohio region."[175]

There was undoubtedly present in France a compelling urge to escape from the impending catastrophe. It was perhaps this fear which in part caused the popularity of Crève-coeur's *Lettres*. The idealization of America was in its positive sense a projection of French aspirations, but in its negative sense it was an imaginary construction of the antithesis of nearly all that constituted French civilization on the eve of

[175] J. F. McDermott, "Guillotin Thinks of America," *Ohio State Archeological and Historical Quarterly*, XLVII (1938), 133.

the Bastille—an escape from reality. The years preceding and during the Revolution, while they were brave with the desperate optimism of Condorcet, were nevertheless also years of profound pessimism and despair. An indication of this was provided by the prize sponsored by the Abbé Raynal for the best essay on the question "Has the discovery of America been beneficial or harmful to the human race?" Eight works inspired by this question have survived, and half of these gave deeply pessimistic answers, reflecting a widely held feeling, as the century drew to its close, that man was losing ground in his struggle to better his lot on earth.[176] The pessimistic answers were not only anti-colonial in their verdicts that the discovery of America had brought economic and moral retrogression to Europe, but they were also pessimistic on the whole course of European civilization since the Renaissance. One of the authors wrote, "Let us not deceive ourselves. The root of the evil we would extirpate is the depravation of the human heart. This depravation has been the same in all centuries. The men of today are in their hearts just what men have always been; and those who follow us will be no different from what we have been. Institutions and laws have not changed men and will never change them."[177] Nevertheless—a most curious fact—all these pessimists and anti-progressionists saw the United States, with its free, happy, and virtuous inhabitants led by philosophers and magnanimous heroes, as the one shining exception in a

[176] Jean André Brun, *Le Triomphe du Nouveau Monde* (Paris, 1785); François Jean, Marquis de Chastellux [?], *Discours sur les avantages et désavantages qui résultent pour l'Europe de la découverte de l'Amérique* (London, 1787); Condorcet, *L'Influence de la révolution de l'Amérique sur les opinions et la législation de l'Europe* [Paris, 1786]; *Dissertation sur les suites de la découverte de l'Amérique* (1787); Henri Carle, *Discours sur la question proposée par M. l'abbé Raynal* (Paris, 1790); Louis Genty, *L'Influence de la découverte de l'Amérique sur le bonheur du genre humain* (Paris, 1787); Justin Girod Chantrans, *Voyage d'un Suisse dans différentes colonies d'Amérique* (Neufchâtel, 1785); Joseph Mandrillon, *Recherches philosophiques sur la découverte de l'Amérique* (Amsterdam, 1784). The last four were pessimistic. See also, *Discours composé en 1788 qui a remporté le prix de l'Académie Française en 1792 sur la question: Quelle a été l'influence de l'Amérique sur la politique, le commerce et les moeurs de l'Europe* (Paris, 1792).

[177] Carle, *op.cit.*, p. 29.

murky world. The American mirage was not only an expression of faith in human progress; it was also a compensation, a fictitious consolation for those who had already lost faith in progress.

To this was added a longing for economic and social security. The anonymous *Lettre de M. de V . . . à M. le C.D.M. à l'occasion des observations publiées sur l'établissement du Scioto* (1790) told how the new reforms directed against the nobles and clergy had, by cutting off the income and privileges of these orders, at the same time thrown into permanent unemployment a large number of functionaries, servants, merchants, and artisans who had depended for their livelihood on the patronage of these classes. To those suffering in the economic dislocation and depression of the Revolution, the Scioto seemed an opportunity to purchase for a modest sum a comfortable living for the present and the possibility of a future fortune with which to return someday to Paris.

To the dispossessed and frightened aristocrats, America seemed to offer still another kind of security. The visionary Marquis de Lezay-Marnésia and his associates in the Compagnie des Vingt-Quatre, the heaviest investors in the Scioto venture, and likewise the subscribers to the equally ill-fated Compagnie de New York, were among this last type of escapists. They were those who dreamed, not of liberty, equality, and democracy (for they had had a bellyful of that), but of founding on the banks of the Ohio or of Lake Ontario benevolent agricultural aristocracies in which they might re-create a France which had forever vanished from Europe.

Thus the decade from 1784 to 1794 was the period of the great dream. There was, it is true, a current of skepticism and even of hostility, but this healthy realism was smothered or ignored by those who insisted on creating an America out of their own hopes and fears. There was much of great human value in the writings of these Americanists; there was even some truth. But in essence the French image of America still remained a symptom of France's own maladies.

CHAPTER V

# THE DISINTEGRATION OF
# THE DREAM

THE counter-revolution of Thermidor, which in July 1794 overthrew Robespierre, marked the death of the American Dream in France. This ideal, which had been so long in elaboration and which for the previous two or three years had been living, as it were, on borrowed time, suddenly disintegrated. It was replaced by a variety of attitudes, which, while not all hostile, were of a very different nature. The abrupt shift in opinion was only one of the results of the ideological revolution caused by the failure of the political revolution.

The very turmoil in the minds of all Frenchmen of these years makes any generalization on the thought of the period extremely difficult. In the matter of attitudes toward the United States, however, there is a clear line of separation between the *Emigrés* who lived in the United States and the remainder of the French people.

The tempests of the Revolution forced a great many Frenchmen to flee to refuge in foreign lands. They streamed out of France in two waves: the first, the "Voluntary Emigration," starting in the summer of 1789, was composed of royalists frightened by the storming of the Bastille and of escapists in search of tranquility and security; the second, the "Forced Emigration," from late in 1791 to mid-1794 or sometimes even later, was the flight of men, often moderate liberals who had collaborated in the early stages of the Revolution, who were literally fleeing for their lives. The majority of these refugees remained in Europe, usually in England

and Germany, but a considerable number—estimated between 10,000 and 25,000—crossed the Atlantic.[1]

Of the first "Voluntary Emigration," relatively few chose America as their haven. Those who did do not appear to have been the intransigent royalists, who naturally gravitated to more compatible political environments. They were more often the escapists, sick of the conditions in France, and therefore political neutralists. Nevertheless, their flight in itself implied a renunciation of the ideals of the Revolution, and, consequently, of the Revolutionaries' idealized image of America. They did not seek political liberty or equality, or a chance to share in the dynamic economic life of a new nation, but rather an asylum from all the stresses of their revolutionary age. Nothing was more revealing than the fact that the Scioto colonists chose as their new home, not Philadelphia, as Voltaire would have done, but the wilderness of Ohio. One of them wrote home shortly after his landing: "We hope soon to arrive at our new territory, where we shall find things in their original state, as God made them and not perverted by the ungrateful hand of man. To some these surrounding woods might appear a frightful wilderness; to me they are a natural paradise. No hosts of greedy priests; no seas of blood to wade through. All is quiet. . . . France shall find herself renovated in the western world, without being disgraced by the frippery of kings or seeing the best blood of the nation spilt to gratify the ambitions of knaves and sycophants."[2]

These were indeed men in search of a mirage. While there were some whom sheer necessity forced to accept the harsh reality of the frontier,[3] those who succeeded in extricating

1 See F. S. Childs, *French Refugee Life in the United States, 1790-1800* (Baltimore, 1940), pp. 9-10.

2 Quoted by T. T. Belote, *The Scioto Speculation and the French Settlement at Gallipolis* (Cincinnati, 1907), pp. 73-74.

3 E.g., the case of Antoine Saugrain (see H. Fouré Selter, *L'Odysée américaine d'une famille française, le docteur Antoine Saugrain* [Baltimore, 1936], and G. Chinard, "Gallipolis and Dr. Saugrain," *Franco-American Review*, I [1937], 201-207), and that of the Viscount de Marlartic (see *The St. Clair Papers*, ed. William H. Smith [Cincinnati, 1882], II, 407-408; *Penna. Mag. of Hist. and Biog.*, XLII [1918], 180-181; *Moniteur universel*, May 13, 1792).

themselves from their American misadventure returned to France with the sour bitterness of frustrated escapists.

Such a one was the Marquis de Lezay-Marnésia, one of the leaders in the Scioto venture, a proud, impractical dreamer who blundered his way from one catastrophe to another. He had hoped to found in the Ohio Valley an aristocratic Catholic agricultural enclave of paternalistic landowners, where the French might find, isolated from the world, a way of life which would be pure and simple yet graced with all the refinements and amenities of Old World culture. He gathered together a group of men and women whom in his innocence he intended to be of the purest moral character. In reality they turned out—according to his son—to be "the most incoherent mixture of persons imaginable—artisans, ex-soldiers, monks, actresses, prostitutes and trouble makers."[4] From the moment he landed in Alexandria he found himself floundering in the legal complications arising from the dubious title to the land he had purchased, and when he finally reached the Ohio he discovered, no Rousseauan Eden, but a tough frontier region inhabited by what seemed to him brutish men who blew their noses with their fingers and lived in hovels—a restless, lazy, improvident, disgusting breed. All the money he had brought with him drained away, his followers deserted him, and he was able to return to France only with the help of a charitable Italian nobleman, the Count Andreani.

It was inevitable that Lezay-Marnésia saw America's democracy as a corrupt, farcical system on the verge of dissolution, and its citizens as gross and immoral men to whom the arts and refinement of taste were unknown. American society, which was the opposite of what his heart craved, revolted him, but the wilderness, undefiled by man, seemed a blessed escape. He was disappointed in everything, he said, except the land itself, and he wrote in his account of his experiences long poetic descriptions of the virgin wilderness with its giant trees and silent glades. Only in the depths of

4 Albert de Lezay-Marnésia, *Mes souvenirs, à mes enfants* (Blois, 1851), p. 11.

*177*

the primeval forest did he find the surcease of conflict he had vainly sought.[5]

Equally typical was the experience of the most famous of all the *Emigrés*, François René de Chateaubriand. This melancholy young man, who in Paris had screamed curses at the revolutionary mob, may have imagined, as he was to claim later, that he came to America in search of the Northwest Passage or to "meditate on the free man of nature and the free man of society dwelling side by side in the same land,"[6] but he was closer to his real motives when he confessed in his old age that the violence of the Revolution "filled me with horror, and the idea of leaving France for some far off land germinated in my mind."[7] When he arrived in July 1791 he had no real interest in observing the workings of a democratic republic, Philadelphia bored him, and he sneered at "the virtuous descendants of William Penn" as "calculating actors who play a continual farce of probity." Each day, he said, saw his illusions vanish one after the other, and that was for him "a most painful experience."[8] It was inevitable that he would conclude, in his *Essai sur les révolutions*, that in the corrupt state of modern society, as he saw it in Paris and Philadelphia, liberty was an impractical ideal. But, like Lezay-Marnésia, he found refuge and comfort in nature. However well he succeeded in his later writings in obscuring the true facts of his American adventure beneath the inventions of his creative imagination, it is clear that his one significant experience was the escape he found at the edge of Niagara Falls, in the depths of the western forest, and in company with the primitive originals of Chactas and Atala.[9]

[5] Claude F. A. de Lezay-Marnésia, *Lettres écrites des rives de l'Ohio* (Paris, an XI).

[6] *Oeuvres complètes* (Paris, 1826), I, 13.

[7] *Mémoires d'outre-tombe*, Part I, Book V.

[8] *Oeuvres complètes*, I, 211-212.

[9] Chateaubriand's American adventure provided material for his *Essai sur les révolutions* (1797), *Atala* (1801), *René* (1805), and *Les Natchez* (1826), and was recounted in his *Voyage en Amérique* (1827) and Part I, Book VI of his *Mémoires d'outre-tombe* (1849). Only the *Essai*, together with the notes added in 1826, gives any reliable indication of Chateaubriand's immediate reactions to America at the time of his voyage. For a summation of the

The second wave of *Emigrés*, however, were a different breed. They were political refugees but not escapists. When they explored the wilderness it was to discover profitable investments in land, not to take refuge from their own world in an exotic asylum. They had left France for the quite practical purpose of saving their lives and most were forced to keep thinking about the practical problem of staying alive. Economic necessity forced them to integrate themselves into American life.

Although many traveled through the frontier regions of the Ohio and Upper New York State and some settled on isolated farms or formed rural communities, such as that of Asylum on the North Branch of the Susquehanna, where preparations were made to receive Marie Antoinette, the majority congregated in the seaboard cities, especially in Philadelphia.[10] The city teemed with Frenchmen of every class and every shade of political opinion, quarreling among themselves and with Americans, publishing rival newspapers, conducting businesses and speculations of every variety— forming, in short, a French community of substantial size within the American capital. Many of these refugees were to be or had already been famous. Around the ex-Constituant Moreau de Saint Méry and his bookshop revolved a colorful group including Talleyrand, Volney, and Démeunier. Other figures in town were such men as the Duke de La Rochefoucauld-Liancourt (the cousin of Franklin's associate); the Duke d'Orléans (later Louis Philippe, King of the French) and his two brothers, the Duke de Montpensier and the Count de Beaujolais; Théophile Casenove, the founder of Casenovia, New York; the Chevalier de Ternant, who had been French minister until 1793; the Count de Tilly, whose marriage to Maria Mathilda Bingham of Philadelphia caused an international scandal; and a host of others. In 1793 their numbers were increased by Santo Domingo colonials fleeing from a Negro uprising.

---

problems concerning Chateaubriand's voyage to America, see P. Martino, "Le Voyage de Chateaubriand en Amérique. Essai de mise au point 1952," *Revue d'histoire littéraire de la France*, LII (1952), 149-164.

10 See Childs, *op.cit.*

It might have been expected that these men and women would arrive with the most favorable prejudices toward their new home. Pro-Americanism was still dominant in France. Most of these "Forced *Emigrés*" had been liberals and supporters of the Revolution in its early stage, and therefore politically aligned with Americanism. Talleyrand, Démeunier, and La Rochefoucauld-Liancourt had been leaders in the Assemblée Constituante. Moreover, they had freely chosen America as their best hope for the future, or else, like Talleyrand, had found the United States the only country willing to give them political asylum. Nevertheless, they soon lost whatever favorable predispositions they may have had and quickly conceived, in most cases, an intense aversion to all things American. The Duke de La Rochefoucauld-Liancourt noted in his diary soon after his arrival in 1794, "All the French I have met so far have little liking for America, and less still for Americans."[11] He even found compatriots who made it a point of pride not to learn English and who boasted of having no American friends.

This widespread and extreme reaction against American life was the central factor in the new complex of attitudes and ideas generated by the Emigration in the United States. It was, however, not a simple phenomenon.

La Rochefoucauld was, of course, exaggerating in saying that none of the *Emigrés* liked Americans. In fact one, a priest, the Abbé J.-Esprit Bonnet, known as Bonnet de Fréjus, published in 1795 a handbook for *Emigrés* entitled *Réponses aux principales questions qui peuvent être faites sur les Etats-Unis de l'Amérique*, which depicted America as an enlightened land of justice, security, and opportunity, ready to welcome the refugee fleeing the corruption and violence of Europe. And there were some who found this promise fulfilled. The Marquise de La Tour du Pin, who later wrote a delightful account of her American experience in *Journal d'une femme de cinquante ans*, arrived with her husband, two children, and a friend in 1794 and bought a farm near

[11] François Alexandre Frédéric, Duc de La Rochefoucauld-Liancourt, *Journal de voyage en Amérique et d'un séjour à Philadelphie*, ed. J. Marchand (Baltimore, 1940), p. 62.

Albany. The whole family cheerfully set about the task of being American farmers, and they made a success of it. The Marquise, who had been lady in waiting to the Queen, got up every morning before dawn to start her chores, did the laundry for the whole household, churned butter, and ate with the hired help like any farmer's wife. She looked at Americans objectively but with sympathy and good humor and enjoyed equally "frolicks" with the neighboring farmers and the hospitality of the Schuylers and the Van Rensselaers. When she was forced to leave, it was with sincere regret, "after having said an affectionate and grateful farewell to all those who for two years had overwhelmed us with friendship, attention and kindness of every sort."[12]

A similar case was that of Brillat-Savarin, the famous gourmet and author of the *Physiologie du goût*. Though obliged to teach French and play the violin in a theater to keep alive, he managed to make his years in America enjoyable, both gastronomically and socially. From Boston he wrote to a friend, "The more I get to know Americans the better I like them. I have often changed my first impressions for the better and rarely for the worse."[13] In his *Physiologie du goût* he gave his recipe for this happy adjustment: "I was leaving the United States after three years, and I had been so happy there that in the moment of emotion which precedes a departure all I asked of Heaven (and my prayer has been answered) was that I should not be less happy in the Old World than I had been in the New. This happiness I had owed principally to the fact that from the first moment of my arrival in the United States I talked like Americans, I dressed like them, I took care not to be cleverer than they, and I approved of everything they did. Thus I repaid the hospitality they offered me with a courtesy which I believe fitting and which I advise to all those who might find themselves in a similar situation."[14]

12 Henriette Lucie de La Tour du Pin, *Journal d'une femme de cinquante ans* (Paris, 1913), II, 103.
13 Jean Brillat-Savarin, "Lettres," *Société littéraire et archéologique de l'Ain. Revue*, IIe année, 1873, pp. 52-53.
14 *Physiologie du goût* (Paris, 1853), p. 351.

The French Catholic priests who came to the United States during these years appear also to have adapted easily and happily to American life. As missionaries they could be expected to be men of charity, but, in addition, they quickly saw that religious toleration—the aspect of American liberalism which most affected them—was a great advantage to a minority sect. They observed that more peace and good feeling existed between Anglicans, Presbyterians, Anabaptists, and Catholics in America than between Jansenists and Jesuits in France. It was baffling to see Protestants donate land and money to build Catholic churches, to be arrested in Puritan New England for travelling on Sunday, to hear American Catholic priests pray God to preserve for the American people "the enjoyment of the divine gifts of liberty and equality," and to learn that Bishop Carroll, the head of the Catholic Church in America, dined on the friendliest terms with Anglican bishops. But they were forced to respect the sort of toleration which honored a man for being faithful to his religious convictions, whatever they were.[15] The largest group of these French priests was at the Sulpician Seminary in Baltimore, but their most distinguished member was Father Cheverus, the first bishop of Boston and later Cardinal, who established the Church in Massachusetts and won great respect and affection from the Yankee Protestants.[16]

In such men and women as these, the successful adaptation to American life came from an inner power, so well defined by Brillat-Savarin, which enabled them to cast off the impedimenta of the past, the elaborate structures of social values under which they had lived, and to accept by an act of free will the new life on its own terms. Their picture of American society, which was the product of a satisfying and happy experience, was necessarily sympathetic, but it was in no sense an illusion, a continuation of the American Dream.

If the American Dream was dead in these friends of America, it had still less chance to survive with men like Talleyrand, who soon after his arrival was writing to Mme de Staël,

15 See Edouard de Mondésir, *Souvenirs*, ed. G. Chinard (Baltimore, 1942).
16 See Huen-Dubourg (A. J. M. Hamon), *Vie du cardinal de Cheverus* (Paris, 1837).

"If I have to stay in this country a year I shall die,"[17] or like Démeunier, who in a letter to Moreau de Saint Méry called the United States "that wretched country we both have such good reason to hate."[18]

It would be natural to suppose that, in these *Emigrés*, the Dream vanished because it was dispelled by reality, but this explanation is not sufficient. Before the Revolution, no amount of contradictory evidence had prevented the liberals from idealizing America. In fact, two of the most extreme exponents of the American Dream, Brissot and Crèvecoeur, had both lived in the United States and were well documented on conditions there. The explanation must lie elsewhere.

The Dream died because it became unnecessary. It had been created, deliberately or not, as a device to prove that certain ideals were universally true and universally practical, that any democratic constitutional republic founded on the principles of political and civil liberty, popular sovereignty, the rights of man, and the enlightenment of the people would produce moral salvation and social and material progress. The French Revolution was intended by its instigators (if not always by its perpetrators) to realize this faith, and, in a certain sense, it was in truth caused by the American Revolution, which provided its moral justification.

But the moment the first stone was wrenched from the Bastille, the American example became superfluous. Those who continued to believe in the Revolutionary creed had no longer any need to look across the Atlantic to find justification for their ideals and their actions. They could now claim that they had produced their own justification.

The American example, however, was becoming for many men something more than superfluous; it was becoming irrelevant. To those who were commencing to question the Revolutionary creed, or who had never accepted it, the American utopia, in such direct contradiction to the violence and

[17] G. Lacour-Gayet, *Talleyrand* (Paris, 1928-1931), I, 199.
[18] Moreau de Saint Méry, *Voyage aux Etats-Unis d'Amérique*, ed. S. L. Mims (New Haven, 1913), p. 255.

injustice before their eyes in Paris, became a very suspicious tale. Either it was a lie, or else it proved that one man's meat could be another man's poison. Montesquieu and Rousseau had warned years before that liberty is possible only for certain nations at certain historic moments, and that the best government is that best fitted to the nature of a people. Condorcet and Brissot had denied this, asserting the universal validity for all mankind of their political and social ideals, and proclaiming that liberty, equality, and fraternity were the birthright of all men everywhere. But the practical failure of these principles in France, together with their apparent success in America, brought a disillusion with such Revolutionary universalism and a return to relativism. This reaction was, naturally, most marked in the *Emigrés* in the United States. Even those who were pro-American insisted on the distinctions between the French and the American problems. De Fréjus wrote, "Equality, which is no less than a blasphemy and an outrage against humanity and reason when it is forced upon empires where rank is the essence of government, is a summons to happiness in states where it was already firmly established before destiny raised them to the rank of world powers."[19] The inevitable conclusion was that the United States, and indeed any nation, was a unique case, the product of a special set of circumstances. Whatever were the virtues of American democracy, there was no need to insist on them, for they proved nothing as far as France was concerned.

Old patterns of thought die slowly, and most of the *Emigrés* apparently landed in America expecting to see all they had read. But they no longer felt any compulsion to idealize, or to deny the evidence of their eyes, and when they discovered a land so different from Crèvecoeur's bucolic idyll they were readily disillusioned. This disillusion had the effect of leaving their minds free to conceive a whole new set of ideas, and also of inducing cynicism, a readiness to find fault, a sort of masochistic pleasure in debunking the Amer-

19 J. Esprit Bonnet de Fréjus, *Réponses aux principales questions qui peuvent être faites sur les Etats-Unis, par un citoyen adoptif de Pennsylvanie* (Lausanne, 1795), pp. xi-xii.

*184*

ican Dream. For instance, when he first landed, Moreau de Saint Méry wrote in his diary, "At last I am come to this hospitable soil, to the land of liberty, this land which, if its inhabitants are wise, is to astonish the Universe with its power."[20] Nevertheless, it was not long before he was zealously collecting the most scabrous anecdotes illustrative of prostitution in the United States and allied subjects in order to demonstrate what he called the American "hypocrisy of virtue."

Though in some cases the *Emigrés* had freely chosen America over Europe as a refuge, they were nevertheless exiles, visitors by compulsion. They therefore tended to lack the curiosity and predilection of free tourists. Talleyrand, who came entirely against his will, was expressing a common feeling when he said, "I arrived full of repugnance for the new sights which generally interest travelers. I found it very difficult to awaken in myself any curiosity."[21]

Since they had been able to take out of France only a limited amount of money, nearly all the *Emigrés* were constrained to live on a reduced scale. The majority had to earn their living, and often by humble tasks. They became schoolteachers, shopkeepers, farmers, musicians. To aristocrats and wealthy bourgeois used to luxury, privilege, and power, this abrupt descent was humiliating and painful. When the irascible Moreau de Saint Méry, who had been for a brief period President of the Electors of Paris, was introduced to the Count de Moré in Philadelphia, he demanded, "You do not suspect, I suppose, who I am or what I have been?"

"My word, no," replied De Moré.

"Well," growled Moreau de Saint Méry, "I was king of Paris for three days, and here I am selling ink, pens and paper to keep alive in Philadelphia."[22]

More painful even than poverty and humiliation was the frustration, the uncertainty, and the insecurity of their lives. The Duke de Moré wrote:

[20] *Voyage*, p. 38.    [21] *Mémoires* (Paris, 1891-1892), I, 232.
[22] Charles Albert de Moré, *Mémoires* (Paris, 1898), p. 148.

*185*

"Alas, I found in the streets of Philadelphia only great men who had become small, ambitious men who had missed their ambitions, fools who had had their rewards, men of yesterday who today were nobodies, parvenus astonished that the wheel of fortune had not stood still for their benefit when their stars reached their zeniths. My friend Du Portail listed for my particular benefit all the French refugees that Philadelphia contained. It was a veritable Noah's Ark. When the vessel of the French monarchy blew up as a consequence of their follies and foolish systems, the explosion hurled a good number of them as far as the United States. Not one of them had been cured or had had his eyes opened or had been restored to saner ideas. And so all of them—Constitutionalists, Conventionalists, Thermidorians, Fructidorians— all saw in their political downfall only an operation which had just missed coming off. They still kept looking back to France as a sort of testing ground to which they would return sooner or later to begin again what every one of them called the 'Great Cause.' There were as many plans and political systems among them as there were refugees of note. In the United States you would have thought you were in the Elysian Fields described in the sixth book of the Aeneid, where in the afterlife every shade feeds upon the hope that he cherished while on the earth."[23]

American life, whether in Philadelphia or on the frontier, was far removed from the existence the *Emigrés* had known in France. They discovered that Americans in their traditions, values, and thinking were fundamentally different from themselves. They had come, they felt, to an alien, not a fraternal land. This feeling of *dépaysement*, when added to all the other sufferings, intensified an awakened affection for their lost homeland and produced in these men a deep and brooding nostalgia. They were sick with longing for France, for French ways and French speech. This was something genuinely new in the century, a true *amor patriae*—an attachment not to one's class, nor one's friends, nor one's *pays*, but to the very soil of France. Wrote one homesick Frenchman,

[23] *Ibid.*, pp. 147-148.

*186*

"Far from my native land, which is still dear to me, and from the friends of my youth, plunged in a sort of constant unhappiness, my imagination delights in the memory of former affections and it is not without effort that I fix my attention on things alien to the emotions which fill my heart."[24] Inevitably this new patriotism worked against any affection or sympathy for a foreign land.

There were a series of unfortunate events. In 1793 Edmond Genêt, the new French minister, attempted to furnish arms to French privateers in American ports and to organize an army of American frontiersmen to attack the Spanish in Louisiana and Florida. When Washington, who had adopted a policy of neutrality toward the European war, refused to support him, Genêt tried to appeal directly to the people, forcing the American government to demand his recall. Then Jay's Treaty with England, negotiated in 1794 in an attempt to settle the thorny problem of neutral rights and other difficulties threatening the peace, caused the French, who had themselves already been violating American neutrality, to unleash their corsairs against American commerce in retaliation. American losses from these French spoliations eventually mounted to over $7 million, a large sum in those days. With grievances against both England and France, the country was split on its foreign policy, the Republicans favoring France and the Federalists England. The Federalists, however, were the majority party, and anti-French feeling became dominant, especially in the seaboard cities where the French congregated. The Naturalization and Alien Acts of 1798 were directed in large part against the French immigrants, and the same year the United States denounced all the French treaties and expelled the French consuls. Undeclared naval war started. These events quite naturally put the French *Emigrés*, whatever their political sympathies, in a most uncomfortable position and rendered them particularly bitter against Washington, Adams, and the other Federalists.

[24] Antoine Jay, "Correspondance inédite d'un Français qui a résidé dans les Etats-Unis, depuis l'année 1795 jusqu'en 1803," *Bibliothèque américaine* (Paris, 1807), no. 4, pp. 1-2. (The first four numbers of this periodical bore the title *L'Amérique du nord, ou le Correspondant des Etats-Unis*.)

Shiploads of French fled from American ports in 1798. Thus political sympathy, already shaken by the French Revolution, was effectively destroyed.

Besides all these circumstances, and more important than any of them, was the simple fact that there was little in the United States to appeal to the accustomed taste of a French aristocrat or cultured bourgeois. He had been bred to certain pleasures and standards—a polished, graceful society, a respect for breeding and artistic and intellectual distinction, an unequaled cultural wealth, a different moral code, and finally that indefinable French ability to enjoy life gracefully. All these were to be found only rarely in America.

Individual reactions to such experiences as these of necessity varied. One people's opinion of another people, when it is generated at a distance from secondhand sources, easily falls into a set of generally accepted clichés, but when it is produced by firsthand experience, as it was in these *Emigrés*, it is chaotically fragmentized. There were a certain number of ideas and interpretations which were apparently current, but it is impossible to find any individual *Emigré* whose total picture of American society corresponded even closely to that of anyone else. Each observer had his own unique interpretation.

There were all shades of antipathy and sympathy. An example of one extreme was Simon Desjardins, sent to the United States in 1793 to develop the holdings of the Compagnie de New York on the Black River near Lake Ontario. Frustrated and disappointed for three years in a hopeless task of developing an inaccessible area into a French colony (to be picturesquely known as Castorland), he felt nothing but bitterness and disgust for all he saw—the lovers on the Albany boat who spent the night amorously picking lice off each other; the slovenly, improvident settlers who sat slouched in the sun in front of their unroofed cabins; the monotonous, ugly appearance of Philadelphia; the cheating innkeepers; the discourteous Jefferson, who grimaced with annoyance at the prospect of more French arrivals. Desjardins summed up his impression neatly: "Grab everything, hang on to everything,

everything for yourself and nothing for the other fellow, that is the great principle of this nation."[25]

Such sentiments were typical of many, perhaps a majority. There were a number of observers who were really more effective in destroying the simplification of the American Dream because of their ability to distinguish objectively between the good and the bad. The Count de Moré, a returned veteran of Valley Forge, revolted by the French Revolution, deplored the false ideas of government and philanthropy "collected by the *jeunes philosophes à talons rouges*" in Rochambeau's army, but he was delighted with a nation which paid him in full for his military services even after ten years, and he was astounded by the economic progress achieved in the United States since his last visit, and pleased by the efficiency and economy of the new government.[26] Philippe Petit-Radel, world traveler and physician, who visited Boston, New York, and Philadelphia in 1797, remarked in his unique Latin autobiography, "Quisque inhiat peculio augendo, languent musae vix a lumine salutatae" (Everyone is intent on increasing his wealth, and the Muses languish neglected on the threshold),[27] but he wrote a most sympathetic article on the Quakers for the *Magasin encyclopédique* and was so impressed by their work in prison reform that he translated and published in Paris Robert Turnbull's *A Visit to the Philadelphia Prison*.[28] The French Quaker Jean de Marsillac, who had come to dwell with his American brethren, wrote a letter to the *Décade philosophique* in which he painted a dark picture of the arts, sciences, and education in the United States, but praised the religious toleration, the legal system, and development of industrial machinery.[29] The three expressions of this sort of mixed reaction which had the greatest impact on contemporary French opinion were Ferdinand Bayard's *Voyage dans l'intérieur des Etats-Unis* (1797), La

25 "L'Amérique au XVIIIe siècle, vue par un Français," ed. B. Faÿ, *La Vie des peuples*, VII (1922), 399-425.

26 Moré, *op.cit.*, pp. 143-169.

27 *De amoribus Pacharitis et Zoroae* (Paris, an IX), p. xciii.

28 *Magasin encyclopédique*, année VI, vol. II, an VIII (1800), pp. 25-40; Robert J. Turnbull, *Visite à la prison de Philadelphie* (Paris, an VIII).

29 *Décade philosophique*, May 19, 1797.

Rochefoucauld's eight-volume *Voyages dans l'Etats-Unis d'Amérique* (1799) and Volney's *Tableau du climat et du sol des Etats-Unis d'Amérique* (1803). Bayard contrasted the simple, virtuous life of the American farmer with the moral corruption created by prosperity in Philadelphia and other cities. La Rochefoucauld, critical as he was of the materialism, pride, and anti-intellectualism of the young nation, retained his admiration for the American constitution and insisted that in spite of their faults "the American people are on the whole a good people."[30] Volney, anticipating Mme de Staël's concept of national psychology, pointed out the complex of cultural traditions and the economic and environmental forces which contributed to the formation of the American character. But, like La Rochefoucauld, he deplored the effects of materialism on the intellectual and artistic life of the nation.

All these men, by their interpretations of American society, were implicitly renouncing the idea of progress. This theory (which summarized the essential concepts of eighteenth-century liberal thought and which justified the French Revolution) had assumed that man's political, economic, moral, and intellectual lives were so intimately united in the essence of his nature that what was (by their definition) "good" in one area of human endeavor would inevitably produce a like "good" in every other area—that is, that man progressed toward perfection on a line of mutually dependent and mutually supporting fronts. Yet, in direct contradiction to these ideas, the conclusion of the *Emigrés* was that America presented a contradictory and confusing picture of simultaneous progress and retrogression—successful liberal government and economic growth, side by side with moral and intellectual failure. Suddenly for these men the contradictions and mysteries of human nature burst through the fragile, rational constructions of the *Philosophes*. In the midst of this unsettling experience, they did not always see clearly what was happening to their own ideas, but all they wrote revealed that they had forgotten their faith in the so-called law of

[30] La Rochefoucauld-Liancourt, *Voyage dans les Etats-Unis d'Amérique fait en 1795, 1796 et 1797* (Paris, an VII), VI, 7.

progress and in the universal efficacy of the Enlightenment. They no longer assumed that man was creating by his own liberated reason a new and ever better world.

This *désaveu des lumières,* as M. Baldensperger has called it,[31] was characteristic of the whole Emigration and was only one manifestation of the new hierarchy of values that was being established. The materialistic utilitarianism of the century and the obvious need for reform of the decaying leviathan state which was France had led men to set the greatest human value on social, economic, political, and moral ideals—on liberty, equality, social virtue, and economic well-being. The *Philosophes* either tended to discount the ideal of artistic excellence, as had Chastellux, or to make of it a symptom of moral degeneration, as had Rousseau. Moreover, in a century which had placed its faith in man's, not God's, reason, the religious experience was incomprehensible to men like Voltaire. The emotions, which had been to the followers of both Descartes and Pascal a source of rational or moral error were, it is true, rehabilitated by Rousseau, but only as a source of social virtue. There was little disposition before 1789 to think, as the Romantics were to do, of evaluating life itself in terms of intensity of emotional experience.

This hierarchy of values, which placed social ideals above the inner emotional, aesthetic, and religious experience of the individual, which denied or ignored the soul, was abruptly overturned in the years of the Emigration. Chateaubriand was to have his religious experience: "I wept, and I believed." Aesthetic values suddenly became very important, and for this reason what impressed the *Emigrés* most was American indifference to the arts. "In general the arts are poorly supported and never encouraged," Moreau de Saint Méry wrote.[32] But he was even more shocked by the vulgarity of taste displayed in what art there was. Of the American theater, in a typical *Emigré* comment, Saint Méry said, "The performances of the interludes are boisterous and even indecent. It

---

[31] See F. Baldensperger, *Le Mouvement des idées dans l'émigration française* (Paris, 1924), II, chap. III.

[32] *Voyage,* p. 361.

191

is by no means rare to hear such words as 'God damn,' 'b----,' 'rascal' and 'son-of-a-bitch.' The women turn their backs to the stage during these interludes. . . . The plays, English or in the English style, are extremely coarse and of a humor repugnant to good taste."[33] This same lack of aesthetic cultivation they saw in the homes of even the most wealthy. "I remember having seen in Mrs. Morris' salon," Talleyrand wrote, "the hat of the master of the house, a rough hat made in America, lying on an elegant table of Sèvres porcelain some American had bought at Trianon. It was a hat a European peasant would scarcely have put on his head."[34] Americans had not grown more vulgar since the days of Valley Forge, but their vulgarity had assumed a new significance in French eyes.

The nostalgia which the *Emigrés* felt for their ancestral soil of France was something more than an emotional barrier preventing an adaptation to American life. It served also to emphasize every difference between French and American ways, and to create a new awareness of how different Americans were from Europeans and of how different France was from all other nations. The rediscovered sense of relativism, the idea that the circumstances were unique for each separate nation and that the problems of one people were irrelevant to those of another people, contributed to this new nationalism. Eighteenth-century cosmopolitanism was replaced by the new concept of national psychologies, and loyalty to mankind gave way to patriotism. The fact that after 1789 the American Philosophical Society virtually ceased its communications with French scientists and philosophers shows how great was the effect of the Revolution in destroying intellectual cosmopolitanism. Volney had come to the United States with rather vague and grandiose hopes of founding in the United States "a second France," an asylum of peace and liberty. Soon after landing he wrote Larevellière Lépeaux, one of the Directors of the French government, "This is less difficult to accomplish than might be thought. Americans have a penchant for our arts, our manners and

[33] *Ibid.*, 374.    [34] *Mémoires*, I, 239.

our language."[35] He even suggested sending to America French artists, writers, teachers, and books to promote what today would be called "international understanding." But he was soon profoundly disillusioned, and on his return to France he confessed that while Northern Europeans found it relatively easy, because of the similarity of political and ethical traditions, to adapt themselves to American life, "the French encounter obstacles in the differences of language, laws, customs, manners and even taste. . . . It cannot be denied . . . that there exists between the two people a conflict of customs and social forms which makes any close union very difficult."[36] Talleyrand put the idea more succinctly in saying, "I have not found a single Englishman who did not feel at home among Americans, and not a single Frenchman who did not feel a stranger."[37] Men of different nations were no longer citizens of the great human republic; they were different sorts of men. And the French sort was the best. "The phlegmatic inhabitants of the New World," Bayard said, "seem to be deprived of that delicacy of sentiment which makes us French so attractive. You must strike hard on their nerves to make them vibrate, while in France it is enough to touch ours with the tip of your finger."[38]

It was on the basis of these new assumptions—relativism, the rejection of the idea of progress, the new romantic hierarchy of values, and nationalism—that the *Emigrés* proceeded to reinterpret American society.

As liberals living in years when France was still groping for a political solution, they were not yet ready to reject the American republicanism. La Rochefoucauld wrote a thorough and approving analysis of the federal constitution and he called the Declaration of Independence "a masterpiece of

[35] A. Mathiez, "Lettres de Volney à La Revellière-Lépeaux (1795-1798)," *Annales révolutionnaires*, III (1910), 174.

[36] Constantin, Comte de Volney, *Tableau du climat et du sol des Etats-Unis de l'Amérique* (Paris, 1803), p. xiii.

[37] Talleyrand, "Mémoire sur les relations commerciales des Etats-Unis," *Mémoires de l'Institut des Sciences et Arts. Sciences Morales et Politiques*, II, an VII, p. 92.

[38] Ferdinand Marie Bayard, *Voyage dans l'intérieur des Etats-Unis pendant l'été de 1791* (Paris, an VI), p. 32.

reason, nobility and courage." They were quite ready to approve of religious toleration and freedom of the press, which Bayard said the Americans rightly cherished as "the shield of civil, religious and political liberty."[39] Humanitarian reforms could interest them, and La Rochefoucauld, like Petit-Radel, wrote a book on the prison system in Philadelphia.[40] But after all that they and their nation had been through, these *Emigrés* felt little inclination to explore further the virtues of democratic republicanism, and many gloomily predicted that this new nation founded on such fine ideals was being destroyed by factionalism and would soon fall into disunion and chaos. In any case they seldom if ever attempted to explain American society by its political institutions, and one of the most striking differences between the *Emigrés* and the pre-Revolutionary Americanists was the sudden loss of interest in the American constitutions.

It was obvious to every *Emigré* that the United States was in the midst of a period of great economic expansion. "The annals of nations offer us no spectacle more extraordinary and imposing than the rapid expansion of the United States in population and power," Antoine Jay wrote.[41] Talleyrand and La Rochefoucauld were particularly impressed by the rapid westward movement of the frontier and the miraculous rise of farms and towns in areas which a few years before had been wilderness.[42] Moreover, as the former wrote Mme de Staël, it was "the best place in the world to make money fast."[43]

Such a rise in population and productivity would have delighted a Physiocrat, but to the men of the post-Revolutionary age the moral and cultural dangers of prosperity were more important than its economic advantages. The accusation that Americans worshiped money was not, as we have seen, new, but never had it been made so loudly or with such unanimity. La Rochefoucauld was told by Beaumetz

[39] *Ibid.*, p. 194.
[40] *Des prisons de Philadelphie* (Philadelphia, an IV).
[41] *Op.cit.*, no. 4, p. 2.
[42] See *Talleyrand in America as a Financial Promoter, 1794-96*, ed. and tr. H. Huthe and W. J. Pugh (Washington, 1942), pp. 145-149, and La Rochefoucauld-Liancourt, *Voyage*, VIII, 59.
[43] Lacour-Gayet, *op.cit.*, I, 192.

when he arrived that the highest praise one American could give another was "Clever fellow, damned sharp,"[44] and he soon came to agree that "the minds of all Americans are continually turned toward the desire to increase their fortunes,"[45] and that the struggle for more and more money was "the dominant idea of everyone in this country."[46] "A Philadelphian," Bayard wrote, "excuses himself from all the obligations of courtesy, and from other duties still more important, in the name of business. The Romans used to say, 'My Gods, my country call me to the Capitol, to the Campus Martius.' A Philadelphia businessman says with the same sense of urgency, 'I am needed down at the shop.' "[47] "The American has no dignity when he has no money," Moreau de Saint Méry said. "There is nothing an American would not do for money, and nothing else he cares about."[48] If there was any trait of the American character on which the *Emigrés* were in practically unanimous agreement, it was this.

It is important, however, to understand precisely what the French meant by this American love of gold. To those who were still ideologically rooted in the eighteenth century, American materialism still appeared as the *luxe* which Rousseau had condemned and which Diderot had warned America to avoid—the moral corruption generated by excess wealth and economic inequality. This was the line of Bayard, who sentimentalized the vanishing innocence and happy simplicity of rural America. "We must not look," he wrote, "in a new country for masterpieces of the fine arts, which bear witness to the wealth of a few individuals and the glaring poverty of the people. I was happy not to find any. Something better invited my contemplation, the happiness of simple men living in an abundance of life's necessities."[49] But in the cities this equalitarian Eden had been destroyed. Philadelphia he described as a class-conscious metropolis in which the prime mark of social distinction was a carriage embellished by a fictitious coat of arms and in

---

[44] La Rochefoucauld-Liancourt, *Journal*, p. 71.
[45] *Voyage*, I, 114.    [46] *Ibid.*, VI, 326.    [47] Bayard, *op.cit.*, p. 250.
[48] Moreau de Saint Méry, *op.cit.*, pp. 290, 291.
[49] Bayard, *op.cit.*, p. 28.

which the wives of working men vied in finery with the wives of shopkeepers, and the wives of shopkeepers with the wives of the carriage aristocracy. American women had sunk to wearing diamonds, and who could doubt that they would soon be bartering their chastity for these baubles?

Thus economic prosperity had brought moral decadence. Crèvecoeur's idyll had not been false, but it had depicted a vanished or vanishing America. This same interpretation was given by Antoine Jay, who spent seven years in the United States. "The transition from mediocrity to opulence was too rapid," he explained. "It is easy to see, especially in the seaboard cities, how much the manners of the people are in conflict with the laws. The spectacle of a nation swept into wealth and luxury by the irresistible force of events yet still restrained by the memory of its ancient virtues and by a lingering attachment to its former institutions merits indeed the contemplation of philosophers."[50] The old integrity and sense of honor were lost, the Sabbath was no longer strictly observed, and women squandered their husbands' money on vain show to outshine their neighbors. Sectionalism had dissolved the national character and party strife raged uncontrolled. Jay believed the destruction of the Union inevitable and he saw an apocalyptic vision of civil war and anarchy. "Thus the hopes of philosophy will vanish forever, and the exalted asylum of liberty will become by the blindness of a people too well favored by fortune the bloody haunt of license, rapine, and tyranny."[51]

But such an interpretation was really already an anachronism. It was to be expected of Rousseauists like Bayard or Jay, but not of a man of the new age, a Talleyrand or a La Rochefoucauld. The latter in fact specifically denied that the pursuit of wealth was necessarily corrupting, and the former was not one to be greatly worried about moral values. Mirabeau had said of Talleyrand, "For money he has sold his honor and his friends. He would sell his very soul for money, and he would be right too, for he would be bartering excre-

[50] Op.cit., no. 4, p. 4.
[51] Ibid., no. 4, p. 36.

ment for gold."[52] When he learned that Alexander Hamilton had resigned as Secretary of the Treasury and had returned to private law practice on the pretext that he needed more income to support his family, he thought the man was either mad or incredibly naive.[53] So if Talleyrand sneered that in America "money is the universal God," this did not mean that he condemned Americans for sacrificing ethical principles to economic profits. What he despised was a nation where "the quantity of money a man possesses is the only measure of distinction," where wealth outweighed birth, breeding, and intellectual or artistic achievement, where men had no interest in any activity that did not produce a tangible return, and where taste and refinement were disesteemed. This was the inevitable reaction of men who were still aristocrats by instinct and already romantics without knowing the name. "For as old Europeans," Talleyrand complained, "there is something gauche about the way Americans spend their money. I admit that our own extravagance is often foolish and frivolous, but American extravagance is such that it only seems to prove that no delicacy in the art of living, even in the art of living frivolously, has yet penetrated the American character."[54] More than a mere political revolution had occurred in the few years since Brissot had written that the Americans were profoundly right in setting street lighting above poetry.

Thus for many of the *Emigrés* the degeneration which prosperity had produced in the United States was not moral but cultural. "Interest in the sciences and their cultivation," Volney wrote, "instead of increasing has instead very markedly declined since the Revolution, and the education of the youth of the nation has fallen into a frightful state of disorder and neglect."[55] Love of money was the root of this American evil.

[52] Talleyrand, *Mémoires, lettres inédites et papiers secrets*, ed. J. Gorsas (Paris, 1891), p. 61.
[53] La Tour du Pin, *op.cit.*, ii, 36-37.
[54] *Mémoires*, i, 240.
[55] *Tableau*, p. 462. See also pp. x-xi.

There was a general agreement on this pessimistic picture. On a trip through New Jersey and Pennsylvania Théophile Casenove found in the schools poor teaching, shoddy equipment, and badly planned curricula.[56] Moreau de Saint Méry, who wrote a textbook used in American schools, was particularly interested in the problem of education. He was, it is true, much impressed by the rate of literacy which he said was higher than that of any European country, and which he thought was of crucial importance for the success of representative government. But beyond the primary level he found American education in a sorry state. The academies he visited enforced no discipline, made the most pitiful pretense of instruction, and seemed designed only to allow parents to get their children out of the house. The colleges were no better. Princeton, he reported, was in a disgraceful condition of neglect and filth. The students, he said, were totally undisciplined and "much more interested in gambling and licentious pleasures than in study."[57] La Rochefoucauld analyzed the problem in some detail. He agreed that primary education was good in Massachusetts, Connecticut, and New Hampshire, but poor in New York, worse still in New Jersey and Pennsylvania, and practically non-existent from Maryland on south. The only academies worthy of commendation he found in New England, and the colleges, with the exception of Yale, Harvard, and Princeton, he described as small, ill supported, and without adequate libraries, qualified teachers, or sound curricula. "This state of imperfection in public education," he concluded, "is wholly the result . . . of that continual preoccupation with making money which is common to all the states and all the professions."[58] The students, infected with this passion for gold, "which they absorb with their mother's milk," and convinced that the only success in this world was one that could be measured in dollars and cents, soon lost all interest in learning. Those Frenchmen who attempted to make a living as schoolteachers found it difficult to make a compromise between their ideal of a

[56] *Cazenove Journal, 1794*, ed. R. W. Kelsey (Haverford, 1922).
[57] *Voyage*, p. 116.    [58] *Voyage*, VIII, 130.

classical education and the demands of American parents for "practical knowledge."[59]

According to most of the *Emigrés*, the compulsion to amass wealth had the same paralyzing effect on all intellectual and artistic effort. "It is certain," La Rochefoucauld wrote, "that men distinguished in the arts and sciences are much fewer in proportion to the population in the United States than in Europe."[60] There were, he admitted, many so-called learned societies, but the members, busy with more important matters, attended the meetings only irregularly. Even the American Philosophical Society, to which he was elected, won from him no more than a passing reference in his book. He reported that there were no literary or scientific journals of any merit, that the American press published nothing but religious books, geographical dictionaries, and reprints of English classics, and that the public read little except the newspapers. He found practically nothing in American art or literature worthy of mention.

The basic cause of this intellectual retrogression, La Rochefoucauld, Volney, and Saint Méry all agreed, was not the inadequacy of American education but the failure of American society to produce professional scientists, scholars, and artists. Their theory was that the universal pursuit of money prevented men from turning their energies to non-material ends, and precluded the emergence of an intellectual class such as existed in Europe.

To this same defect they attributed the absence, even among the best-educated and wealthiest Americans, of that refinement of taste which produced what was known in France as "society" and which was the soil necessary to nourish intellectual and artistic excellence. Commenting on the lack of true hospitality in Philadelphia, La Rochefoucauld wrote: "The real reason for this is the struggle, more constant and more general in Philadelphia than elsewhere, to make more money, even when one already has a large

[59] See E. Philips, *Louis Hue Girardin and Nichols Gouin Dufief and Their Relations with Jefferson* (Baltimore, 1926); L. H. Girardin, *Education* (Richmond [?], 1798 [?]).
[60] *Voyage*, VIII, 130

fortune. This is the dominant idea of every one in this country. This mercantile spirit, which is so general, necessarily produces selfishness, isolates the individual, and leaves him with neither taste nor time for society. So what we call society does not really exist in Philadelphia. People are vain about their possessions; they like to display to the newcomer from Europe their handsome furniture, their fine English glassware, their beautiful porcelains. But once he has seen all this at a formal dinner party they prefer someone new who has not yet witnessed the magnificence of the house and has not yet praised the old Madeira which has made two voyages to India. And then a new face is always better than an old one for someone who does not have much to say to either the one or the other."[61]

Nevertheless, in spite of this pessimistic picture, none among the more intelligent French commentators found America an utter wilderness culturally. A number of the *Emigrés* and diplomatic officers were elected to the American Philosophical Society, and Moreau de Saint Méry, for one, was notably faithful in attending the meetings; he donated a variety of gifts, including copies of his own works, a cocoanut, and "a ball of hair found in the stomach of a mule."[62] Both Volney and La Rochefoucauld had the greatest admiration for Jefferson and for other American leaders, but they all insisted that something was causing the United States to lag behind Europe intellectually and artistically, and perhaps even to be retrogressing. While the pursuit of money might be the immediate evil, those who gave real

61 *Ibid.*, VI, 326-327.
62 *Amer. Philos. Soc. Transactions*, IV (1799). Members elected between 1794 and 1800 were La Rochefoucauld-Liancourt; Volney; Adet, the French minister; the Doctors Grassi and Jean Devèze, who had settled in Philadelphia; Louis Etienne Duhail, French consul in Norfolk; Théodore Charles Mozard, consul for Massachusetts, Rhode Island, and New Hampshire; Alexandre Leribours, a resident of Philadelphia; Jacques Marie Le Fessier de Grandpré; M. F. H. Le Comte; and A. J. Laroque. See "Old Minutes of the Society, from 1743 to 1838," *Proc. Amer. Philos. Soc.*, XXII (1885), part 3, no. 119; *Amer. Philos. Soc. Transactions*, IV (1799); G. Chinard, "The American Philosophical Society and the World of Science (1768-1800)," *Proc. Amer. Philos. Soc.*, LXXXVII (1943), 1-11; J. G. Rosengarten, "The Early French Members of the American Philosophical Society," *ibid.*, XLIV (1907), 87-93.

thought to the problem sensed that there must be a more fundamental cause. The explanations they offered varied greatly but they were all significant, for they contained the germs of nineteenth- and twentieth-century European interpretations of American society.

The old theory of American degeneration from climate naturally occurred to some. Bayard suggested that there might be more to the idea than Jefferson had been willing to admit, and Moreau de Saint Méry claimed that American indolence could be explained by the climate.[63] This explanation, however, found only infrequent acceptance and it was categorically denied by both Bonnet de Fréjus and La Rochefoucauld. The latter wrote: "The ridiculous assertion advanced by some that the New World is incapable of producing the same genius and talents as the Old has been so clearly shown to be absurd by the mere mention of the names of certain American citizens whose genius and wisdom would do honor to any nation on earth that we may suppose this error will never be repeated. The American people are intelligent, intellectually alert, and easily taught."[64]

The effect of an equalitarian social system on a nation's intellectual and artistic life, which was to be so brilliantly analyzed by Alexis de Tocqueville in his *De la démocratie en Amérique,* was a problem of which the *Emigrés* were aware, even though they did not perceive all the implications. Brissot had pointed out that in the United States the absence of an aristocratic class with excess income prevented private support of scientific inquiry and artistic creation. The *Emigrés,* impressed by the wealthy families who entertained them in Philadelphia, could not accept this argument that Americans were too poor to patronize the arts and sciences, but they certainly agreed that Americans did not do so. The only solution Volney could offer was the foundation of a national institute with an annual budget of $100,000 to subsidize American scientists and artists.

Antoine Jay, however, who was later to be a leading literary critic and a member of the French Academy, an-

[63] *Voyage,* pp. 352-353.    [64] *Voyage,* VIII, 129-130.

ticipated De Tocqueville in seeing that the replacement of the traditional aristocratic audience by the mass audience of the new equalitarian state would force art into a different mold.[65] He deplored the fact that in Boston plays were written and produced to please what he called the ignorant and stupid populace and not, as in France, "educated and intelligent persons." France's established pre-eminence in the arts was due, he claimed, to her tradition of the aristocratic audience, and popular art, art created to please the masses, could be only vulgar and inferior. He illustrated his point by describing a performance he witnessed at which the audience shouted and booed an actor for his failure to register surprise in the accepted manner by falling flat on his face, and kept screaming, "The fall! The fall! Damn the fellow! He will not fall!" until the unhappy actor yielded to their will by flinging himself to the boards, whereupon they generously applauded his obedience saying, "He did it very handsomely."[66]

But social equality was only one explanation for the state of the arts and sciences in America. Another far more frequently advanced, and one which was to continue to appeal to both the European and American mind, was the concept that the United States was a "young nation." The newness of the New World in a geological, biological, and anthropological sense had already been firmly established in both popular and philosophic thought in the eighteenth century. But the curious thing is that the Americanists before 1789— for instance, men like Chastellux and Lacretelle—had insisted that America was not culturally a new civilization, but rather an extension and integral part of the European Enlightenment. This was the "Greek colony concept." Under the impact of the French Revolution, this theory vanished practically overnight.

The coming of Romanticism has been explained as the transition from a static-mechanistic-uniformitarian concept of the cosmos to a new affirmation of its meaning in terms

65 See my "Antoine Jay and the United States," *American Quarterly*, IV (1952), 235-252.
66 Jay, *op.cit.*, no. 8, pp. 156-157.

of the contrary principles of dynamism, organicism, and diversitarianism.[67] It was precisely such a *Weltanschauung* which seemed to govern the *Emigrés'* interpretation of the United States. They tended to see the new nation as a society inherently alien to their own and they instinctively spoke in terms of "we Europeans" and "you Americans." They thought of American civilization as a distinct organism in the process of growth, of becoming. "This is a country which is growing up," La Rochefoucauld wrote. "What is true today of its population, its institutions, its prices, its trade was not true six months ago and will not be true six months hence. America is a young man just leaving childhood and entering upon manhood."[68] But they did not mean merely that the cities were recently founded and the political system newly organized; they also meant that the people were somehow spiritually and psychologically young. The equating of economic expansion with a sort of biological immaturity provided plausible explanations for the dominant traits of Americans. Their energy and growth, manifested in the swift exploitation of the frontier, were the natural attributes of youth. "The population . . . increases at an almost unbelievable rate, and the American people are not stopped in the task of clearing new lands either by attachment to their homes or by great distances, or in short, by any difficulty whatsoever."[69] Similarly, American pride was the arrogance of adolescence. La Rochefoucauld cited the incredible presumption of a Congressional committee which in 1796 had debated long on whether they should officially designate the United States as "the most enlightened nation in the whole world," and had abandoned the phrase only reluctantly. "I cite this example," he continued, "only as the most striking and national. As a matter of fact, almost all the books printed in America and conversations of individual Americans furnish similar examples every day. This trait, which no one who has known the United States will deny, characterizes

[67] See M. Peckham, "Toward a Theory of Romanticism," *Publ. Mod. Lang. Assoc.*, LXVI (1951), 5-23.
[68] *Voyage*, I, xi.
[69] *Ibid.*, VIII, 59.

all Americans, but it is an extravagance of youth and will disappear with it."[70]

If immaturity could explain American energy and self-confidence, it could also account for American materialism, and hence her cultural inferiority. The numbers of gifted men the United States had already produced and the advances made along certain lines, notably in penology, proved that there was no inherent defect in the American mind. All that was needed was that the nation outgrow its childish love of gold. "Time will reduce this to reasonable dimensions," La Rochefoucauld wrote, "and the United States will surely take their place among the older nations in learning and in the sciences as well as in political power. But there is no doubt that the rapidity of this important and certain progress still depends on the rate at which the character of the people changes."[71]

Talleyrand placed even greater insistence on this curious idea that the length of time a locality has been inhabited and the perfection of its physical structures are in direct ratio to the cultural maturity of the inhabitants. He claimed he saw the principle graphically demonstrated by the contrast between the seaboard cities and the frontier: "It is a new experience for a traveler to leave one of the principal cities where society is perfected and to traverse successively all the stages of civilization and industry, which sink progressively lower and lower, until he arrives after a few days at the shapeless rude cabin constructed of newly felled logs. Such a trip is a sort of practical and living analysis of the origin of peoples and states. One departs from the most complex social organization to arrive at the most simple. Each day one loses sight of some of those inventions which our requirements as they have multiplied have made into necessities. One feels as though he were traveling backward over the progress of the human mind."[72]

One of the most applauded passages of a memoir he read before the National Institute was on the American woods-

---

[70] *Ibid.*, VIII, 128-129.    [71] *Ibid.*, VIII, 133-134.
[72] "Mémoire sur les relations commerciales des Etats-Unis," p. 100.

man: "The American woodsman is interested in nothing; any sensitivity is foreign to him. Those branches yonder arched by nature, that lovely clump of foliage, that bright spot of color lighting up a dark part of the wood, this deep green darkening another—all that is nothing, it means nothing to him. His only thought is the number of strokes it will take him to chop down the tree."[73] What applied to the frontier in relation to the seaboard, obviously applied to the United States as a whole in relation to Europe.

A curious contradiction existed, incidentally, between Talleyrand's and La Rochefoucauld's interpretations, for the former found that "society in its first origins," as he witnessed it on the frontier, was not characterized by pride and energy but by laziness and immorality. As he said, "Indolent and grasping, poor but without desires they still resemble too closely the savage natives whose places they have taken . . . [and] all their vices are made worse by ignorance."[74] This picture of the shiftless, vicious and brutish frontiersman was often given by French travelers.[75]

Volney alone, apparently, saw the "romantic error of those writers who call a 'new and virgin people' what is in fact a mixture of peoples from old Europe—Germans, Dutch and especially British from the three kingdoms."[76] As his *Tableau du climat et du sol des Etats-Unis* was one of the foundation stones of modern systematic geography, so his projected but unfortunately unwritten work on American civilization might well have been an equally important contribution to modern sociology, for he clearly saw the importance, in the study of the American character, of both the various cultural traditions transplanted from Europe and the impact of the new environment on these traditions.[77] At Vincennes in Indiana Territory, for instance, he wit-

[73] *Ibid.*, p. 101.
[74] *Talleyrand in America as a Financial Promoter*, pp. 82-83.
[75] E.g., "Portions of the Journal of André Michaux," *Proc. Amer. Philos. Soc.*, XXVI (1889), 1-145.
[76] *Tableau*, p. v.
[77] See V. Jeanvrot, "Volney, sa vie, ses oeuvres," *La Révolution française*, XXXV (1898), 278-286, 348-375; G. Chinard, *Volney et l'Amérique* (Baltimore, 1923).

nessed what he claimed was an example of the superiority of the Anglo-Americans over the French in meeting the challenge of the frontier. American stiffness, taciturnity, grossness, and lack of consideration for others, which to most Europeans seemed a sort of national incivility, he explained as a consequence of the peculiar American individualism produced by the enforced isolation and independence of a frontier existence.

No other *Emigré* perceived so well the complexities of the problem, but many agreed with Volney's statement that the United States was "a second edition of England, but reproduced on a much larger format than the original."[78] To these men, who had been told by *Philosophes* like Condorcet that rationalism and political liberalism would suffice to unite all men in an indissoluble fraternity, it was a rude and unpleasant surprise to discover that in spite of the recent war, American values and mores were much closer to those of England than those of France. Bayard, a violent Anglophobe, claimed that "All the errors and vices of England have flooded the cities of America."[79] Jay condemned American subservience to the dictates of English taste and fashion, the perverse American admiration for Shakespeare, and in particular the production of plays written in another land for another audience which neither portrayed American manners nor presented ideas and sentiments adapted to American society. Talleyrand made this Anglicization of America the subject of a long letter to Lord Lansdowne, leader of the English opposition,[80] which he later rewrote as the paper read before the National Institute in Paris in 1797. His thesis was that British success in controlling the American trade was due not only to American economic self-interest, but also to similarities of language, political institutions, law, education, and manners. This imposition of English customs and patterns of thought on the United States explained to him why the two peoples responded to reason rather than

[78] *Tableau*, p. 346.    [79] Bayard, *op.cit.*, p. 262.
[80] *Correspondance diplomatique de Talleyrand. La Mission de Talleyrand à Londres, en 1792. Ses lettres d'Amérique à Lord Lansdowne*, ed. G. Pallain (Paris, 1889).

to emotion, why they were the only modern nations without "society," and why both were essentially incompatible to the French.

Thus the new sense of nationalism and the rejection of universalism produced the belief that an unbridgeable chasm divided the Frenchman and the American, that each must inevitably remain a stranger in the other's land. The last years of the century have been called the period of "the great schism" between France and America. The schism, however, was not basically political or diplomatic but cultural and ideological. The death of eighteenth-century universalism caused the French to see America as an alien organism at a stage of development different from that of French civilization and developing according to different principles. The very fact that the new republic, so long spiritually and economically dependent on the European motherland, was now turning its face westward and energetically accepting the challenge of its own unique destiny only served to confirm this belief. The de-europeanization of America had begun in the French mind.

The *Emigrés* appear to have been especially sensitive to the new forces acting on men's minds in the 1790's and to have anticipated the directions the new thinking was to take. Therefore there was an appreciable lag in the appearance in Paris of the complex of new attitudes which was to produce anti-Americanism. The popular idealization of the United States, as long as it was not disturbed by contradictory evidence or international political conflicts, endured by a sort of inertia. By 1793 the compulsion to idealize life in America in order to justify liberal reforms had long since vanished, and interest in American political theory and practice was steadily declining. Even those writers like Roederer and Adrien de Lezay-Marnésia who still cited American examples did so to illustrate specific controversial points rather than to suggest models for imitation.[81] Yet there were at first few voices which denied the official government line

[81] Pierre Louis Roederer, *Du Gouvernement* (Paris, 1795); Adrien de Lezay-Marnésia, *Qu'est-ce que la Constitution de 1793? Constitution de Massachusetts* (Paris, an III).

of French-American fraternity. The main force which kept alive this good will to as late as 1795 was the hope for economic and military support from across the Atlantic against the power of England. For instance, the *Décade philosophique*, the first literary and intellectual periodical to emerge after the Revolution, was prompted to declare in 1794, "Americans are united with the French not only by bonds of gratitude but even more by their love of liberty." But it was clear that it was tangible expressions of gratitude rather than mere community of ideas that the writer was interested in, for he amplified this sentence by discussing American shipments of wheat and the chances of an armed alliance.[82] Reports were printed frequently of American celebrations in honor of French military victories, and the news of General Mad Anthony Wayne's victory at the Battle of Fallen Timbers was optimistically hailed as the outbreak of a new American war against England.[83] Such expectations found expression in the enthusiastic reception given James Monroe by the Convention in August 1794 and the presentation to Congress of a Tricolor in return for Monroe's gift of an American flag.

The signature of Jay's Treaty with England in November 1794 did not arouse any immediate reaction, for the terms were kept secret, and Monroe, as American minister, assured the French government that if the treaty turned out to be inimical to French interests it would never be ratified. But in November 1795, when the news reached Paris that the treaty had indeed been ratified by the Senate and when simultaneously the full text of the document became known, the government and newspapers did an about-face. They burst forth in outraged protests against what they considered a shameless betrayal. America, the cherished ally, had sold out her benefactor to the implacable enemy across the Channel. Washington, who as late as 1794 was still revered as a republican saint,[84] became the object of the most vitriolic

[82] 30 prairial, an II.    [83] *Moniteur universel*, Dec. 1 and 22, 1794.
[84] E.g., J. M. A. Servan and P. Guilbert, *Correspondance entre quelques hommes honnêtes* (Lausanne, 1794), pp. 59-60.

attacks. It is true that the line taken by the newspapers was that this act of treachery was the work of the reactionary Federalists (who were reported to be triumphantly chopping down the Liberty Trees all over New England),[85] and that the American people were still loyal and true friends of France. This construction, however, had the effect of destroying what tatters still remained of the American Dream, for to say that the people were good but the government was bad was to deny the very essence of the *Philosophes'* vision of America.

The diplomatic break, which rapidly grew more serious until it ended in the Undeclared War, had the effect of generating a strong and broad wave of anti-Americanism. This popular reaction, emotional and chauvinistic, was a natural product of the new nationalism spawned by the Revolution, but it was no doubt increased by the sudden release of the concealed current of anti-Americanism which had existed even before 1789.

Once the tide of opinion began to set in the opposite direction, everything seemed to accelerate its course. The activities of the various American land companies, for instance, were a recurrent source of trouble. One group, headed by the financier Robert Morris, was circulating in 1794 and 1795 pamphlets written by Thomas Cooper and Joseph Priestley in promotion of the sale of 300,000 acres along the Susquehanna,[86] in competition with the Compagnie de New York and other agents selling lands in Kentucky, Pennsylvania, and northern New York.[87] Advertisements posted in the streets of Paris and published in newspapers and in *Les Petites affiches*, an advertising sheet, offered a variety of tempting bargains.[88] Whatever good effect the extravagant

[85] *Moniteur universel*, April 4, 1796.

[86] *Plan de vente de trois cent mille acres de terres situées dans les comtés de Northumberland et de Huntington dans l'état de Pensylvanie* (Philadelphia, 1794); *Notes sur les défrichements en Amérique à l'usage des Européens* [1794?]; Thomas Cooper, *Renseignements sur l'Amérique* (Paris, an III and Hamburg, 1795).

[87] See *Plan de vente*, pp. 45-47.

[88] See Jacques Mignard, *Quelques escrocs anglais démasqués, ou les déserts de l'Amérique du nord présentés tels qu'ils sont* (Paris, an VI); *Annonces, affiches et avis divers*, Sept. 22, Oct. 12, Oct. 13, 1797, etc.

prospectuses had was more than offset by the complaints of disappointed purchasers. The *Moniteur* gave publicity to these protests and in 1794 published a letter from Fauchet, minister in Philadelphia, to the French government, denouncing fraudulent American land sales to French emigrants and enclosing a letter from one Jonas Fauche of Greensboro, North Carolina, which named Robert Morris as the arch-villain.[89] Similar warnings were given by other papers.[90] An indication of the violent feeling which could be aroused by these alleged frauds is seen in the pamphlets published by a Paris printer and patent medicine vendor named Jacques Mignard, who denounced the sales as a vile English plot to drain France of money and population, and said the lands offered in New York were inhabited by fierce Indians, covered by snow three-quarters of the year, and separated from Albany by impassable mountains. Mignard asserted that the emigrants became slaves, that the tyranny of Catherine of Russia was preferable to American "liberty," and that Americans were "vile vermin" and "cannibals," who were all infected with venereal diseases and habitually sold their daughters into prostitution.[91] Such prejudices found support in the traditional bad reputation of American businessmen and received ample confirmation from returning *Emigrés* like Talleyrand.

Against these political and economic forces for ill will there was no diplomatic counterweight in Paris. Monroe, successor to the aristocratic Gouverneur Morris, seemed to be a minister whose political views and whose personality would make him compatible to the Convention and would permit him to carry on the interrupted work of Franklin and Jefferson, but Jay's Treaty and his recall by Washington cut the ground from under him, and the Directory refused even to accept the credentials of his successor, C. C. Pinck-

[89] Jan. 5, 1795. See also a similar letter, June 17, 1795.
[90] E.g., *Bibliothèque britannique*, II (1796), 30-47; *Décade philosophique*, July 28, 1796.
[91] J. Mignard, *op.cit., Apperçu des crimes commis par les Anglo-Américains envers les Français* (Paris, an VIII), and *Réponse de Jacques Mignard à la diatribe de Pocheux* (Paris, an VIII).

ney. Then came the unsuccessful joint commission of Pinckney, Gerry, and Marshall and the disastrous XYZ Affair. It was not until a new commission was sent in 1800 to settle the French imbroglio and Robert R. Livingston was appointed minister by Jefferson in 1801 that the United States had an official spokesman in Paris. Thomas Paine was still in France, but he had been deprived of his seat in the Convention, was for a time imprisoned, and was without money and leading a disordered life. His violent attack on Washington and his recommendation that the French government refuse to receive Pinckney in order, as he said, to make Washington look ridiculous and to preserve democratic principles, may have helped to justify him personally to the Directory but these were no contributions to French-American amity.[92] Joel Barlow too had remained in Paris, but he withdrew from French politics in 1793 to devote himself to the accumulation of almost $200,000 in "commerce and speculation."[93] It is true that in December 1799 he submitted to the French government a memoir proposing a declaration of neutral rights and the outlawing of privateering, and also published letters urging a settlement of the "misunderstanding" between the two nations and the establishment of a European federation and world court to regulate international trade.[94] But such efforts had as little effect on opinion and on diplomatic relations as Paine's remarkable *Pacte Maritime* (in which Barlow and Skipwith, the American consul, collaborated), which proposed a congress of neutral nations with the power to assure neutral rights.[95] Equally ineffective were the efforts of John Skey Eustace to counter-

[92] Thomas Paine, *Letter to George Washington* (1796). See also B. Faÿ, *L'Esprit révolutionnaire en France et aux Etats-Unis à la fin du XVIIIe siècle* (Paris, 1925), p. 260. A long anonymous article published in the spring of 1796, attacking Jay's Treaty and Washington, and praising Jefferson, may well also have been the work of Paine, though it has not hitherto been attributed to him. (*Moniteur universel*, March 29, 1796, and *Mercure français*, 30 ventôse, an IV.)
[93] R. F. Durden, "Joel Barlow and the French Revolution," *William and Mary Quarterly*, 3rd series, VIII (1951), 327-354.
[94] *Letters from Paris, to the Citizens of the United States of America* (London, 1800).
[95] *Pacte maritime, adressé aux nations neutres par un neutre* (Paris, an IX).

act the effects of Jay's Treaty,[96] of Thomas W. Griffith, who in 1798 published a book entitled *L'Indépendance absolue des Américains* in an attempt to justify American policy and to promote better understanding,[97] and of the Quaker pacifist George Logan, who arrived in Paris as a self-appointed emissary to try to heal the breach and who was greeted as "the envoy of the patriotic party of the United States."[98]

In the totality of French opinion must be included the many royalist *Emigrés* living in England and on the Continent, for they were soon to be reintegrated in the nation's thought. If there were some aristocrats who could still praise the American Revolution by contrasting its moderation with the excesses committed in France, there were also many, like Chateaubriand, who blamed the Americans and their fatal example for all the catastrophes they themselves had suffered. Lafayette wrote Washington that the hatred of the aristocratic party for America dated from the beginning of the French Revolution.[99] Joseph de Maistre, perhaps the most eloquent defender of the royalist position, attacking the principle of democratic republicanism, wrote in irritation, "People give the example of America. I know nothing so exasperating as the praises bestowed on that babe in swaddling clothes; wait till it grows up."[100] He was willing to bet a hundred to one that the projected city of Washington never would be built.[101]

While the new interpretations of American civilization offered by royalists abroad and by republicans in France did not duplicate those of the *Emigrés* in the United States, they were the result of the same relativistic approach. As early as 1792, Necker had written, "It would be a great fallacy to imagine that liberty, equality, and all our other

96 J. S. Eustace, *Traité d'amitié, de commerce et de navigation entre S. M. Britannique et les Etats-Unis d'Amérique* (Paris, an IV).

97 *L'Indépendance absolue des Américains des Etats-Unis prouvée par l'état actuel de leur commerce avec les nations européennes* (Paris, 1798).

98 *Moniteur universel*, Aug. 28, 1798.

99 Lafayette, *Mémoires, correspondance et manuscrits* (Paris, 1837-1838), IV 436.

100 *Considérations sur la France* (London, 1797), p. 65.

101 *Ibid.*, p. 120.

new institutions will make us similar to Americans."[102] De Maistre made the same point in insisting that traditions and circumstances in the United States were so different that it was impossible to draw any analogies with France.[103]

Even those who still had faith in the ideals of the French Revolution were forced to admit that those principles had had very different success on the two sides of the Atlantic. Charles Pictet (who was, perhaps significantly, not a Frenchman but a Genevan) expressed in the introduction to his *Tableau de la situation actuelle des Etats-Unis* (1795) the greatest admiration for American prosperity, political stability, and domestic order, and for the success of the American Revolution in avoiding political excesses and any violent disruption of the social structure. But he could no longer, like a pre-1789 *Philosophe*, attribute these achievements to the application of universally valid principles of government; instead, he tried to discover the special circumstances which had produced them. These circumstances he listed as the long-established traditions of liberty and representative government; the strength of religion in the United States; the continuity of leadership; the predominantly agricultural population, which he regarded as favorable to good order and moderation; and, lastly, the deep-rooted American sense of civic responsibility.

The same relativistic approach was later used by apologists for the Consulate to produce quite different conclusions. Pierre Victor Malouet, a former member of the Constituent Assembly, attempted to explain the apparent contradiction of the economic and political success of the American democracy and the unscrupulous dishonesty of American businessmen. Brissot, he said, had made the error of interpreting the United States according to an absolute formula which blinded him to the mixture of good and bad in American life. Malouet pointed out that there were certain special circumstances, particularly the deep-rooted traditions of self-government, which made democracy successful in the United

[102] Jacques Necker, *Du pouvoir exécutif dans les grands états* (Paris, 1792), II, 7.
[103] *Op.cit.*, p. 118.

*213*

States, but that there were other circumstances, particularly the lack of capital and the need for financial daring and enterprise, which made Americans so tolerant of unethical business practices. Fraudulent bankruptcies and the like, which would ruin a European state, did little harm, he claimed, to a nation in the process of rapid economic expansion. Thus there was no essential connection (as the Progressionists had assumed) between politics, economics, and morality. "We must distinguish," Malouet wrote, "two persons in the moral make-up of the American: one who is sincerely devoted to democracy because he has found agreement between its principles and his own material interests, and another who pursues fortune by every means at his disposal."[104] American democracy was an American product for Americans only. "It was madness to suppose the American example applicable to France. . . . An enthusiast like Brissot could not see that America is like a chessboard on which all the squares are laid out to be filled as they stand, while Europe is a battlefield on which the various prejudices, passions, and vices would be in perpetual chaos and conflict were it not for some dominant governing force. This does not mean," Malouet concluded, "that servitude is necessary in Europe, but only that democracy is no good here; only force can maintain liberty among us, supposing, of course, this force to be subject to the control of justice and reason."[105]

Thus, whatever were his politics and prejudices, the observer in France seemed compelled, just as the *Emigrés* who had crossed the Atlantic, to interpret the United States from the assumption that the character of any nation is the product of a unique set of circumstances and that there are no, or few, universal social principles binding on all mankind. The inevitable conclusion from this new relativism was that America's case was to a great degree irrelevant to France's problems. The natural result was an abrupt loss of interest. Pictet wrote in 1795, "Little is known in Europe about exist-

[104] J. B. A. Suard, *Mélanges de littérature* (Paris, 1803), pp. 166-167. See *Décade philosophique*, 10 fructidor, an XI, on Malouet's authorship of this unsigned essay.
[105] *Ibid.*, pp. 164-165, 170.

ing conditions in the United States. Just when that republic was emerging from the crisis which raised it to the rank of a free nation, more immediate concerns drew the attention of Europe."[106] In this the journalists agreed, and the following year the *Moniteur* observed, "The story of events of the American War is well known, but shortly after that time our attention was transferred to the great movement which has shaken Europe, and we have paid little attention to what has been happening in the United States since they became independent."[107] Thomas Griffith complained in 1798 that most Frenchmen knew so little about the United States that they were continually confusing it with the West Indies or South America.[108]

An illuminating index to the loss of interest is provided both by the quantitative decline in the publications on the United States and by the new character of those that were printed. Apart from the *Voyages* of La Rochefoucauld and Bayard, the only French work of those years which attempted to give a comprehensive view of the United States was Pictet's *Tableau*. An even more significant clue to the drop in popular interest was the disappearance of the American and the United States from creative and popular French literature— three plays on American themes in 1795, 1796, and 1797,[109] a new edition of Nougaret's *Honorine Clarens* in 1796, Billardon de Sauvigny's *Recueil d'apologues* in 1797 (containing tributes to Washington and Franklin, probably written earlier), a few scattered references in novels like Mounier's *Adolphe* (1795), and that was all. A lingering concern with American politics was indicated by new editions of *The Federalist* in 1795 and of Ramsay's *History of the American Revolution* in 1796, but what interest there was in the United

106 Charles Pictet, *Tableau de la situation des Etats-Unis de l'Amérique d'après Jedédiah Morse et les meilleurs auteurs américains* (Paris, an III), p. 13.
107 *Moniteur universel*, Mar. 28. 1796.    108 Griffith, *op.cit.*, pp. 7, 14.
109 Alexandre Vincent Duval, "Bella, ou la Femme aux deux maris," in *Oeuvres complètes* (Paris, 1822), II, 237-318; first performance, 27 prairial, an III (June 15, 1795); see *Décade philosophique*, 10 messidor, an III. Marsollier de Vivetières, *Arnill, ou le Prisonnier américain* (Paris, 1797). Benoît Michel Decamberousse, *Asgill, ou le Prisonnier anglais* (Paris, an IV).

States was directed mainly either to the exotic element, represented by translations of William Bartram's *Travels* in 1799 and of Timberlake's *Memoirs* in 1797, or to special topics, such as a work of Robert Fulton's on canals,[110] John Paul Jones's *Memoirs*, La Rochefoucauld's and Petit-Radel's reports on the Philadelphia prison system, occasional items in the *Décade philosophique* and the *Bibliothèque britannique* on American finances and reports on American flora[111] and agricultural techniques.[112] The only enduring favorite was Benjamin Franklin. The second part of his *Autobiography* was first printed in the *Décade philosophique* in 1798 and was republished the same year in book form by Castéra. Editions of *La Science du Bonhomme Richard* continued to appear, and the *Décade* from time to time printed some of his letters and essays.

But Franklin, for all his continuing appeal, was dead. The only living American who was succeeding in reaching the French public was, curiously, the Congregational clergyman and geographer, Jedidiah Morse. Charles Pictet's *Tableau* was in fact in large part nothing more than a translation of Morse's *American Geography*. Morse also reached French readers indirectly through the English geographer William Guthrie's *New Geographical Grammar*, which borrowed heavily from Morse for its section on the United States and was translated in numerous French editions from 1799 on.[113] The *Bibliothèque britannique*, published in Geneva by Pictet, also printed selections from Morse,[114] and the *Encyclopédie méthodique* made use of long passages from the American geographer without acknowledgment.[115] This influence was not without importance, for Morse's work, besides describing physical features, covered in some detail the man-

110 R. Fulton, *Recherches sur les moyens de perfectionner les canaux* (Paris, an VII).

111 Efforts were made to introduce into France the bayberry, locust, and sugar maple. See *Décade philosophique*, 30 nivôse, an III; 10 vendémiaire, an III; 30 frimaire, an VI.

112 *Ibid.*, 30 thermidor, an II; 20 vendémiaire, an V.

113 *Nouvelle géographie* (Paris, an VII) and many subsequent editions.

114 Jan. 1803, pp. 366-377.

115 *Encyclopédie méthodique. Géographie physique* (Paris, 1803), II, 416.

ners, customs, morals, education, institutions, agriculture, industry, and government of the various sections of the United States and reflected the Yankee prejudices of the author, particularly in his descriptions of the Southern states. The sum total, however, of these publications relating to the United States was small indeed when compared to what had appeared before 1794, and the decline clearly confirms the loss of public interest in American civilization as such.

The only aspect of the United States which attracted real attention was the question of diplomatic relations between the two nations, and during the Directory there was much public debate on the question of the increasing tension. Since the United States was the only nation sharing the principles and ideals of the French Revolution, French-American relations were a moral issue involving the prestige of the Republic. There were many heated arguments in those cafés where political matters were discussed,[116] and the problem was debated in the newspapers and the Conseil des Cinq Cents.

Since the Directory throughout its existence held to a truculent policy toward the United States and since this attitude was accompanied by increasing anti-Americanism on the part of the general public, and among both the royalist exiles and many of the republican intellectuals, it was natural that whatever new attempts were made to re-evaluate American civilization were usually pessimistic.

The old idea of American degeneration, which was discussed by such *Emigrés* as Bonnet de Fréjus, La Rochefoucauld, Bayard, and Moreau de Saint Méry, was still far from dead and was even regaining intellectual respectability. Aubin Louis Millin, the archeologist, did not hesitate to write in the *Magasin encyclopédique* in 1799, "In America one becomes older sooner than in Europe. The influence of climate is even more evident in its effects on women and is very marked in the case of animals, which are much smaller than in the Old World."[117] Thomas Griffith felt it necessary

---

[116] See Faÿ, *op.cit.*, p. 261.    [117] I, an VII (1799), 476.

to refute the statement made by Raynal twenty-eight years before that America had never produced a single man of genius,[118] and Pictet likewise included a discussion of the theory and a quotation of Jefferson's refutation.[119]

A more prevalent idea, however, and one with obvious political origins, was the alleged affinity of Americans for England and things English. This was the theme of Talleyrand's *Mémoire* and of Fauchet's *Coup d'oeil sur l'état actuel de nos rapports politiques avec les Etats-Unis* (1797), and it was the idea which Griffith's book was written to refute. The accusation appeared frequently in the newspapers. It contradicted of course the thesis that the pro-English American foreign policy was the work of a small minority of Anglomaniacs, but as diplomatic relations deteriorated such subtleties were ignored. In 1797 the *Décade* was saying, "The United States are bound to England by the same traditions and language, by extensive commercial relations, and by long-standing habits which the conflicts between the two nations have failed to erase. In vain have we hoped for some time that gratitude, or at least self-interest, would make of that federal republic a loyal ally of France. Now Washington has concluded with our most implacable enemies a treaty wholly inimical to our interests."[120] Instead of interpreting American foreign policy as mere expediency, as an effort to adjust as well as possible to the momentary power situation, French commentators, thinking always in terms of national cultures and national characters, insisted on seeing it as a manifestation of a spiritual and cultural orientation toward England and hence as evidence of a fundamental incompatibility with France.

Jay's Treaty, condemned as a sort of collective act of national ingratitude, appeared as only one more manifestation of American unscrupulousness in any matter involving monetary profit. This vice was sometimes seen as the corruption, which the Rousseauists had feared, of an originally virtuous and equalitarian society by wealth and *luxe*. In a play produced in 1793 an American Quaker announced

[118] Griffith, *op.cit.*, p. 9.   [119] Pictet, *op.cit.*, pp. 18off.   [120] April 19, 1797.

Hélas, déjà le luxe altère nos succès;
Et l'or, qui corrompt, a rompu l'équilibre
De cette égalité recouvrée à grands frais.[121]

More often, however, the prejudice was simply the product of the reports of the returning *Emigrés* and of the accumulation of unfortunate French experiences with American land agents and importers. In 1798 Griffith reported that the idea that Americans were dishonest and untrustworthy in commercial dealings was very common.[122]

However low an opinion the French had of American business ethics, they were nevertheless well aware of the rapid growth of the United States in population and wealth. French papers published tables of figures showing the growth of American foreign trade and the rapid increase in population revealed by the census.[123] The *Moniteur* printed articles in 1795 and 1796 showing that the United States had the lowest public debt per capita of any civilized nation and was enjoying the benefits of a sound currency, thriving foreign trade, and a booming shipbuilding industry.[124] This dynamic growth was both a reason for envy and a source of worry. As early as 1770 Raynal had warned of the threat the United States might be to European colonies, and Fauchet repeated the same warning to his government in 1795.[125]

An inevitable corollary to the loss of faith in the idea of progress, to the sense of the irrelevancy of the American political experiment, and to the disillusion with the American moral character was the sudden and complete evaporation of that faith in the American Enlightenment which had filled the *Philosophes* with such hope. When Millin reviewed the new volume of the *Transactions* of the American Philosophical Society of 1793, he was critical and condescending,

---

[121] "Alas, luxury is already debasing our triumph, and corrupting gold has upset the balance of that equality which we won by such great sacrifices." Beffroy de Reigny, *Allons, ça va, ou le Quaker en France* (Paris, 1793), p. 24.

[122] *Op.cit.*, pp. 16-29, 143.

[123] E.g., *Bibliothèque britannique*, 12 nivôse, an VII.

[124] April 13, 1795 and Feb. 28, 1796.

[125] Jean J. A. Fauchet, *Mémoire sur les Etats-Unis d'Amérique*, ed. C. L. Lokke, Amer. Hist. Assoc., 1941.

and a comparison of the tone of this article with the enthusiastic notices given the first volume in 1771 is a good indication of the change that had taken place.[126]

There existed, however, an ideological current running counter to those who insisted on decrying the United States. In spite of the Terror, some men still persisted in their love of liberty, and for them America proved that even if the freedom of man was a difficult ideal it was not an impossible one. Pictet wrote: "O Liberty! Liberty! Daughter of Heaven! Precious gift granted only to the wise! Source of virtues, glory and prosperity! Thou fleest in horror far from these lands where men profane and calumniate thee, from these countries that men bathe in blood and tears in thy name. Thou art content to dwell only among those people who lead pure and simple lives, who love labor and order, who respect the law, cherish justice, and adore one God who punishes and rewards mankind."[127]

In spite of the relativistic character that French thought was rapidly assuming, the great current of materialistic, deterministic liberal ideology created by the *Philosophes* and the Encyclopedists was not dead, nor was it to die. In the last decade of the century it was kept alive by the group of men later to be known as *Idéologues*, who had originally gathered in Mme Helvétius' salon and who included such old friends of Franklin and Jefferson as Volney, Cabanis, J. B. Say, and Destutt de Tracy. These men were to fulfill their most important function in French-American relations during the First Empire, but under the Directory they were also important in maintaining a small but persistent body of admirers of American liberalism.

Through 1794 the *Décade philosophique*, the organ of the *Idéologues*, remained pro-American in the old Philosophic tradition. In reporting the Fourth of July celebrations of that year in the United States it commented, "What must interest us especially is the love the American people expressed for the French and for the principles which we sup-

126 *Magasin encyclopédique*, III, an III (1795), 289-302.
127 Pictet, *op.cit.*, pp. 35-36.

port."[128] After the publication of the terms of Jay's Treaty, the *Décade,* as we have seen, joined in the general chorus of denunciation of Washington and later of Adams. J. B. Say, in an article in this paper, went so far in 1798 as to accuse Washington of being a crypto-royalist and an Anglophile and of having supported the American Revolution only in the expectation of being able to sell out to the English at a good price.[129] But the *Décade* drew a sharp distinction between the Federalists and the true friends of liberty and France—Jefferson and his followers. Commenting on the election of Adams and Jefferson as President and Vice-President, it said, "France will have in these two men an evil genius and a good genius; but unfortunately the evil genius is the more powerful of the two."[130] Consequently the editors attempted to adopt an ambiguous attitude, alternating between attacks on the American government and praise of the virtues of American democracy, in particular religious freedom and universal public education, and between condemnations of Washington and attempts to excuse his foreign policy.[131] The picture of Jefferson as France's secret ally had received powerful confirmation in the French mind from Jefferson's famous letter to Mazzei denouncing the Federalists as pro-English, which Mazzei had imprudently translated and published in an Italian paper and which the *Moniteur* gleefully republished in January 1797, with the addition of a spurious final paragraph condemning American ingratitude and injustice to France.[132] Franklin, too, continued to be revered as a true friend of France and an apostle of liberty. When Rousseau's body was transferred to the Pantheon in 1794, a bust of the American patriarch was carried in the procession. Throughout the Directory a café on the Rue Faubourg-Montmarte was decorated with his life-sized portrait, beside those of Rousseau, Voltaire, Helvétius, and Marat. In 1800 a fête was celebrated in Franklin's memory

128 *Décade philosophique,* 20 vendémiaire, an III.
129 *Ibid.,* 10 vendémiaire, an VII.
130 *Ibid.,* April 29, 1797.
131 *Ibid.,* July 28, 1796 and Nov. 30, 1796.
132 Jan. 25, 1797.

in the Temple de la Victoire (Saint Sulpice).[133] In his review of Franklin's *Autobiography*, J. B. Say repeated the frequent comparison with Rousseau's *Confessions* and used Franklin as a weapon to attack Washington and Adams. Quoting a letter from Franklin to Dr. Mather advocating the maintenance of the French-American alliance against England, he wrote, "If Franklin were, as he ought to be, the oracle of his nation, which now has revealed itself to be so unworthy of him and of his services, would America then be permitting her government, bribed by British gold, to sell her out to the tyrant of the seas?"[134]

If we read between the lines, it is possible to guess that the *Idéologues'* attacks on the Federalists were perhaps little more than an acceptance of the popular chauvinism and that their admiration for Jefferson came more directly from the heart. In 1795 the *Décade* said, "America appears destined to be the asylum to which will flee that peace which practically all the governments of Europe seem to be striving to banish from the Old World. . . . When from that happy land we turn our eyes to our own continent, what a grievous spectacle oppresses our hearts."[135] And two months later: "Already that interesting nation [the United States], thanks to its wisdom, industry, and courage, is enjoying the fruits of its revolution. It is advancing in great strides toward national prosperity, toward the highest degree of social well-being, while in the other half of the globe war and discord must soon bring about the dissolution of all government and plunge the nations of Europe once more into poverty and barbarism."[136] In the first years of the Consulate, in commenting on La Rochefoucauld's report on American prisons, J. B. Say rather pointedly expressed the hope that the new regime would be able, like that of the Americans, to bring the principles of the Revolution to successful application. "Let us hope," he wrote, "that the liberal ideas diffused in so many fine books and on which our Revolution was

133 See Faÿ, *op.cit.*, p. 298.
134 *Décade philosophique*, 10 vendémiaire, an VII.
135 *Ibid.*, 10 pluviôse, an III.
136 *Ibid.*, 20 germinal, an III.

founded will at long last descend from their theoretical eminences, so that the world may finally see that we French can act as well as think and that we too may have institutions worthy of serving as models to other nations."[137]

Such sentiments, which were frequently echoed by Pictet's *Bibliothèque britannique*,[138] show that a new form of Americanism was beginning to take shape among those liberals who still remained true to the ideals of the French Revolution, though they decried the perversions these ideas had suffered. As the tide of reaction crept back over Europe, they were to look longingly to America as the one land in which the principles of the previous century had triumphed and survived.

Perhaps this sort of sentiment had a broader base than has been supposed, for even during the darkest days of the Undeclared War there remained a constant minority pressure for appeasement. In 1797 a number of papers sought to excuse the conduct of the American government on the grounds that French naval weakness left the Americans at the mercy of English privateers.[139] In April and May of the same year, Louis Philippe de Ségur, who had served in America under Rochambeau and had returned an enthusiastic Americanist, took up the defense of the United States in two vigorous articles.[140] In June, Emmanuel Pastoret, the ci-devant Marquis de Pastoret, who had been closely associated with Americanists in both the Musée and the Société de 1789, attacked, as a member of the Conseil des Cinq Cents, the anti-American decrees of the Directory as unconstitutional and pled eloquently for a rapprochement.[141] Such efforts as these were strongly opposed by the government, but the friends of America persisted, and the next year L. Hauteval, who had been in the United States and had formed attachments there, published a pamphlet apologizing for the errors of both nations and pleading in the name of their mutual interests

[137] *Ibid.*, 20 nivôse, an VIII.
[138] III (1796), 17, 37.   [139] Faÿ, *op.cit.*, p. 267.
[140] *Nouvelles politiques*, April 25 and May 17, 1797.
[141] *Motion d'ordre d'Emmanuel Pastoret sur l'état actuel de nos rapports politiques et commerciaux avec les Etats-Unis de l'Amérique Septentrionale* (Paris, an V).

and past friendship for a reconciliation.[142] In September 1797 Louis Otto, who had first gone to America in 1779 as secretary to La Luzerne and had remained at the legation in Philadelphia in various capacities until 1792, submitted a vitriolic memorandum to the Directory condemning the blundering, stupidity, impolicy, and transgression of prerogatives of which he said Genêt and Fauchet had been guilty, defending the actions of the United States, and urging reconciliation.[143] Then in December 1798 Jean Antoine Rozier, who had been French consul in New York since 1795, wrote a report to Larevellière-Lépeaux of the Directory indicating that there was the possibility of a third-party split under Washington and Hamilton and urging the re-establishment of diplomatic relations.[144]

These efforts prepared the way for Napoleon's abrupt shift in policy and the settlement of the imbroglio. But no change in diplomatic relations could restore the American Dream in France. This was a new age and the Dream had outlived its function. Every aspiration creates its own myth. As the Spanish lust for gold created the myth of El Dorado, so the Philosophic search for liberty had created the myth of the American Utopia. When that search came to its end in the nightmare of the Terror, the myth vanished like a morning mist. Henceforth French attitudes to the United States were to be divided chaotically by all the divisions rending French thought. Reactionaries were to execrate the American example, democrats were to gaze at it longingly though dubiously, nationalists were to scorn it, and romantics were to forget it. That precious sense of fraternity, so aptly symbolized by the friendship of Voltaire and Franklin, which Philosophic cosmopolitanism, for all its delusions, had at least brought to momentary realization, was gone.

[142] L. Hauteval, citoyen français, au gouvernement et au peuple américains (Paris, an VI).

[143] Considérations sur la conduite du gouvernement américain envers la France, depuis le commencement de la Révolution jusqu'en 1797, ed. G. Chinard (Princeton, 1945).

[144] "Mémoire sur la relation des Etats-Unis d'Amérique avec le gouvernement directorial adressé par Rozier, consul-général à New York, au directeur Larevellière-Lépeaux," in L. M. Larevellière-Lépeaux, Mémoires (Paris, 1895), III, 179-189.

224

# CHAPTER VI

## THE CONSULATE AND THE EMPIRE, 1799-1815

Just as the Fall of the Bastille and the Thermidorian reaction had produced radical changes in French opinion of the United States, so the *coup d'état* of Brumaire, by which Napoleon seized power in 1799, likewise created a new political and ideological situation which was inevitably reflected in a new set of attitudes toward the American republic. The new relativism and nationalism, which first manifested themselves during the Emigration, continued to operate in French thought, but the violent anti-Americanism of the Undeclared War quickly disappeared, to be replaced by both an official pro-American policy and a revival of Americanism among the liberals and intellectuals. These new attitudes, however, by no means constituted a rebirth (except in rare cases) of the American Dream. Admiration for the United States was now moderated by many reservations and was denied by many voices. The totality of the French image of American civilization was a confusion of contradictory and divergent ideas which reflected the chaos of French thought in this period of transition.

The series of dramatic events which marked both French internal politics and foreign relations had immediate impact on the attitudes of Frenchmen toward the United States. Talleyrand's clumsy attempt in 1797 to extract a bribe from the American envoys sent to liquidate the imbroglio had produced the XYZ Affair and a virtual state of war. His reliance on the Francophile Republicans to divide America proved ill founded, and his devious tactics had served only to strengthen and unite American hostility. The United States was seriously preparing for war, naval attacks on armed French ships increased, and there rose the specter of a joint Anglo-American attack on the French and Spanish colonies. Then in 1798 Victor Du Pont, the returning consul general, presented Talleyrand with a report of a confidential conversation with Vice-President Jefferson, who had indicated that continued spoliations would throw American naval power to the side of the British and threaten the French and Spanish colonies, but that a policy of appeasement might bring the pro-French Republicans into power in the next elections. This argument was particularly effective, for Talleyrand was at that very moment working for the re-cession of Louisiana to France from Spain and he feared that an Anglo-American operation down the undefended Mississippi would destroy his dream of rebuilding the French empire in America.[1]

Consequently, Talleyrand abruptly shifted his policy. It was made clear to the American government that an envoy would be courteously received, and the newspapers began suggesting that the "good sense of the American people" would prevent war with France.[2] Napoleon, upon his seizure of power in November 1799, fully endorsed the new policy, further implementing it by revoking decrees hostile to American shipping. Now the official newspaper line became that the quarrel had all been the fault of the discredited Directory and that a friendly settlement could be easily arranged.[3]

President Adams, anxious for peace, sent a commission, which was cordially received in March 1800. The negotiations, however, were dragged out, principally because Napoleon was anxious first to get a firm hold on Louisiana. At last, on September 30, the Treaty of Mortefontaine was signed, ending French spoliations and freeing the United States from the entangling obligations of the Treaty of 1778. The signature was hailed in Paris as the happy restoration of friendship between the two republics, and Joseph Na-

[1] See J. A. James, "French Opinion as a Factor in Preventing War between France and the United States, 1795-1800," *Amer. Hist. Review*, XXX (1925), 44-55; S. E. Morison, "Du Pont, Talleyrand, and the French Spoliations," *Mass. Hist. Soc. Proceedings*, XLIX (1916), 63-79.

[2] *Décade philosophique*, 20 ventôse, an VII.

[3] *Ibid.*, 20 germinal, an VIII.

poleon held a brilliant fete in honor of the American envoys.[4] The very next day, October 1, in the secret Treaty of San Ildefonso, Spain promised to cede Louisiana to France.

An additional motive lay behind the French policy of conciliation. While satisfying the nation's yearning for internal order and stability, Napoleon at the same time wished to avoid any semblance of counterrevolution. His assumption of Americanism was calculated to associate in the public mind the new regime with the men of 1789 and Philosophic liberalism.

A new source of friction appeared when the imminent transfer of Louisiana to France finally became known in the United States, and it was sharply aggravated when the Spanish *Intendant*, acting presumably on French orders, blocked American settlers in the Mississippi and Ohio Valleys from access to the sea by suspending the right of deposit in New Orleans. Jefferson had difficulty restraining American hotheads who demanded the use of force.

But once again the English threat made appeasement of America the best French policy. The precarious Anglo-French truce negotiated in the Treaty of Amiens (1802) could not last long, and Napoleon suddenly realized that a Louisiana under the French Tricolor would fall an easy victim to English invasion from Canada or from the sea, particularly if the Americans supported the aggression. He decided it would be far more advantageous to sell the territory to the Americans, who were possible allies, for a good price than to let it fall gratis into the hands of the English.

So when Monroe arrived in Paris to attempt the purchase of New Orleans, he was astounded to be offered the whole territory. With the enthusiastic help of the old Americanist Barbé-Marbois, Monroe, assisted by Robert R. Livingston, the American minister in Paris, quickly closed the historic sale. French liberals, pleased both by the addition to the American republic and by the rare spectacle of the transfer of territory by friendly negotiation, applauded the cession. Certain chauvinists, however, not grasping the strategic ne-

⁴ *Ibid.*, 20 vendémiaire, an IX.

cessities, bitterly regretted the loss of so rich a colony. Moreover, the friction caused in Louisiana by the imposition of a new legal and political system and by the rapid influx of Americans which threatened to overwhelm the French Creoles caused bitter resentment in New Orleans, and echoes of this resentment were heard in Paris.[5] Such grievances, however, were soon forgotten, at least in France.

During the next nine years, from 1803 to 1812, new diplomatic conflicts arose over the question of neutral rights. England tried to control neutral shipping to its own military advantage, and Napoleon countered with his Continental System, designed to sever British trade from Europe. The United States, as the leading neutral maritime power, was caught in the middle and had ships seized by both sides. Three facts, however, dictated that the War of 1812 was fought against England and not against France. One was the Battle of Trafalgar, which by giving England control of the sea made it difficult for France to act against neutral ships unless they entered a continental port. The second was the British manpower shortage, which led to the impressment of American sailors. The third was American westward expansion, perhaps more responsible for the declaration of war than the maritime conflicts.[6] At the same time Napoleon, while he did not hesitate to seize American ships in pursuance of the basic purposes of his Continental System, was for obvious reasons anxious to see the United States at war with England and consequently avoided an overtly anti-American policy. French newspapers reported with virtuous indignation all the British aggressions against American shipping and kept predicting that the Americans would soon be fighting by the side of their old allies against tyrannical England. Americans were continuously presented by the controlled press as friends of France and supporters of the Continental System. The only unfavorable items were occasional

[5] E.g., Claude C. Robin, *Voyages dans l'intérieur de la Louisiane* (Paris, 1807); Pierre C. Laussat, "Letters from Prefect Laussat to Decrès," in J. A. Robertson, *Louisiana under the Rule of Spain, France and the United States, 1785-1807* (Cleveland, 1911), II, 29-59; *Décade philosophique*, Dec. 1, 1804.

[6] See S. F. Bemis, *A Diplomatic History of the United States* (New York, 1942), p. 156.

expressions of impatience at American hesitation to com-mence hostilities. When Congress finally did declare war in 1812, all the hopeful predictions at last seemed fulfilled. The Americans were fighting, the French press said, a "second war of independence." American victories were hailed en-thusiastically and American defeats glossed over.

The lifting of the restrictions on travel and communica-tions between France and the United States was an important and immediate result of the reestablishment of friendly rela-tions in 1800. Americans, who had been relatively rare in France during the Undeclared War, began to reappear in increasing numbers. There were four American ministers during the Empire: Robert R. Livingston, an old Franco-phile; General John Armstrong, minister from 1804 to 1810 and brother-in-law of his predecessor: the poet Joel Barlow, who returned to Paris to take up his post in 1811 and died a year later in a Polish inn while returning from a fruitless trip to Vilna to conclude with Napoleon the commercial agreement he had been named to negotiate;[7] and William H. Crawford, who succeeded Barlow in 1813. Barlow, who had lived in France from 1788 to 1804, appears to have been highly regarded by the intellectuals, and according to La-fayette was "remarkably well received by the Emperor and all the people about the Court."[8] Pierre Samuel Du Pont de Nemours, the former Physiocrat, was particularly active in supporting him and, after Barlow's tragic death, extolled his friend as the author of "the only epic America yet possesses" and as a diplomat, orator, philosopher, and friend of France.[9] The following year, Barlow's *Columbiad* was published in Paris both in English and French versions.[10] The *Mercure étranger* translated his preface, which affirmed that the goal of American poetry must be to instill the love of liberty.[11]

[7] See L. Howard, "Joel Barlow and Napoleon," *Huntington Lib. Quarterly*, II (1938), 37-51.
[8] *Letters of Lafayette and Jefferson*, ed. G. Chinard (Baltimore, 1929), p. 331.
[9] Pierre S. Du Pont de Nemours, *Notice sur la vie de M. Barlow* (Paris, 1813).
[10] *The Columbiad* (Paris, 1813); *La Columbiade* (Paris, 1813). The latter, translated by C. E. Oelsner, contains only the first canto.
[11] I (1813), 384-386.

More influential than Barlow was the Irish-born David B. Warden, who arrived in Paris in 1804 as General Armstrong's secretary and who served from 1808 to 1814 as American consul in Paris.[12] He enrolled in the Ecole de Médecine de Paris, where he studied under such men as Georges Cuvier, Geoffroy Saint-Hilaire, and Joseph Louis Gay-Lussac. Warden's friendships with the leading scientists in Paris and his position as secretary to the minister made him a natural link between French and American men of science. He translated into English works of Cuvier, Gay-Lussac, Jean-François Callet, Antoine L. Thomas, and the Abbé Grégoire[13] and published in English and French a book of his own, *On the Origin, Nature, Progress and Influence of Consular Establishments* (Paris, 1813).[14] President Jefferson, whom he admired greatly, made use of him as a correspondent to obtain scientific information and publications and as intermediary in dealing with French scientists. For instance, in 1808 Warden presented Jefferson's gift of fossil mammoth bones to the French Imperial Institute.[15] In like manner, Warden served as correspondent for Dr. Samuel L. Mitchill, professor at Columbia College, U.S. Senator, and one of the founders of the *Medical Repository*, forwarding to New York scientific news and acquainting his French friends with Dr. Mitchill's activities.

Warden's most used medium during the Empire for publicizing American scientific news was the *Bibliothèque américaine*, a periodical published in 1807 by Henri Caritat, a friend of Thomas Paine, who had been from 1797 to 1804

12 See F. C. Haber, "David Bailie Warden, A Bibliographical Sketch of America's Cultural Ambassador in France, 1804-1845," *Bulletin de l'Institut Français de Washington*, new series, no. 3 (1953), 75-118.

13 Georges Cuvier, *Historical Eulogium on Joseph Priestley* (Paris, 1807); J.-F. Callet, *Tables of Logarithms* (Paris, 1809); Henri Grégoire, *An Enquiry Concerning the Intellectual and Moral Faculties, and Literature of Negroes* (Brooklyn, 1810); A. L. Thomas, *Eulogium on Marcus Aurelius* (New York, 1808).

14 The French version: *De l'origine, de la nature, des progrès, et de l'influence des établissements consulaires* (Paris, 1815). For French opinion of the book, see *Mercure*, Oct. 23, 1813 (article by J. B. Say) and *Mercure étranger*, II (1813), no. 10, 221-223.

15 See H. C. Rice, "Jefferson's Gift of Fossils to the Museum of Natural History in Paris," *Proc. Amer. Philos. Soc.*, XCV (1951), 597-627.

a bookseller in New York.[16] To this journal Warden contributed a number of articles forwarded by Dr. Mitchill as well as productions of his own pen. Caritat, who was liberal, Jeffersonian, and anti-mercantile in his sympathies, likewise published articles on the United States by Camille Saint Aubin, an expert on government finance and a former member of the Tribunat, and by Antoine Jay, Moreau de Saint Méry, and others, and printed reviews on current works, both French and English, on the United States, biographical sketches of American figures, political documents, government reports, statistical tables, articles on American trade, industry, and politics, excerpts from American periodicals, news of American literary activities, translations of American scientific and medical papers, and news items of American scholarly work. All in all, it presented a favorable and reasonably rounded picture of American cultural, scientific, political, and economic activities.

After the demise of the *Bibliothèque américaine,* the *Mercure* occasionally carried American scholarly and scientific news. The *Mercure étranger,* founded in 1813, was also supplied with American news forwarded by Dr. Mitchill to Warden. It printed numerous items on American scholarly, scientific, and literary publications and investigations, and it reported to the French public in 1814 the first news of "a very talented young man" by the name of Washington Irving.[17]

William Lee, American consul in Bordeaux, who during the Restoration was to make himself *persona non grata* to the Bourbons by his undisguised Bonapartist sympathies, undertook to defend American foreign policy in his *Les Etats-Unis et l'Angleterre* (1814), translated by Antoine Jay, the former *Emigré,* now editor of the *Journal de Paris.* Besides cataloguing the English acts of aggression, Lee depicted the United States as a peace-loving nation without territorial

16 See *N.Y. Pub. Lib. Bulletin,* XLIII (1939), no. 10, p. 717 and C. Evans, *American Bibliography* (Chicago, 1931-1934), XI, 392; XII, 410. The *Bibliothèque américaine* was published in nine issues in 1807, the first four bearing the title, *L'Amérique du Nord, ou le Correspondant des Etats-Unis.*
17 III (1814), 434.

ambitions and his countrymen as a frugal, tolerant, and hospitable people who had offered asylum to fugitives from every land. He stressed the important point that American commercial expansion would be beneficial, and not dangerous, to France's interests.

Besides such diplomatic representatives, there were various other Americans in Paris, though they were not as numerous as they were to be after the end of the Napoleonic Wars. Robert Fulton, who had arrived during the Directory, in addition to publishing his work on canals, developed an experimental submarine for Napoleon (which functioned successfully even though it failed in its attack on British naval ships) and built a steamboat which made a successful run in the Seine on August 9, 1803 (four years before the launching of the *Clermont* on the Hudson), witnessed by a committee from the National Institute and a large crowd of spectators. In 1812, with the help of Warden he published in Paris a work on submarine torpedoes.[18] The artist Benjamin West, who still remained very much an American, was in Paris for the Salon of 1802, at which Napoleon complimented him on his "Death on a Pale Horse," and he gave a large dinner for his fellow artists, men of letters, and connoisseurs of painting.[19] When he returned in 1804, hailed as the representative of the avant-garde of historical painting, he advised Napoleon to follow the example of George Washington, who had also "liberated a continent," a remark his English colleagues thought so unsuitable to his position as president of the Royal Academy that they suspended him from that office for several months.[20] There were many more Americans in Paris: Ferdinand Hassler, appointed by the American government for carrying out a coastal survey;[21] David Humphreys, poet, soldier, and former minister to

[18] *Recherches sur les moyens de perfectionner les canaux de navigation* (Paris, an VII) (on which see J. B. Say's comment in *Décade philosophique*, 20 ventôse, an VII) and *De la machine infernale* (Paris, 1809).

[19] F. Kimball, "Benjamin West au Salon de 1802," *Gazette de beaux arts*, series 7, VII (1932), 403-410.

[20] E. Wind, "The Revolution of History Painting," *Journal of the Warburg Institute*, II, no. 2 (Oct., 1938), 116-127.

[21] Haber, *op.cit.*, p. 102.

Spain; Robert Morris, later president of the American Philosophical Society;[22] and many lesser figures.[23]

American creative literature was not to attract much attention in France until the vogue of Irving and Cooper, which started in the 1820's, but it was during the Empire that such works began to be published in Paris. The first American novel translated into French was probably Charles Brockden Brown's *Wieland* in 1808,[24] and samples of American poetry appeared occasionally in the *Mercure étranger*.[25] Unquestionably the best-known American poet was Barlow. The Abbé Grégoire published a pamphlet paying the most effusive tribute to his friend's *Columbiad*,[26] and one reviewer ventured to proclaim Barlow as a genius of the first rank and to assure him a place among the great epic poets of all time.[27]

American writings with the greatest appeal to the French public, however, continued to be either those of exotic interest or else political and historical works. A second edition of Bartram's *Travels* appeared in 1800, followed in 1810 by a translation of Patrick Gass's account of the Lewis and Clark expedition,[28] and in 1812 by Zebulon Pike's narration of his western expeditions.[29] Such periodicals as the *Annales des voyages* and the *Bibliothèque britannique* published translations of American accounts of western explorations.[30] A continuing interest in the American Revolution was evi-

22 *Correspondence of Jefferson and Du Pont de Nemours*, ed. G. Chinard (Baltimore, 1931), p. 172.

23 E.g., see *Mercure de France*, Jan. 4, 1812.

24 *La Famille Wieland, ou les Prodiges*, tr. Pigault-Maubaillarcq (Calais, 1808).

25 E.g., II (1813), 74-76; III (1814), 360.

26 *Observations critiques sur le poème de M. Joël Barlow "The Columbiad"* (Paris, 1809); *Critical Observations on the Poem of Mr. Joel Barlow, The Columbiad* (Washington, 1809); see also Joel Barlow, *Letter to Henry Gregoire, in Reply to His Letter on the Columbiad* (Washington, 1809).

27 *Bibliothèque américaine*, no. 9, p. 365.

28 P. Gass, *Voyage des capitaines Lewis et Clark* (Paris, 1810). See also reviews: *Annales des voyages*, XI, 236-264 and *Mercure*, Nov. 3, 1810.

29 Z. B. Pike, *Voyage au Nouveau Mexique* (Paris, 1812).

30 E.g., *Annales des voyages*, XXII (1813), 274-291 (translations from the *National Intelligencer* of Washington, D.C.); *Bibliothèque britannique*, XXII (1803), 366-377; *Encyclopédie méthodique. Géographie physique*, II (Paris, 1803), p. 416.

denced by translations of both John Marshall's and David
Ramsay's lives of Washington.[31] Marshall's work was as much
a history of the United States as it was a biography and was
the principal source for Carlo Botta's important *Storia della
guerra dell'independenza degli Stati Uniti*, published in
Paris in 1809 and translated into French three years later.[32]
These works revealed the renewed attention French liberals
were giving the American republic and they were supplemented by the publication of Jefferson's Message to Congress
of December 8, 1801[33] and by his two inaugural addresses.[34]
Letters from the American president also appeared in various
periodicals.[35] A most interesting item was a translation, which
appeared during the First Restoration in 1814, of Jefferson's
*Manual of Parliamentary Practice*, by L. A. Pichon, who had
served as French consul general in Washington.[36] Pichon's
introduction and notes not only reflected his admiration for
Jefferson but also revealed, significantly, French ignorance
of parliamentary procedure. The Royalists too could make
use of the Americans and a speech Gouverneur Morris delivered in New York in 1814 hailing the restoration of the
Bourbons and condemning "philosophy" and democracy was
also translated.[37]

Petit-Radel's translation of Robert Turnbull's *A Visit
to the Philadelphia Prison* appeared in 1800, and new editions of La Rochefoucauld-Liancourt's *Des Prisons de Philadelphie* were published in 1799 and 1800. The latter work
attracted lasting interest, was republished in 1819, and was

31 J. Marshall, *Vie de George Washington* (Paris, 1807); D. Ramsay, *Vie de
George Washington* (Paris, 1809).
32 C. Botta, *Histoire de la guerre de l'indépendence des Etats-Unis d'Amérique* (Paris, 1812-1813).
33 *Discourse of Thomas Jefferson for the Opening of the Session; Discours
de Thomas Jefferson pour l'ouverture de la dernière session du Congrès*
(Paris, an X). This book, containing both English and French versions, may
have been translated by Thomas Paine. The Bibliothèque Nationale copy is
inscribed, "From Thomas Paine to his good [friend] the Citizen Grégoire."
34 *Décade philosophique*, 10 floréal, an IX and July 29, 1805.
35 *Ibid.*, 10 pluviôse, an IX and 10 prairial, an XI; *Annales du Muséum
National d'Histoire Naturelle*, v (1804), 316.
36 *Manuel du droit parlementaire* (Paris, 1814).
37 *Discours prononcé à Ney-York* [sic] *à l'occasion du rétablissement de la
maison de Bourbon* (Paris, 1814).

an important factor in instigating the French study of American penology which was to lead to De Tocqueville's and Beaumont's investigation of American prisons.

Perhaps the most significant thing is the variety of American writings that were printed in Paris. Franklin's *Science du Bonhomme Richard* continued to be republished;[38] the *Décade* published a letter by Samuel Adams on the philosophy of Kant;[39] in the same periodical appeared an amusing commentary on Parisian manners by an anonymous Bostonian;[40] John Quincy Adams's *Letters on Silesia* were translated in 1807; and various American scientific and medical contributions appeared in book form[41] and as articles in the *Bibliothèque américaine* and in the *Mercure étranger*.

Thus Americans, both by their physical presence in Paris and through the printed word, were beginning once more to make their existence known, though still in a very modest way. Compared with the interest the French were displaying in England, Germany, Spain, Italy, and other lands, the attention they gave to the United States was relatively small. Nevertheless there existed a steady and increasing curiosity about all phases of American civilization.

French comments on the United States during the Consulate and Empire are intelligible only if we separate opinion generated in Paris from the reports of travelers who viewed American civilization with their own eyes. The former was almost uniformly favorable and sympathetic; the latter displayed all the chaotic fragmentation which is typical of first-hand experience and included every extreme of opinion and interpretation.

A number of the men who published their impressions of the United States during this period were returned *Emigrés*. La Rochefoucauld's *Voyages* first appeared in 1799, and

---

[38] G. Peignot, *Principes élémentaires de morale, suivis de la Science du Bonhomme Richard* (Paris, 1809); *La Science du Bonhomme Richard* (Lyons, 1811); *Frankliniana, ou Recueil d'anecdotes de B. Franklin, par un Américain* (Paris, 1800).
[39] 30 frimaire, an X.    [40] July 29, 1805.
[41] E.g., Mark Leavenworth, *Essai sur l'influence de nos vents variables sur la température des saisons* (Paris, 1807); Benjamin Rush, *Recherches sur les fonctions de la rate* (Geneva, 1807).

Volney's *Tableau* in 1803; Bayard's *Voyage* was republished in 1799, and Bonnet de Fréjus' *Réponses* was reissued in 1802 under a new title, *Les Etats-Unis de l'Amérique à la fin du 18e siècle*. The mixed reports of these observers were continued by others who had emigrated to the United States in the 1790's and were now returning. In general, however, such men, who usually had stayed in the United States from choice and had had more time to become Americanized, spent less time in condemning American materialism and barbarism and more in expressing admiration for American prosperity and the security and liberty afforded by American equalitarianism. As Europe became engulfed in the Napoleonic Wars, the advantages of life in America became more distinct.[42]

This, however, did not apply to the diplomatic representatives of Napoleon in the United States. In spite of the pro-American line which the Emperor had laid down for domestic consumption, men like Turreau de Linières, the French minister from 1804 to 1811, and Félix de Beaujour, appointed French consul-general at the same time, saw clearly the fundamental contradiction between Bonapartism and Jeffersonian democracy. They were frank in their contempt for the latter, but at the same time the phenomenal rise of American maritime commerce worried them greatly, and they saw the adolescent colossus of the West as a real danger to the Emperor's hegemony.[43] Diplomatic officers on the lower echelons, however, were apparently less prejudiced.

42 See Louis Simond, *Voyage d'un Français en Angleterre pendant les années 1810 et 1811* (Paris, 1816); Jean Bridel, *Le Pour et le contre, ou Avis à ceux qui se proposent de passer dans les Etats-Unis d'Amérique* (Paris, an XII-1803); Victor Collot, *Voyage dans l'Amérique Septentrionale* (Paris, 1826) (this work was printed in 1804 but not published until 1826); "Extrait d'une lettre d'un habitant des Etats-Unis," in J. B. A. Suard, *Mélanges de littérature* (Paris, 1803), III, 175-184; Jean Devèze, *Dissertation sur la fièvre jaune* (Paris, an XII); "Notes sur les Etats-Unis d'Amérique; Philadelphie, 1806," *Bibliothèque américaine*, no. 8, pp. 193-211, and no. 9, pp. 352-362; "Extraits de diverses lettres écrites d'Amérique en 1812," *Mercure étranger*, I (1813), 63-66; Jean Antoine Le Clerc, *Mémoire, ou Coup d'oeil rapide sur mes différens voyages et mon séjour dans la nation Crëck* (Paris, 1802).
43 Louis Marie Turreau de Linières, *Aperçu sur la situation politique des Etats-Unis d'Amérique* (Paris, 1815); Louis Auguste Félix de Beaujour, *Aperçu des Etats-Unis au commencement du XIXe siècle, depuis 1800 jusqu'en 1810* (Paris, 1814).

A certain number of political refugees also came to the United States, either Bonapartists who had fallen from power, like General Moreau, the victor of Hohenlinder, who lived for eight years in Morrisville, across the Delaware from Trenton, or royalists who refused to accept the Empire, like Hyde de Neuville, future French minister to the United States, who spent seven years in exile in America. This self-styled "fiery royalist," in reaction against Bonapartist absolutism, came to feel a sincere admiration for American-style equality and liberty, and when he returned home he did not hesitate to praise to Louis XVIII "that fine and wise [American] constitution which protected every liberty and infringed upon none."[44]

Travelers to Louisiana gave very different reports, depending on whether they had visited the colony before or after annexation by the United States. Those who saw the region under Spanish control were impressed chiefly by the contrast between the lethargy and economic stagnation produced by the repressive rule of the Spanish *Intendants* and the vigorous, dynamic expansion of the American West under a free constitution.[45] But the French Creoles were "stupefied and disconsolate" at having their homeland sold from under them to an alien power. They foresaw that French culture and language would be submerged by the flood of Americans, and they claimed they were being subjected to political and legal discrimination, and that they were at the mercy of the drunken and incompetent American administrators, who made "blunder after blunder and mistake after mistake"[46] and of the swarms of unscrupulous lawyers who descended on the unhappy Creoles to take advantage of the legal confusion. As we have seen, their protests found their way into the Parisian newspapers and were sympathetically and indignantly repeated by French officials and by the

44 Jean Guillaume, Baron Hyde de Neuville, *Mémoires et souvenirs* (Paris, 1888-1892), II, 184-185.

45 Berquin-Duvallon, *Vue de la colonie espagnole du Mississippi* (Paris, 1803); *Mémoires sur la Louisiane et la Nouvelle-Orléans* (Paris, 1804); François Marie Perrin Du Lac, *Voyage dans les deux Louisianes* (Paris, 1805).

46 Robertson, *op.cit.*, II, 52-53.

botanist Claude C. Robin, in Louisiana at the time of the cession.[47]

The activities of French missionary priests continued to expand. Father Cheverus became Bishop of Boston in 1808 and in 1810 Benoît Joseph Flaget, who had first come to the United States in 1792, was consecrated Bishop of Bardstown in Kentucky with a diocese which embraced most of the United States west of the Alleghenies. A group of French Trappists under Father Urban arrived to make an establishment in 1803, to be followed by a second group under Father Durand in 1805.[48] The missions were to an extent dependent on French contributions and the fathers reported frequently to French Catholics on their efforts. In spite of the successful extension of the church, their task was not easy. Life in the West was rough, and the priests had to expect hardships, including, as they warned new recruits, "very coarse and ill-seasoned food and no wine on the table."[49] Moreover, toleration could be a two-edged sword: though the "infidels and heretics" contributed generously to building Catholic churches, Father David, father superior of the seminary established in Kentucky, complained of the difficulty he had in holding his seminarians. "In this land of liberty and trade," he wrote "young men soon grow tired of obedience and mortification."[50]

The reports of English travelers, which were read both in the original and in translation, were also a factor in shaping French opinion. These could be liberal and sympathetic in tone,[51] but the best-known, Isaac Weld's *Travels through the*

47 Robin, *op.cit.; Décade philosophique*, Dec. 1, 1804.
48 "Epistle or Diary of the Reverend Father Marie Joseph Durand," tr. E. M. E. Flick, *Amer. Cath. Hist. Soc. of Philadelphia Records*, XXVI (1915), 328-346 and XXVII (1916), 45-64; M. J. Spalding, *Sketches of the Life, Times and Character of the Rt. Rev. Benedict Joseph Flaget, First Bishop of Louisville* (Louisville, 1852); *Amer. Cath. Hist. Soc. Records*, XVIII (1907), 12-43; XXIX (1918), 37-59, 153-169, 231-249; *Cath. Hist. Review* I (1915), 305-319; J. H. Schauinger, *Cathedrals in the Wilderness* (Milwaukee, 1952).
49 Fr. G. I. Chabrat, in *Benoît-Joseph Flaget, Evêque de Bardstown dans le Kentucky, à ses compatriotes de France* (n.p.n.d.), pp. 12-13.
50 *Journal des voyages*, I, 319.
51 E.g., "Journey from New York to Philadelphia," *Bibliothèque britannique*, X (1799), 341-355; XI (1799), 477-503.

*States of North America* (1799), translated in 1800, emphasized such aspects of American life as the poor educational system, the ostentation of the rich, the vulgarity of the poor, and the great American vice—love of money.[52] To an extent these criticisms benefited America's reputation in France, for there was no better recommendation to a Frenchman than to suffer criticism from the English. The dark picture painted by Richard Parkinson in his *Tour in America* (1805) was refuted in detail and ridiculed by Charles Lasteyrie-Dusaillant, a strongly liberal agronomist.[53] There also existed the common bond of Anglophobia among the French, the Americans, and the Irish nationalists. A powerful and widely read piece of anti-English literature of the day was the *Memoir* of William Sampson, an Irish nationalist refugee in New York;[54] and the *Bibliothèque américaine* gleefully translated and published an excerpt, a letter addressed by Sampson to Lord Spencer, which ironically compared the prosperity, liberty, and justice reigning in America with the poverty, tyranny, and injustice with which England was "blessed."[55]

None of the travelers of these years, with the exception, perhaps, of Hyde de Neuville, possessed the talent necessary to permit him to make a significant new contribution to European interpretations of American civilization. These men are of interest chiefly as they may have influenced the development of the image in France. It is difficult, however, to say what was the net effect of their diverse and contradictory reports. Jean Bridel, a Swiss who had spent twenty years in the United States, published in 1803 a handbook for emigrants, apparently subsidized by the Holland Land Company, which promised to men of every station and profession who were willing to work hard, unlimited opportunities in a free and enlightened society.[56] But the land he depicted was unrecognizable as the same one described by

[52] *Voyage au Canada et dans la partie septentrionale des Etats-Unis* (Paris, an VIII). See *Décade philosophique*, 20 frimaire, an IX.
[53] *L'Amérique du Nord (Bibliothèque américaine)*, nos. 1-2, pp. 72-123.
[54] *Memoirs of William Sampson* (New York, 1807).
[55] No. 9, pp. 287-305.    [56] Bridel, *op.cit.*

a Frenchman who called himself Milfort and who had been for twenty years a *tustennuggee* or war chief of the Creek Indians in Georgia. His book, written in 1802, in an effort to persuade Napoleon to appoint him as a sort of viceroy to the Creek nation, out of which he planned to make a buffer state between the United States and a French Louisiana, told of a race of lazy, arrogant, thieving, ignorant, vicious men known as "Crakeurs" or "Gaugeurs" who gouged out each other's eyes with soot-hardened fingernails and wore their spurs to bed. He doubted that there could exist on the whole earth a viler race of men than Americans.[57]

On one point, however, practically all agreed: the prosperity of the United States. The image of the energetic, growing adolescent inevitably came to their minds. The author of *Mémoires sur la Louisiane* wrote in 1804, "One must have witnessed, as I have, the energy and industry of Americans, both in manufacturing and agriculture, to have a true idea of what this new people are capable of becoming as a result of the prodigious growth of their population, which will double three or four times in the course of the century."[58] Similarly, Perrin Du Lac, impressed by the well-fed and well-clothed people, the handsome, thriving cities, the busy factories, the fertile farms, and the swelling population, wrote, "Let us have no doubts. This nation, young but already full of ambition, is feeling its strength in the world."[59]

To Hyde de Neuville, a man gifted with prophetic vision, this prosperity was dramatic and exciting. America, it was true, was a land "without a past," a land without poetry, incapable of appealing to the romantic imagination. But the imagination, he said, was not stimulated precisely because the mind was forced everywhere to come to grips with stark reality. Everything man could achieve in the material sphere was presented to the astounded eyes of the observer. Hyde de Neuville found something magic and almost theatrical about America. It was a nation driven by phenomenal energy and dedicated to the cult of material progress and positive

[57] Le Clerc, *op.cit.*    [58] *Op.cit.*, p. 54.    [59] *Op.cit.*, pp. 437-438.

success. "A prodigious vitality animates this great body, newly born yet already full of strength. . . . It has attained in one leap the civilization which usually is the property only of nations which have reached a certain maturity."[60] In another place he said, "This land is truly one of miracles: one cannot conceive of such an astonishing and rapid prosperity."[61] Areas which a few years before had been occupied by wild animals and roving Indians were now dotted with thriving settlements. The fields were still full of blackened stumps and the homes were still crude cabins, but within these cabins he found, not miserable and starving peasants, as he would have expected in Europe, but well-clothed, well-fed, and well-educated citizens. "Under that roof of planks and bark you discover nothing that does not bespeak affluence, urbanity, and sometimes even luxury!"[62] In a letter to the Princess de La Trémouille, he wrote, "These rebel colonists are in the process of becoming a strong and powerful people among the nations of the world. They are climbing with rapid strides toward the greatest of destinies."[63]

André Michaux, the botanist, whose father had explored the West before him, like other French travelers who crossed the Alleghenies, saw this astounding growth in its most energetic form in the Ohio Valley. This was a land of tough, violent men; in the inns he sometimes found "the rooms, the stairs, and the yard strewn with men dead drunk." The settlers' cabins teemed with children; and an endless procession of flatboats loaded with immigrants descended the Ohio. It was a beautiful, fertile region. Land was cheap, taxes negligible, and a man could earn enough in a day to live for a week. The Ohio, Michaux predicted, would someday be the richest and most populous region in the United States.[64] General Collot, who knew both the eastern seaboard and the West, declared that the combination of high wages, low cost of living, and plentiful land constituted a standard of

---

[60] *Op.cit.*, I, 467.    [61] *Ibid.*, I, 455.    [62] *Ibid.*, I, 456.
[63] *Ibid.*, I, 466. See also F. Monaghan, "The American Drawings of Baroness Hyde de Neuville," *Franco-American Review*, II (1938), 217-220.
[64] François André Michaux, *Voyage à l'ouest des monts Alléghanys* (Paris, 1804).

living "far superior to any which ever fell to the lot of any nation ancient or modern."[65]

The Bonapartist diplomats alone, unwilling or unable to admit the success of a democratic government, denied this prosperity, or, rather, admitted its apparent existence but denied its reality. Turreau de Linières, who had risen to the rank of general in the Revolutionary armies and who had distinguished himself chiefly by his pitiless ravaging of the Vendée in 1794, had espoused without reserve Napoleon's absolutistic principles and was rewarded by appointment as American minister and by elevation to a baronage in 1811 upon completion of his services. The vitriolic quality of his anti-Americanism was partly a reflection of his opposition to equalitarianism and liberalism, but it was also generated by his fear of America's growing maritime power, by his personal dislike of Americans, perhaps partly due to the attacks against him in the American press, and by the bitterness he felt against American maritime interests, which preferred English control and the insult of impressment to war and loss of the profitable neutral trade.[66] He consequently painted as dark a picture as he could of American society. He was forced to admit that a foreigner arriving in the United States was struck by the great prosperity, "a new sight to a European."[67] But this prosperity, he claimed, was an illusion because it was based on foreign trade alone. Turreau decried international commerce, not on economic but moral grounds. "Commerce," he wrote, "corrupts both the moral and physical character of a people. . . . It destroys neighborly feelings, weakens even family bonds; essentially the enemy of liberal principles, it corrupts all minds, denatures all characters, depraves all sentiments."[68] By multiplying foreign contacts, it denationalized citizens and destroyed patriotism. It became a corrosive, destructive power within the state, controlling the government, corrupting magistrates, and sapping the national will. Turreau clearly saw that interna-

[65] *Op.cit.*, pp. 222, 250.
[66] See Bemis, *op.cit.*, p. 156.
[67] Turreau de Linières, *op.cit.*, p. 18.
[68] *Ibid.*, p. 43.

tional finance and trade was a political danger to any absolutistic national government. In order to prove the falsity of American prosperity and growth, he shamelessly misrepresented population statistics and claimed that the unhealthy living conditions and the corrupt morals of the United States made it impossible to attribute to natural growth an increase that was due almost wholly to immigration induced by the false promises of American agents.[69] (Modern authorities state that of the increase of 3,310,667 between 1790 and 1810, only 3.6 per cent was due to immigration.[70]) American agriculture, he reported, was in a sorry condition because of high wages, unscientific methods, poor soil, insufficient population, and the constant migration of farm labor. Manufacturing was no better off, for it suffered from the same excessive wages, plus dependence on English supplies and the "indiscipline and laziness of the workers."[71]

Turreau's assistant, Félix de Beaujour, who, curiously, seems to have relied more on published sources, principally Jay, Volney, and Talleyrand, than on his own experiences, took a similar line. He made greater admissions of the apparent American prosperity, conceding that the American working man was incomparably better fed and clothed than the European, that the total national wealth was increasing rapidly, that investments produced a return of 15 per cent, even after leaving large rewards for both management and labor, and that a continued rapid increase in population could be expected. But he claimed, like Turreau, that all this growth came from immigrants attracted by cheap land, who found only "poverty and death." He also repeated all the minister had said about the deficiencies of American agriculture and manufacturing.

Beaujour's chief criticism, however, was directed toward the expansion of foreign trade. Americans had made themselves "the peddlers of the world," and he predicted for them

[69] *Ibid.*, 38-39. His figures for the current U.S. population and that "twenty-five years ago," 6,000,000 and 2,000,000, were about 1¼ million and 2 million below those of the 1810 and 1790 censuses.
[70] See H. U. Faulkner, *American Economic History* (New York, 1943), p. 296.
[71] Turreau de Linières, *op.cit.*, p. 81.

a brilliant but brief career. But brief or not, American economic expansion seemed to Beaujour a specter haunting Europe. If the United States continued to expand westward and southward and if the Spanish colonies, with the support of their northern neighbor, succeeded in achieving independence, he foresaw that the center of world trade would shift to the western hemisphere, and with it the center of political power and eventually of western culture. The arts and sciences would be taken from the Mediterranean area, where "nature has placed the loveliest lands and the finest race of men and where the human race has developed in all its beauty." Pre-eminence would be given to peoples refused these gifts by nature, and the world would retrogress to barbarism. The arts and sciences would be neglected and die, and the scourge of ignorance would descend again upon the world.[72]

This fear of the American colossus was widespread and was voiced by other travelers. Milfort warned that if the United States should gain control of Louisiana, they would form a "colossal power" capable of dominating Spanish America and dictating to Europe. Pierre Laussat, appointed colonial prefect by Napoleon to receive the transfer of Louisiana from Spain, warned his Ministry of Foreign Affairs, even before he learned of the Purchase, that "Americans are the most dreaded rivals of the world in trade."[73] And after the transfer of sovereignty, Claude C. Robin in his *Voyages dans l'intérieur de la Louisiane* (1807) predicted that unless rapid action were taken by France these "active and ambitious" Americans would invade the vast, rich, and unoccupied territory west of the Missouri, from whence they could attack Mexico and South America, thus barring European powers from these great colonies. The threat to Europe of American expansion, which had been seen as early as 1770, was looming larger and larger in the French mind.

It should be noted, however, that there were those who deprecated such fears. Louis Simond, an *Emigré* who had remained until 1810 and had become a successful shipowner

[72] Beaujour, *op.cit.*, pp. 243-244.    [73] Robertson, *op.cit.*, ii, 34.

and a staunch Federalist, claimed that sectionalism, the weakness of the Federal Government, the unwillingness of the people to support a large military establishment, and the absence of a pauper class, the normal European source of recruits, all contributed to make the United States essentially a pacifistic state. "Each new generation born in America," he explained, "enters life only to enjoy it, to be born, multiply and grow old in obscurity, peace, security and abundance, and finally to end a happy life at the bidding of nature alone, without great torments and without great delights, without glory and without sacrifices."[74]

It was indeed these blessings of peace, security, and civil liberty which most impressed the average Frenchman newly arrived from war-torn Napoleonic Europe. He was not so much interested in the abstract principles of the American political system as he was in its concrete and evident benefits. Michaux the botanist, who called the American government "one of the best in the world," wrote: "From no matter what part of the world you come, you can enter any city or port in the United States and stay there as long as you please or travel about as long as you wish and go wherever you like, and you will never once meet an officer or official to ask you who you are or what your business is."[75] It was this freedom of the individual from governmental control and supervision, in such sharp contrast with the centralization of the French government, which had increased with each successive regime from Richelieu to Napoleon, which most impressed the French visitor. "There is scarcely a nation in the world," one man wrote, "where the individual is required to sacrifice a smaller share of his natural rights to the social order, or where the citizen has to give up a smaller portion of his natural liberty and of his property in order to safeguard the remainder. You hardly see or feel the presence of government."[76] As one Frenchman said, Americans, living under a government "scarcely seen and never felt," were "as happy as it is possible to be in a political society."[77] There were some, like Perrin

---

[74] Simond, op.cit., I, 343.  [75] Michaux, op.cit., p. 211.
[76] Suard, op.cit., III, 183.  [77] Mercure étranger, I (1813), 63.

Du Lac, who in spite of their admiration for American civil liberty deplored the violence of party strife and the demagoguery engendered by political liberty.[78] But these seemed small sacrifices for the benefits of freedom. Not the least of such benefits was the stimulation of economic activity. Berquin-Duvallon, a former Santo Domingo colonist, in his *Vue de la colonie espagnole du Mississippi* (1804), extracts from which had previously appeared in the *Mercure de France*, stressed the point that the economic superiority of the American West over Louisiana was due, in large part at least, to the freedom of individual enterprise possible under the American political system.[79]

The contrast of American democracy with Bonapartism naturally struck most forcibly the political refugees, and Hyde de Neuville, whose grandfather had been an English Jacobite and who himself had remained loyal to the Bourbons throughout the Revolution, confessed, "I have not been able to live several months among Americans without having all my ideas affected by the spectacle I am witnessing, and especially my ideas on liberty and on the sum of benefits and dangers it may produce."[80] Equality too, he discovered, had a new meaning in America. Here the gross and ignorant laborer of the Old World did not exist. The inhabitant of the rudest hut would be considered a gentleman in France; he could read and write; he studied the newspapers and followed on a map the progress of the war; his wife was better dressed than a *petite bourgeoise* of the French provinces. Yet no American regarded manual labor as degrading. The farmer's wife whom he found in her beribboned dress reading Young's *Nights* nonetheless milked her own cow. The judge or colonel led his own horse to the watering trough. This young nation, vigorous and free, might have a great meaning for old Europe. "Born yesterday," he wrote, "this nation is not shackled by prejudices, by traditions, by those dreams which are the heritage of the past and form the swaddling

[78] Perrin Du Lac, *op.cit.* See also Louis Pitou, *Voyage à Cayenne, dans les deux Amériques, et chez les anthropophages* (Paris, 1805).
[79] Duvallon, *op.cit.*, pp. 62-63.
[80] Hyde de Neuville, *op.cit.*, I, 466.

clothes of other nations. . . . I may be wrong, but as I view America at first hand I feel something unknown stirring in the future. I sense that the tyranny which weighs down our unhappy country is not the last word of the new century, and that a new wind is blowing across the world, at once the cause and the product of our Revolution. The precise consequences are difficult to predict and will be slow in developing, but I am beginning to think that America has discovered the secret and anticipated the hour."[81]

It was only the diplomats who, of course, could see no good in American democracy. Turreau de Linières resurrected Montesquieu's theory that democracy was practical only in small states, and he claimed it was an absurdity in large, wealthy, commercial nations. As a good Bonapartist, he affirmed that the people had the right to determine their form of government by plebiscite, "but once the political system is recognized and approved, the people can no longer have will, power, or action; for the code of laws which they have imposed on themselves is the result and necessarily the extent of their powers. . . . The people are not capable of reasoning, and still less of analyzing, and it is a fraud to call upon their authority and to provide their influence in the direction of public affairs."[82] The Bill of Rights was, he said, the cause of the progressive anarchy overwhelming the United States. "The legislature has not enough ability or enough energy to throw off the yoke of the people and to seize the independence necessary for the exercise of its functions."[83] The badly planned, decentralized federal Constitution, handicapped by a scattered and sectionalized population, gave the United States a weak government, rendered impossible the existence of a "national will," and delivered the nation over to political corruption and party strife.[84]

Beaujour, likewise arguing against the weakness of democratic and decentralized government, recommended that the power of the people be restricted, the executive be strengthened, senators be elected for life, and that the House be

[81] Ibid., I, 467-468.    [82] Turreau de Linières, op.cit., pp. 137-138.
[83] Ibid., p. 121.    [84] Ibid., p. 130.

composed exclusively of landed proprietors. He was convinced that the present American government could not long endure and would soon collapse into either disunion or despotism.

While practically all the travelers agreed, as had the *Emigrés*, that Americans displayed an inordinate love of money, they condemned this and other American moral and cultural faults with leniency or severity, depending on their relative sympathy for the American form of government and their admiration for, or fear of, the economic progress of the United States. As one contemporary commentator said, "Between the exaggerations of enthusiasts and the ill humor of disappointed immigrants it is difficult to discern the truth about the United States. Travelers judge foreign countries with the prejudices they bring with them. Their descriptions of the soil and climate of the country are as contradictory as their observations on American manners, character, and intelligence."[85] Hyde de Neuville, for instance, was forced to concede that he had reservations about a society where a man was esteemed not for his merit but for the size of his fortune, and where, as he said felicitously, "the habit of more or less successful speculation has somewhat altered the strict notions of probity."[86] But he could not believe, for he was no philosophic absolutist, that one defect marred the whole man, and in fact he found the domestic morals of the American people, particularly of the women, exemplary. To this, a man like Beaujour could not agree, and he said, "[The American] weighs everything, calculates everything, and sacrifices everything to his own self-interest. He lives only in himself and for himself, and he regards disinterested action as folly. He despises the purely agreeable talents, and is a stranger to any idea of heroism or glory."[87]

The question was whether the pursuit of gold debased the whole American character, and there was no agreement on the point. Perrin Du Lac claimed that nineteen-twentieths of the Santo Domingo refugees who had fled to the United

[85] *Bibliothèque américaine*, no. 8, p. 193.
[86] Hyde de Neuville, *op.cit.*, I, 453.
[87] Beaujour, *op.cit.*, p. 155.

States in 1803 (after Napoleon's disastrous attempt to regain control of the island) had been fleeced by the Americans; Duvallon said the Americans had flocked to the wharves to receive them with open arms and had "disputed who should have the joy of taking in the numerous families and of showering on them all the attentions which humanity could suggest."[88] Du Lac described the typical frontiersman as little better than a savage—a vicious, indolent derelict who inhabited a crude hovel, lived by occasional farming and hunting, and found his only pleasures in stupendous drunken orgies. Michaux in his travels beyond the Alleghenies found the inhabitants hospitable, friendly, literate, religious, and intensely proud of their independence. The one aspect of American morals on which there was any sort of agreement at all was the high standard of sexual morality among women.

Differences of temperament and different experiences can partly explain these various interpretations of American character, but there was also much genuine misunderstanding caused by incompatible ethical codes. The frequent complaints that Americans were crafty, unscrupulous, and suspicious (even to the extent of not trusting their own wives with the money for the family marketing) suggest the source of much of the bitterness. The American attitude, exemplified by the classic myth of the Yankee horsetrader, was that a business transaction was a duel of wits into which a man entered with full knowledge of the risks and in which he was expected to use every stratagem within the letter of the law to mislead and outmaneuver his opponent. To the European, however, a transaction was, in principle at least, a contract based on good faith and mutual confidence. When a deal between a Frenchman and American ended to the former's disadvantage (as was apparently usually the case), the American thought the Frenchman a simpleton and the Frenchman thought the American a scoundrel. This point was clearly seen by Louis Pitou, a political exile to French Guiana released by Napoleon, who spent some time in Newport and New York. Even if there were many fraudulent bankruptcies

---

[88] Duvallon, *op.cit.*, p. 230.

and many cases of bad faith in American business, Pitou said, the European who suffered from them had no cause for complaint, for he had come to America expecting to make a quick killing, and if he was outsmarted he had only himself to blame. Pitou pointed out that Americans scorned a man who cheated on his taxes and that they received the destitute with kindness and generosity.[89]

There was also the effect of nationalistic prejudices evident in those travelers who did not like Americans. Thus Pierre Laussat wrote to his government, "The Americans in general hate us. Even the least English of them is, in spite of his magnificent and hypocritical protests, much more English than French."[90] "What sort of men are these Americans?" asked Robin. "Tall, feeble, lethargic, pallid men, unused to hard work, living on watery food and heavy bread, never enjoying the sustenance of healthy fermented beverages, preferring to the rich juices of fresh meat their tough and foul smelling salt pork, revealing in their pale gums a thin and impoverished blood. . . . What comparison is there between these creatures and our robust and vigorous Frenchmen?"[91] Such nationalistic prejudices were not likely to be dissipated by American arrogance, and one may imagine how the French must have bridled at being told that Napoleon's victories were all very fine but nothing a handful of American militia could not have done.

Whatever were the contradictions of opinion about American morals, there was general agreement on the national indifference to the arts. It was conceded that the rate of literacy was high, that elementary education was excellent, and that Americans showed talent in law and might even someday excel in the sciences. But as the *Emigrés* of the 1790's had already said, Americans were too materialistic a people to produce an art or a literature. The argument, however, was not that money-making absorbed all the national energy; rather, it was that materialism had brutalized the American spirit.

[89] Pitou, *op.cit.*
[90] Robertson, *op.cit.*, II, 55, 57.
[91] Robin, *op.cit.*, III, 127-128.

Turreau naturally identified materialism with equalitarianism and the mercantile spirit, and he claimed that these
two evils were responsible for the neglect of higher education
in the United States. "A young man leaves school only to
enter a shop or a lawyer's office, and it is there that he is
supposed to acquire a knowledge of ethics, law, philosophy,
and especially politics."[92] For Beaujour the great American
vice, the love of money, was the root of that ugliness and vulgarity which for him characterized American civilization.
"Everywhere a hideous land, a harsh sky, a dark, crude nature."[93] American cities were rectilinear and monotonous;
American architecture "the Dutch style married to the
Chinese."[94] This nation was a transplanted society which had
made the transition from barbarism to civilization at one
leap. It had no character of its own; the only truly national
traits were vanity, coldness, and lack of imagination. The
pleasures of social intercourse were unknown; there was no
amenity of manners, no delicacy of sentiment. The American
cared for nothing but money; he judged men only by the size
of their fortunes; he thought and talked of nothing but business. Such a nation could achieve a high literacy and excel
in medicine, natural history, and mechanics, but, Beaujour
said, "we cannot foresee the same success in literature and the
beaux arts. We may presume Americans will never have, or
will have after only many years, a national literature, for they
have no national language, and English literature, so rich
in every genre, will for a long time supply their lack. Moreover a nation, no matter how enlightened, can scarcely hope
to have a literature until it has a distinctive character, of
which the literature is a faithful expression. Americans still
do not have any such character, and they still form less a
people than an amalgam of several peoples."[95]

Other men were most repelled by the vulgarity of Americans or by their appalling lack of sensitivity. Perrin Du Lac
said that in the state legislatures the members sat with their
feet on their desks and swilled from a common jug. In the

[92] Turreau de Linières, *op.cit.*, p. 122.    [93] Beaujour, *op.cit.*, p. 41.
[94] *Ibid.*, p. 83.    [95] *Ibid.*, pp. 143-144.

theaters men kept their hats on, smoked noisome black cigars, and never dreamed of yielding a seat to a lady. "All of which proves," he remarked, "that politeness and liberty do not go easily together."[96] The delights of social intercourse and an appreciation of nature were unknown in America. "Do they go to the country to rest from their labors? It is only to be able to drink without interruption; it is not to enjoy the beauties of nature nor the charms of woods and fields. A brook, were it worthy of the muse of Virgil or Delille, is nothing to them but just so much pure water, so of no value. A good Havana cigar, a newspaper, and a bottle of Madeira— those are the joys of an American's life."[97]

The assumptions underlying these criticisms were the same as those made by the *Emigrés* of the previous decade: that an equalitarian bourgeois society must be culturally inferior to an aristocracy; that culture can exist only if there are professional artists and scholars supported by a leisured class; that the United States was still culturally dominated by England; and that Americans were an immature people.

Not all the comments were so harsh, but there was substantial agreement on American artistic and cultural inferiority, despite the high rate of literacy. Yet it is never safe to generalize. Hyde de Neuville sensed in the American farmer who studied Napoleon's campaigns and in his wife who read Young's *Nights* the possibilities of a new sort of mass culture, "something unknown stirring in the future." Bridel, quoting Jefferson's refutation of Raynal's statement that America had never produced a man of genius, reaffirmed like a good *Philosophe* his faith in an enlightened America.[98] Nor was it true that America had no aristocracy. The young Count de Caraman, whose uncle had accompanied Lafayette in America in 1784, came to the United States in 1811 as secretary to the new minister, Sérurier. If we may trust his account, written forty years later but from notes taken at the time, he found in the society of such men as Gouverneur Morris, who reminisced reverently of Marie Antoinette, Chancellor Livingston, an inveterate Francophile, and John

96 Du Lac, *op.cit.*, p. 53.     97 *Ibid.*, p. 99.     98 Bridel, *op.cit.*, p. 58.

Izard Middleton, painter, archeologist, and intimate of Mme de Staël, "the most refined manners allied with all that European society formerly could offer in the way of pleasures and even of luxury."[99] As for American women (whom even the most adverse critics admired for their beauty as well as their virtue) he remembered as particularly charming "Mrs. Rewbell, the daughter-in-law of the former Director, and Mrs. Patterson, who has since become the Marchioness of Wellesley."[100] Nor was De Caraman the only Frenchman to succumb to the charms of American womanhood, for in 1803 had taken place the famous marriage of Jerome Bonaparte, Napoleon's youngest brother, to Elizabeth Patterson, the daughter of a wealthy Irish merchant in Baltimore.

This complex and contradictory image (if it may be called an image) produced by the travelers, which was an immediate reflection not only of diverse personalities and dissimilar experiences but also of the complex of ideological and political forces at work, was in sharp contrast to the relatively simple and uniform picture of America evolving in France itself. This picture, which was the work both of Napoleon and of the covert liberal opposition, was a most favorable one.

The death of Washington in 1799 gave Napoleon his first chance to implement his policy of identifying his new regime with American republicanism. The American hero, who a couple of years before had been reviled by the press of the Directory as a traitor and as a stooge to British tyrants, was all at once rehabilitated as the beloved leader who had brought order and stability to the American Revolution. On February 7, 1800 Napoleon issued an order of the day to the Army of the Republic, decreeing ten days of official mourning: "Washington is dead. That great man fought against tyranny; he consolidated the liberty of his country. His memory will forever be dear to the French people, as to all free men of the two worlds, and especially to the soldiers of France who, like him and the soldiers of America, are fighting the battle

[99] Georges Joseph Victor de Caraman, *Les Etats-Unis il y a quarante ans* (Paris, 1852-1854), II, 6.
[100] *Ibid.*, I, 10.

for liberty and equality."[101] At the same time he ordered that Washington's bust be placed in the Grand Gallery of the Tuileries beside those of Hannibal, Caesar, Turenne, Condé, Mirabeau, and the other heroes of ancient and modern times. Talleyrand, the foreign minister, submitted an effusive "Report" paying homage to Washington as "the man who first dared believe he could inspire degenerate nations with the courage to rise to republican virtues," and to the United States as "the wisest and happiest nation on the face of the earth."[102] Numerous eulogies, both spontaneous and officially inspired, were pronounced on the American hero. The Lycée des Sciences et Arts de Marseille offered a gold medal for the best oration on Washington.[103] Jean François Dubroca, in a eulogy delivered before a meeting of the Theophilanthropes, a deistic society organized during the Directory, praised Washington as a champion of the Enlightenment.[104] Faulcon delivered another eulogy in the Chambre des Représentants. The most famous tribute was that of Louis de Fontanes in the Temple de Mars on February 8. Without explicitly comparing Washington and Napoleon, Fontanes underlined so heavily the parallels between the two men that it must have been difficult to tell whether he was eulogizing the American president or the French consul. He dwelt on the many similarities between the French and American Revolutions, on the fact that Washington assumed power not through ambition but in answer to the voice of the people, and on his great contribution of consolidating the Revolution and bringing order and security to the country. "It often happens," he said, "that after great political crises there arises an extraordinary man who by the sheer power of his character restrains the excesses of all parties and brings order out of chaos."[105]

This obvious attempt to disguise Napoleon in Washing-

101 *Moniteur universel*, 19 pluviôse, an VIII.

102 H. C. Lodge, *George Washington* (Boston, 1889), I, 1-3; Archives Nationales, Affaires étrangères, Etats-Unis, vol. 51, nos. 172-173.

103 *Magasin encyclopédique*, I (an VIII), 199.

104 *Eloge de Washington* (Paris, an VIII).

105 *Eloge funèbre de Washington* (Paris, 1800).

ton's mantle was repeated in the newspapers and the governmentally inspired literature of the day. Charles Antoine Saladin in his *Coup d'oeil politique sur le continent* (1800) defended Napoleon against charges of political ambition by recalling that the same accusations had been made against Washington, and by drawing parallels between France's struggle against English "tyranny" and the American Revolution.

This inspired resurrection of French-American fraternity created a mild revival of popular interest in the United States. In 1801 was produced the first play on an American theme to be seen on the French stage in several years, Mayeur de Saint Paul's *L'Héroïne de Boston*, a pantomime based on Nougaret's novel *Honorine Clarens*, recounting the love stories of two French officers and two American girls during the American war. As was the rule in French-American romances, the villain was a lascivious English officer.[106] It was at this time that Bonnet de Fréjus added a new title-page and introduction to the unsold copies of his *Réponses* of 1795 and republished them as *Les Etats-Unis à la fin du XVIIIe siècle*. Two hack writers, Chas and Lebrun, by borrowing from publications of the 1780's and early 1790's— principally Morse, Crèvecoeur, and the *Mercure*—threw together a work which recreated almost integrally the idealized image of America of those earlier years, *Histoire philosophique et politique de la révolution de l'Amérique Septentrionale* (1801). But the book revealed the significant difference of this revived Americanism, for the dedication was to Napoleon and the authors were careful to explain that American liberty meant respect for the law, not license, and that the doctrine of the social contract and the principle of equality were not to be misinterpreted as signifying pure democracy or an unrestricted franchise.

After the coronation of the Emperor in 1804, parallels between Washington and Napoleon were no longer politically desirable, but the War of 1812 brought a second revival of

---

[106] François Marie Mayeur de Saint Paul, *L'Héroïne de Boston, ou les Français au Canada* (Paris, an X). Théâtre de la Gaieté, 20 vendémiaire, an X (Oct. 12, 1801).

the shopworn mirage. The traditional theme of French-American amity was taken up again, and the brave Americans were presented once more as heroes fighting for their independence against English oppression.[107] Once more "the sword of Washington was drawn." The old Asgill legend was revived in a play by Henri Verdier de Lacoste, *Washington ou Les Représailles*, which portrayed a heroic and magnanimous Washington and recreated the character of the simple and virtuous American Quaker.[108] It was also at this time that Antoine Jay undertook to translate William Lee's *Les Etats-Unis et l'Angleterre*. The curious uses to which French propagandists could put Americanism were shown by a work published in 1813 and entitled *Anecdotes anglaises et américaines*, attributed to the Chevalier de Langeac. The author's avowed purpose was to show the merits of absolute monarchy and reveal "how vile is that English constitution, half royal and half popular and always oppressive." For this purpose he related a long list of incidents of the American Revolution to illustrate the cruelties and injustices inflicted by the English on the simple, virtuous, and courageous Americans. The author drew from a variety of sources, but principally from Crèvecoeur, Ramsay, Franklin, and the *Courier de l'Europe* of the 1770's. He retold as historic facts Franklin's hoaxes "The Sale of the Hessians" and "The Boston Independent Chronicle."[109] Thus was recreated integrally in the dying days of the Empire the enthusiasm for Franklin and the *Insurgents* of the 1770's and Crèvecoeur's bucolic idyl of the 1780's.

The double support of Americanism by both Bonapartists and liberals generated a disposition not necessarily to idealize the United States but at least to regard them in the best possible light. An article in the *Mercure* in 1811 typified this attitude perfectly:

107 E.g., *Mercure de France*, Feb. 15, Feb. 22, Aug. 1, Sept. 26, Nov. 14, 1812; Jan. 23, 1813.
108 H. V. de Lacoste, *Washington, ou les Représailles* (Paris, 1813). Théâtre de l'Impératrice, Jan. 5, 1813.
109 On the French publications of "The Sale of the Hessians," see my " 'The Sale of the Hessians.' Was Benjamin Franklin the Author?" *Proc. Amer. Philos. Soc.*, XCVIII (1954), 427-431.

"Although North America cannot be compared with Europe in the beaux arts, literature, and sciences it is nevertheless every day making great progress, especially in the mechanical arts. The circumstances in which the inhabitants of that part of the New World find themselves do not yet permit them to devote themselves to the promotion of the sciences with the enthusiasm and success characteristic of a people who have already arrived at a high level of population, wealth, and civilization. Personal fortunes, which are smaller than those in Europe and are more equitably distributed among the various classes, the spirit of commercial and agricultural enterprise, the need to increase individual fortunes and the facility with which this may be done, all these factors are retarding the progress of knowledge among this newly constituted people. The delay, however, is more apparent than real, and it must not be confused with that apathy and inertia still to be found in certain European countries. There exists among Americans a very intense intellectual activity, but it is applied to their immediate and most pressing needs. A young civilized people must direct their first efforts to their social organization and to their domestic, agricultural, and industrial requirements."[110]

The "young nation" concept, appearing in the last sentence, had by now become a commonplace.

This general pro-American prejudice still contained a strong element of relativism, and the *Décade*, in commenting on Malouet's essay on the United States, said, "Those who have gone to seek their fortunes in the United States and have not succeeded, those who feel the need of the excitement, diversions and debauchery of our great cities, those who have emigrated to the United States without any fixed plan or purpose—all such have nothing but bad to say of the country. On the other hand, certain enthusiasts have perhaps exaggerated the virtues of America. The ones to whom we should listen are those judicious minds who can bring together and compare all the positive information available."[111] The weighing of information, however, usually came out in America's favor.

[110] Nov. 2, 1811.  [111] 10 fructidor, an XI.

For one thing, the economic progress of the United States impressed observers in France as much as it did the travelers. The new volume of the *Encyclopédie méthodique* published in 1803 contained articles on America refuting the theory of American degeneration as applied to the problem of America as a human habitat and stressing the fertility and prosperity of the United States.[112] Schoolbooks and elementary geographies likewise described the United States as a fertile and prosperous agricultural nation in which manufacturing and commerce were fast developing.[113] Various periodicals throughout this period, but especially around 1812, printed reports and tables of figures on American population, finances, and foreign trade, which demonstrated the healthy economic condition of the country.[114]

Camille Saint Aubin's articles in the *Bibliothèque américaine* used American prosperity as a demonstration of the soundness of a free-trade policy and a laissez-faire economy. He particularly called attention to American progress in the mechanical arts and light industry, in which, he said, these so-called "young people" equalled or surpassed Europeans. The mechanical ingenuity of the Americans, which was already becoming well known, he attributed to the economic independence of the farmers and the high rate of literacy. Perhaps Saint Aubin was the first Frenchman to attempt to discover the secret of American productivity; and he claimed the answer was high wages and shorter hours.[115]

An interesting index to French attitudes is provided by reviewers' comments on current books about the United States. Volney's *Tableau*, for instance, occasioned a series of articles by Pierre Louis Roederer, the Ideologue, who censured Volney for his harsh criticisms of "our friends the Americans." American manners, Roederer granted, might

112 *Géographie physique*, II (Paris, 1803), 357-445.
113 E.g., J. H. Hassenfratz, *Géographie élémentaire, à l'usage des jeunes gens de l'un et de l'autre sexe*, 4e édition (Paris, 1800), 5e édition (Paris, 1809); Guthrie, *Nouvelle géographie*, 2e édition française (Paris, 1800), and *Abrégés* (Paris, 1800, 1805, and 1813).
114 E.g., *Décade philosophique*, June 1, 1806; *Annales des voyages*, XVII (1812), 139 and XXIII (1814), 231-234; *Mercure de France*, Jan. 25, 1812 and April 25, 1812.
115 No. 6, p. 145.

be "a little cold and even callous," but he thought Volney unjust in condemning on a few isolated instances a people who were so sober, frugal, enterprising, and industrious.[116] Another review, in the pro-American *Décade philosophique*, left the reader with the impression that Volney had found nothing wrong in America except the climate. "This great nation," the *Décade* said, "merits the study of all true friends of liberty. Destined by its constitution and laws and by its particular circumstances to a progress and prosperity whose limits we are unable to fix, the United States now arouses in us an even greater interest because of the character of that philosopher [Jefferson] now governing it, whose moderation and virtue have disarmed the passions of his enemies."[117]

Claude Robin's *Voyage*, so bitterly critical of Americans, received the same treatment. Lerenaudière gave it an extremely unfavorable review in the *Mercure*, avoiding any mention whatsoever of Robin's attacks on the United States or the friction caused by the cession of Louisiana.[118] The review in the *Annales des voyages* made only slight reference to these questions, devoting itself to quoting Robin's exotic descriptions.[119] Beaujour, no doubt because of his official status, received more favorable reviews of his *Aperçu des Etats-Unis*, but Marcel de Serres in the *Mercure* prudently confined himself to reproducing Beaujour's ideas in diluted solution.[120] The *Décade* in commenting on Perrin Du Lac's *Voyage* concentrated on reproducing his reports on American progress, prosperity, and civil, political, and economic liberty. Moreover, the reviewer sharply attacked Du Lac for making unfavorable comments on Jefferson and for his predictions of disunion, adding for good measure a warm tribute to the American president.[121] The *Décade* in reporting on Michaux's *Voyage*, ignoring the drunken orgies and

---

[116] *Journal de Paris*, Jan. 9, 10, 11, 14, 15 and 20, 1804.
[117] 10 frimaire, an XII, p. 397.
[118] Jan. 30, 1808.
[119] II (1809), 116-121.
[120] LX (1814), 412-423. See also *Annales des voyages*, XXIII (1814), 231-234.
[121] LII (1807), 455-463.

other unsavory aspects of the frontier, painted an idyllic picture of life in the West as one of complete security and liberty, saying that in this land, where crime was so unknown that doors were never locked, government scarcely existed and the citizen was free to enjoy absolute political, civil, and economic freedom.[122]

It almost appears as though there were a conspiracy on the part of the intellectuals to present America in its most favorable aspects. This was certainly true, as we shall see, of the *Idéologues*, Napoleon's silent opposition. Moreover, it was quite possible for men who accepted Bonapartism either out of conviction or prudence to feel a sincere admiration for the American republic.

Jean François Dubroca's eulogy of Washington in 1800 lauded with obvious sincerity the American president as a champion of freedom and an apostle of the faith that the foundation of political liberty is the enlightenment of the people.[123] Saint John de Crèvecoeur's new book, *Voyage dans la haute Pennsylvanie* (1801), was another example. This work, which was in large part copied from Bartram, Carver, and Imlay and gives every indication of hasty composition, was obviously tailored to the current vogue of Americanism. The dedication to Washington followed the party line, and the introduction offered fulsome praise to Napoleon and stressed the theme that France and the United States were the two nations of true liberty. Moreover, Crèvecoeur was careful to temper his liberalism with a warning that unlimited freedom and excessive democracy were destructive of "true liberty" and the welfare of the state.

Despite these obeisances, prudent or sincere, to Napoleon, the work was a genuine liberal document and an eloquent and convincing defense of the American experiment. Crèvecoeur's thesis was that, although the United States were admittedly in many ways still inferior to Europe, they were making great progress, and their faults were merely those of a new and as yet unfinished civilization. Manpower was lacking for the many tasks at hand, and the young nation

[122] XLII (1804), 534-538.  [123] Dubroca, *op.cit.*

still had to create its implements—to build roads, bridges, mills, and houses, to drain marshes and clear fields, all things which Europe had long ago accomplished—before it could turn its energy to the cultivation of the arts and sciences. But these tasks, he said, were rapidly being done. Americans, a mixture of many races, were young and hence vigorous and enterprising. Their numbers were fast increasing, and they possessed a fertile and rich land. America was founding schools and colleges, for as a child of the Enlightenment she knew that knowledge is the foundation of human perfection. Most important of all, the American constitution assured her citizens liberty, religious freedom, equality, and justice, and, instead of restricting the individual, protected his person and property, encouraged his will, and left him free to work for the common welfare.

The important political implications of Crèvecoeur's new book were underlined by the *Décade*. It seemed to the reviewer that America had found that point of maximum happiness between the violence of savagery and the corruption of civilization for which the eighteenth century had so long sought. "It is in that happy land that have taken refuge true liberty, equality, and fraternity." The reviewer drew a contrast between "the absurd and barbaric feudal customs" of Europe and American safeguards of life and property, and between European religious persecutions and American toleration—"which is not toleration but simple justice, since it is based not on opinion but on natural law." There had been of late some, he said, who had been declaiming against equality. But America could teach such men the nature and precious worth of true equality, which was equality before the law to protect the individual from whatever injustices and abuses he might have to fear from natural moral, physical, and intellectual inequalities.[124]

An even clearer case of the union of Bonapartism and an admiration for American liberalism was the case of Antoine Jay. Jay had been an *Emigré* but no royalist, and when he returned from the United States in 1803 his former teacher

[124] 20 thermidor, an IX.

Joseph Fouché, who during the Terror had lined up dissident Lyonnais on the banks of the Rhone and mowed them down with grape shot and who was now Napoleon's Minister of Police, called him to Paris and made him tutor to his two sons, confidential friend, and assistant at his Ministry. Jay weathered his patron's fall from power in 1810 to become translator for the Emperor and in 1812 editor of the *Journal de Paris*. In his subsequent career as critic, academician, and journalist he was to be one of the leading Americanists of the Restoration.[125] His philosophic novel *Le Glaneur ou Essais de Nicolas Freeman* (1812) was a curious example of how a consistent disciple of Voltaire and the *Philosophes* could at the same time be a loyal Bonapartist, and of how a police spy could be a fervent admirer of Jeffersonian democracy. The book was a complete reversal from the harsh criticisms of American society made in his "Letters" written ten years before.

Jay still held to his theory that the original virtue of Americans had been corrupted in the eastern cities by the too sudden influx of wealth. He said that "commercial speculations are the principal subject of Americans' conversation and thought,"[126] and he warned his readers to put no trust in the romances of M. de Crèvecoeur, "who has deceived many readers and gives only a false and exaggerated idea of the United States."[127] But it was of rural America, where he supposed the antique American virtues still endured, that he wrote—the virginal charm of the country girls, the innocent pleasures of village dances and husking bees, the joys of life on a New England farm blessed with liberty, simplicity, goodness, and happiness.

Even more interesting was Jay's complete silence on the subject of American literary taste (which before had moved him to write so many vitriolic pages) and his new emphasis on social and political questions. He praised particularly the practice of universal education, open to rich and poor alike,

[125] See my "Antoine Jay and the United States," *American Quarterly*, IV (1952), 235-252.
[126] *Le Glaneur, ou Essais de Nicolas Freeman* (Paris, 1812), p. 342.
[127] *Ibid.*, p. 87.

THE CONSULATE AND THE EMPIRE

which made of the American farmer a literate and well-informed citizen. He also revealed a strong sympathy for Protestantism. Few men anywhere, he said, were better educated, more tolerant, or more virtuous than the ministers of New England. "Happy the people," he exclaimed, "where religion finds such interpreters."[128] And he had an equal admiration for the Quakers: "The fundamental principles of the Society of Friends are simple Christianity in its primitive purity."[129] Their tolerance he thought their greatest virtue, and he claimed that religious freedom in America had had a profoundly beneficial effect on the morals of the nation and the national respect for constituted authority. Here was, then, no nation torn by internal dissension and corrupted by wealth, which he had described before, but "a land where the individual counts, where liberty reigns without license, and where no man is above the law."[130] Most significant was Jay's admiration for Thomas Jefferson, whom he called "a philosopher and friend to humanity,"[131] for the hallmark of a liberal throughout the Empire was the hero-worship of the American president. The radical shift in Jay's attitude consisted in his playing down those cultural aspects of American society which he had before found so unattractive and in his new affirmation of faith in American liberalism.

For all his enthusiasm for Jeffersonian democracy, however, Jay remained, even after Waterloo, loyal to the Emperor. But in the case of some Bonapartists, Americanism was symptomatic of a growing restiveness under Napoleon's authoritarianism. Carlo Botta, a Piedmontese who had enthusiastically embraced the French Revolution, had served in the French Armies in Italy and had been named in 1804 Deputy from the Department of Doire, but in 1814 he voted for the dethronement of Napoleon. This defection was perhaps foreshadowed by his *Storia della guerra dell'indepen-denza degli Stati Uniti*, which, in spite of its effort for objectivity, revealed a great admiration for the liberty and equality achieved in America. He was a relativist in his stress on the peculiar historic circumstances which had permitted

128 *Ibid.*, p. 84.    129 *Ibid.*, p. 153.    130 *Ibid.*, p. 328.    131 *Ibid.*, p. 137.

these blessings and had produced the "good morals, frugality, temperance, and chastity" he believed characteristic of American life, but he was also a *Philosophe* in his belief that the American Revolution had been preceded and accompanied by remarkable progress in philosophy, sciences, and the arts.[132]

The success of Botta's history revealed a movement to idealize American liberalism, almost a re-creation of the American Dream, which, while avoiding any explicitly unfavorable comparisons with Bonapartism, was unquestionably motivated by a covert resentment against the repressions of the Empire. Arsène Thiébaut de Berneaud, an agriculturist and writer, in his review of the *Storia* in the *Annales des voyages*, wrote that the Continental Congress had been "wiser than the amphictyonic council of ancient Greece."[133] Ginguené, the *Idéologue*, in the *Mercure* said Botta's "predilection for the American cause is obvious; so is it in all straight-thinking and honorable men." He declared the United States was the only nation in ancient or modern times which had approached the ideal of a free people and had achieved "that precious liberty which, leaving the citizen in the full enjoyment of all his rights, allows him the exercise of all his faculties and protects him by a good government from factionalism, which has hitherto been the deadly plague and poison from which no republic has escaped." He averred that prosperity had destroyed neither the simplicity nor love of liberty of Americans, protected as they were by absolute civil equality and complete religious liberty. No war in history had been more justified, even more sacred, than the American Revolution.[134] It was difficult to miss the implications of such statements.

The presence of fervent Americanists in positions of power and influence within the Napoleonic regime was of considerable diplomatic advantage to the United States. This fact is clearly seen in the activities of François Barbé Marbois, who had figured in French-American relations since his ap-

132 Botta, *Histoire*, I, 8, 20; IV, 97-98.
133 XI (1810), 111-124.
134 May 12, 1810.

pointment as La Luzerne's secretary in 1779. Placed by Napoleon in charge of the Louisiana Purchase negotiations, he maintained the most cordial relations with the American agents, his old friends James Monroe and Robert Livingston, and was an important factor in the success of their mission. In 1816 he published an account of Benedict Arnold's treason, *Complot d'Arnold*, which he prefaced by a lengthy "Discours sur les Etats-Unis d'Amérique" (dated June 10, 1815, one week before Waterloo). This gave the first complete and organized statement of Barbé Marbois' Americanism; he was some thirteen years later to express the same ideas in his *Histoire de la Louisiane*. His thesis was that the experience of the United States demonstrated to France the value and practicability of a liberal and representative government. He did not suggest that France should blindly imitate the United States, for Americans benefited from special traditions and circumstances which had schooled them for successful democracy, but he did believe that America offered profitable lessons to the Old World. In spite of slavery, commercialism, cultural inferiority, and other admitted faults, the American experiment had been a great success. The happiness, prosperity, and strength of the American people were the product of a number of great achievements: a constitution conceived in wisdom, justice, and moderation and founded on the traditions and will of the people; liberty under the law; true equality, which created a nobility of merit to replace the old nobility of privilege; religious toleration; freedom of the press; and the education and enlightenment of the people. On these foundations had been erected, he claimed, a stable society in which crime was rare, property secure, and public order respected. Moreover, the nation's finances were extremely sound. Such a combination of prosperity and liberty had fashioned a people who could, no matter how acrimonious their debates, always submerge their private differences for the good of the nation and accept the expressed will of the majority. He denied the predictions of disunion and despotism, for both eventualities, he said, were incompatible with the American spirit. One of the great internationalists of his age, Barbé Marbois argued that American wealth and power did not threaten Europe, and he insisted that the prosperity of any nation contributes to the prosperity of all.

More important than these Bonapartist liberals like Crève-coeur, Jay, Botta, and Marbois were the men and women who took a less equivocal position. There were many who remained convinced, in spite of Robespierre and the Terror, of the permanent value of the liberal ideals of the eighteenth century. As soon as they understood the real directions of Bonapartism, they renounced the Emperor (though seldom openly) and many turned to the United States, just as the previous generation of *Philosophes* had done, as the only nation which had actually realized and confirmed the ideal of a liberal representative republic. America became once more, for them, "the hope of the human race." As Franklin had been the symbol of liberal constitutionalism under the Bourbons, now Jefferson (who even during the darkest days of Imbroglio had been trusted as a friend of France) became the new hero of freedom-loving men; behind him stood the great figure of Washington, the ideal of republican integrity.

Mme de Staël, the daughter of Necker and one of the most brilliant women of her age, preferred exile to compromise with Bonapartism. Her devotion to the cause of liberty inevitably made her sympathetic toward the United States, in which she was already interested because of her Protestantism, her many friends who had visited America—such as Le Ray de Chaumont, Talleyrand, La Rochefoucauld, and Chateaubriand—and her extensive and successful speculations in American land.[135] In her great work *De la littérature* (1800) she affirmed her faith in progress and in the doctrine that the enlightenment of man is necessary to the establishment and preservation of his liberty, just as liberty and toleration are indispensable to the propagation of "philosophic reason." America appeared to her as the only nation which presented the spectacle of an enlightened people enjoying liberty and equality. If an American literature had

[135] See R. L. Hawkins, *Madame de Staël and the United States* (Cambridge, 1930).

not yet taken shape, nevertheless the words of American orators revealed to her the simple and moving eloquence which was the mark of a free and enlightened people. In 1804 and again in 1807 she considered coming to the United States, where she had many friends. In her letters to Thomas Jefferson she told him that his name was sacred to her and to her associates. If America could only solve the problem of slavery, she said, "there would be at least one government in the world as perfect as human reason can conceive." In the same letter she confessed, "Our family is still a little intellectual island where Franklin, Washington, and Jefferson are revered as in their own land."[136]

Lafayette was another who refused to accept the principles of the Empire. Throughout these years he corresponded with Jefferson, for the President had thought of appointing him governor of Louisiana, and there was also the long and complicated affair of the grant of certain public lands by Congress to the impoverished hero in long-delayed payment for his services. Lafayette remained a devoted supporter of the American republic, which he saw as the one surviving stronghold of the ideals for which he had fought all his life. In America, he said, the cause of mankind had been won and guaranteed by the liberal American constitution and by Jefferson's patriotic and enlightened administration. He still had faith that the principles of 1789 would finally triumph in France and in Europe. America was for him a torch in the darkness, keeping alive this hope and proving its reality.[137]

One of the firmest and most active friends of the United States during the Empire was Samuel Pierre du Pont de Nemours, who, as a leading Physiocrat, had been interested in America ever since Franklin's first visit to Paris in 1767. In 1776 he asked Vergennes to send him as a secret agent to America,[138] and in 1778 he collaborated with Mirabeau in drawing up the Treaty of Amity and Commerce with the

[136] G. Chinard, "La Correspondance de Mme de Staël avec Jefferson," *Revue de littérature comparée*, Oct. 1922, pp. 621-640.
[137] *Letters of Lafayette and Jefferson*, pp. 213, 227-228, 232, 253, 331, 337, 344.
[138] D. Aimé, "L'Année critique: Vergennes, Du Pont et l'Amérique," *Franco-American Review*, II (1937), 1-9.

United States. In 1789, as a member of the Assembly of Notables and later as a deputy of the Third Estate, he was one of those to favor the American Constitution over the English as a model for France. During the Revolution he fled Paris and was for a time imprisoned, but under the Directory he returned to political power and was a member of the Conseil des Anciens and founded *L'Historien*, the organ of the Constitutional Party. However, after the *coup d'état* of Fructidor, his paper was suspended and he himself just missed exile to Cayenne. Discouraged and disgusted, he conceived the plan of emigrating to the United States to form there with his two sons Victor and Eleuthère Irénée and his son-in-law Bureaux de Pusy a land and trading company through which he might achieve not only financial security but also a realization of his economic theories.[139] In 1798 he added to these objectives a charge by the National Institute to conduct scientific research in America.

Finally, after many delays, he arrived in the United States in 1799 and bought a house, christened "Good Stay," on Staten Island. Soon he and Jefferson, to whom he had been writing of his plans for the past two years, were in touch and in April 1800 Du Pont was elected to the American Philosophical Society, to which he submitted several papers, one of which, "Sur la théorie des vents," was published in the *Transactions* of the society.[140]

That spring Jefferson wrote simultaneous letters to Du Pont and Joseph Priestley, asking these two distinguished new Americans for recommendations on a curriculum for an American university. Du Pont replied by composing a small book, *Sur l'éducation nationale dans les Etats-Unis d'Amérique* (Philadelphia, 1800 and Paris, 1812), which Guizot serialized in his *Annales de l'éducation.*[141] In 1802 Du Pont returned to Paris, temporarily he thought, as a sort of unofficial personal representative of Jefferson. He cooperated

139 See *Life of Eleuthère Irénée Du Pont from Contemporary Correspondence, 1778-1834*, ed. B. G. Du Pont (Newark, 1923-1927), v, 141-150.
140 *Amer. Philos. Soc. Transactions*, VI (1809).
141 III (1812), 158-172, 222-232, 286-292, 356-366; IV (1812), 36-43, 98-108, 158-163, 228-241, 283-294, 348-357; V (1813), 35-46, 96-106.

with Robert Livingston, the American minister, and was delighted by the success of the Louisiana Purchase. For thirteen years he was to remain in France, maintaining an active correspondence with Jefferson and later with Madison, welcoming American visitors to Paris and seizing every opportunity to express his admiration not only for American political principles but also for the scientific and literary achievements of his adopted country. Finally he returned to the United States in 1815, to end his days there two years later.[142]

It would be wrong to picture Du Pont, in spite of his warm feeling for the United States, as a complete convert to American democracy and American ways. For instance, he once warned Bureaux de Pusy, "One must be careful of Americans when they are too amiable; their nature is cold and indifferent."[143] He by no means favored universal franchise and he advised Jefferson to keep political power in the hands of the landed and well-educated citizens. "Cabaret elections," he said, filled him with horror and disgust.[144] Jefferson himself well defined Du Pont's attitude when he once wrote him, "We both consider the people as our children, and love them with parental affection. But you love them as infants whom you are afraid to trust without their nurses, and I as adults, whom I freely leave to self-government."[145]

Du Pont's Americanism was a reaction to his own frustrations. He wrote much more about what America could be and should be than about what it was; he loved his "second country" less for itself than as a proving ground for his beloved theories. In 1804 he wrote Jefferson, "Europe is no longer a fitting abode for Philosophy. For a time, more or less long but which in all probability will last longer than I shall, it will be the prey of press gangs, priests, generals,

[142] See G. Schelle, *Du Pont de Nemours et l'école physiocratique* (Paris, 1888); G. Chinard, *The Correspondence of Jefferson and Du Pont de Nemours, with an Introduction on Jefferson and the Physiocrats* (Baltimore, 1931).

[143] *Life of E. I. Du Pont*, IV, 287.

[144] Chinard, *Correspondence of Jefferson and Du Pont de Nemours*, pp. 194, 261.

[145] *Ibid.*, p. 258.

Jesuits, corruption, shameless dishonesty, vexatious, iniqui-
tous and ruinous taxation, and every possible error in politics, trade, finance, and administration."[146] He feared that
the endless wars were bringing the ruin of education and
were impoverishing men's minds. "Now it is America's turn,"
he proclaimed.[147] There only could philosophy thrive, for
this was the "land of liberty, ruled by a true philosopher,"[148]
a land where "liberty is not only in the laws, good or bad
and well or ill enforced as they may be, but in the blood and
traditions of the people."[149] This representative republic, the
guardian of the freedom of the press, the protector under the
law of personal liberty and property, was now "the last republic in existence, the last hope of the republics yet to be
born."[150] "I love your American republics," he wrote Jefferson, "and the serious philosophy of your sober nation."[151]
But he loved more their chief executive, whom he revered
as the champion of philosophy and whom he called "the
magistrate of Mankind."[152] He told Jefferson, as soon as he
had read his Second Inaugural Address, which had created
a flurry in France by attacking "the anti-philosophers who
find an interest in keeping things in their present state,"[153]
that his words must be published as widely as possible
through the world. He planned a translation and said the
Abbé Morellet was going to quote the American president
in an address before the Institute.[154]

Du Pont's greatest interest was in American education,
or rather—to be exact—in the possibilities of American education. In *Sur l'éducation* and in repeated letters he insisted
on the supreme importance of primary schools. Even though
America had the highest literacy rate in the world, he urged
still greater progress. The curious thing, however, is that
he saw such education not as a means of equipping the individual to meet his own problems but as a device by which
the state molded the "right" sort of citizens and instilled in

[146] *Ibid.*, pp. 87-88.   [147] *Ibid.*, p. 326.   [148] *Ibid.*, p. 94.
[149] *Ibid.*, p. 7.   [150] *Ibid.*, p. 172.   [151] *Ibid.*, p. 77.
[152] *Ibid.*, p. 172.
[153] *Works of Thomas Jefferson*, ed. P. L. Ford (New York, 1904), VIII, 345.
[154] Chinard, *Correspondence of Jefferson and Du Pont de Nemours*, p. 94.

them while yet young the correct notions (*préjugés* was the word he used) to control—in default of reason—their moral and political conduct. In addition to this universal primary education, he proposed to offer to gifted youths, rich or poor, the secondary and university training necessary to develop fully their talents and render them wholly useful to the state. He dreamed of a great national university in Washington which would not teach the "vain and useless" traditional curriculum of European universities (theology, arts, literature, metaphysics, ancient tongues, etc.) but instead such subjects as medicine, engineering, chemistry, government, law, economics, and navigation. It would produce not polished gentlemen but doctors, engineers, and statesmen. "The sciences are the keys to the treasures of nature," he wrote. "Hands must be trained to use them rightly. A single day of an educated man of genius is of more value to mankind than the labor of a hundred thousand average men for a year."[155]

If Du Pont's ideas leaned sometimes more to statism than to Jeffersonian democracy, he was nevertheless in practical agreement with Jefferson and the historic trends of American idealism in his belief in universal education as a training for good citizenship, in equal intellectual opportunity for all, and in social utilitarianism.

In the midst of these various liberals was a core of fervent Americanists constituted by that group of thinkers known as the *Idéologues*. These important men, perhaps too neglected by historians until recently, were more than mere disciples of Condillac's sensualism, as they have sometimes been represented. They constituted a vital link in the history of French positivistic thought, uniting the eighteenth century with the Positivists of 1840 and the Naturalists of 1880. As the direct heirs of the *Philosophes* and Encyclopedists, they maintained the faith in man's capacity to refashion and improve his environment and to progress indefinitely. They taught a doctrine of monistic materialism, scientific, experi-

[155] *Sur l'éducation nationale dans les Etats-Unis d'Amérique* (Paris, 1812). Quoted from *National Education* (Newark, 1923), p. 55.

*271*

mentalist, and mechanistic, and directly opposed to that Christian dualism best exemplified by Chateaubriand, which was so antipathetic to the apparent trends of Americanism. They still believed in the salvation of mankind by liberty and knowledge. Bullied and disillusioned by Napoleon, they turned, like the *Philosophes* before them, to the American example as a justification of their faith. By a happy coincidence they found in Thomas Jefferson, the American President, a colleague thinking along parallel philosophic and political lines. He confirmed their Americanism and created for them an intimate and intellectual bond with the United States.[156]

Ideology, of which the founder was Condorcet and the chief exponents were Destutt de Tracy and Georges Cabanis, included in its ranks such men as Volney, Garat, Roederer, Sieyès, J. B. Say, Laromiguière, Daunou, Lakanal, and De Gerando. Its strongholds were the Class of Moral and Political Sciences of the National Institute and the *Décade philosophique*, edited by Ginguené until 1796 and later by Boisjolin and Say.

Jefferson had first met the *Idéologues* when, as minister in Paris, he frequented Mme Helvétius' salon in Auteuil, later to be the headquarters of the group. There he knew Condorcet, the Abbé Morellet, Cabanis, Destutt de Tracy, and Volney. During the Undeclared War of 1798, Jefferson's contacts with these men were severed, but he remained high in their esteem, and, as we have seen, they regarded him as the friend of France and the defender of revolutionary republicanism in the United States. With the restoration of good relations in 1800 he once more was free to write to his old friends and receive letters from them.

As president of the American Philosophical Society, Jefferson was able in some degree to restore that organization to its former function as a conduit between French and American thinkers. The French members elected between 1800

---

156 See F. Picavet, *Les Idéologues* (Paris, 1891); E. Cailliet, *La Tradition littéraire des Idéologues* (Philadelphia, 1943); G. Chinard, *Jefferson et les Idéologues, d'après sa correspondence inédite avec Destutt de Tracy, Cabanis, J. B. Say et Auguste Comte* (Baltimore, 1925).

and 1815 were Baptiste Joseph Delambre, the astronomer; Destutt de Tracy; Constant Duméril, the zoologist; E. I. Du Pont de Nemours; Pierre Samuel Du Pont de Nemours; Pierre Joseph Letombe, French consul general; François André Michaux, the botanist; and Philippe Rose Roume, of the National Institute.[157]

In several ways 1801 was a crucial year. The Treaty of Mortefontaine between France and the United States was ratified, the *Idéologues* began to turn against Napoleon, and Jefferson was inaugurated as President. In his inaugural address Jefferson defined his political creed: a government by and for the people achieved through a representative federal constitution; the preservation of the liberties of press, religion, and person; equality before the law; majority rule; governmental economy; encouragement of agriculture and commerce; and free enterprise. Such principles were like a breath of fresh air from across the Atlantic. The *Décade*, the *Idéologues'* paper, printed a translation, prefaced by the following comment: "While in some countries of Europe continual efforts are being made to relegate to the land of fantasy and even to render odious any system of government founded on liberal and philosophic ideas, it is heartening to see the first magistrate of a great people, of a people who have always distinguished themselves by their wisdom and virtue, openly profess these maxims elsewhere decried and proclaim them as the only ones proper to raise a nation to its highest prosperity and felicity. All those called to govern republics could if necessary draw from this speech useful lessons."[158]

The last sentence was pointed, at least. Lafayette wrote his old friend the American president a letter of warm congratulation, saying, "The example of a government founded upon and supported by the plain principles of liberty never has been so necessary as it is now to recover the ideas of

---

[157] "Old Minutes of the Society from 1743 to 1838," *Proc. Amer. Philos. Soc.*, XXII (1885), pt. 3, no. 119; *Amer. Philos. Soc. Transactions*, V (1804); VI (1809); new series, I (1818).

[158] 10 floréal, an IX.

mankind. How much they are altered in France you can hardly conceive. . . . Your speech has had among the friends of Liberty, and the pretenders to be so, the great success it deserves. Every eye is fixed upon you and from my rural retirement the heart goes with them."[159]

On November 26, 1801 Jefferson was nominated for membership in the Class of Moral and Political Sciences of the National Institute, which included among its members Volney, Cabanis, Crèvecoeur, Garat, Du Pont de Nemours, and Destutt de Tracy. Du Pont had already written from the United States, proposing Jefferson's name and saying, "You would find few men in Europe, even for the other sciences, and none anywhere in the world for our Class of Moral and Political Sciences, who could be compared to President Jefferson."[160] However, the Institute did not even wait for this letter to make the nomination.

Jefferson's letter of acceptance, written in November 1802 and printed in the *Décade,* emphasized an idea he often stressed in his letters abroad, namely the international brotherhood of science. He accepted the honor "as a proof of the spirit of fraternity which unites in a single family all those who cultivate the arts and sciences, in whatever part of the globe they may dwell."[161] In the same vein he wrote Faujas de Saint Fond, the director of the Paris Museum of Natural History, in a letter published in the Museum's *Annales,* concerning the Lewis and Clark Expedition. "It would be a great pleasure for me," he said, "if these voyages procured for us materials which could extend the boundaries of our knowledge and enable us even to bring to our elder brothers in science a tribute of our gratitude for the knowledge they have been communicating to us for so many centuries."[162] Such a spirit found sympathetic echoes in Paris, and in January 1803 the American Philosophical Society received a letter signed by the president and secretaries of the Insti-

159 *Letters of Lafayette and Jefferson,* p. 213.
160 Chinard, *Correspondence of Jefferson and Du Pont de Nemours,* p. 39.
161 10 pluviôse, an XI.
162 *Annales du Muséum National d'Histoire Naturelle,* v (1804), 316.

tute, expressing their desire, as successors to the French Academies, to renew the correspondence initiated years before.[163]

It was inevitable that the *Idéologues* sought to renew their former friendship with Jefferson. In October 1802 Cabanis wrote recalling himself to his old friend's memory and expressing his admiration for his "truly republican administration."[164] Meanwhile, Lafayette had been writing Jefferson about Destutt de Tracy, for his son, George Washington Lafayette, was engaged to Tracy's daughter. Tracy himself wrote, sending copies of his *Eléments d'Idéologie* and his *Grammaire*.[165] In 1803 J. B. Say, who had been so devoted an admirer of Franklin, sent Jefferson a copy of his *Traité d'économie politique* with a remarkable enclosing letter, saying in part:

"The happiness which your country enjoys under your administration is such as to excite the envy of the nations of Europe; however your prosperity will be perhaps the source of theirs. They will see to what degree of happiness a human society can aspire that consults good sense in its legislation, economy in its expenses, morality in its politics. These counsels of wisdom can no longer be represented as pure theories not susceptible of application. It is likewise your task to demonstrate to the friends of liberty throughout Europe how great an extent of personal liberty is compatible with the maintenance of the social body. It will then no longer be possible to defile by excesses the noblest of causes; and it will perhaps finally be perceived that civil liberty is the true goal of social organization, and that we must consider political liberty only as a means of attaining this end. The United States are the children of Europe; but the children are greater than the parents. We are old parents raised in foolish prejudices, chained by a mass of ancient fetters, and bound by a quantity of puerile considerations. You will show us the true ways to free ourselves from them. For you have done more than win your liberty; you have established it."[166]

[163] "Old Minutes of the Society from 1743 to 1838," *Proc. Amer. Philos. Soc.*, XXII (1885), pt. 3, no. 119.

[164] Chinard, *Jefferson et les Idéologues*, p. 23.

[165] *Ibid.*, pp. 34-37.     [166] *Ibid.*, pp. 14-15.

In his treatise, Say used the American example to prove that a representative republic is the least expensive form of government and that population is a direct index to the prosperity and productivity of a nation.[167]

Volney in the spring of 1803 also wrote Jefferson in the same tone. "Happy is the land," he said, "where the principles of government are economy of blood and money, moderation in private and public expense, respect and love for justice, and, if not esteem, at least compassion for the poor human race, and for that portion called the common people, who are here despised only so that they may be oppressed. Poor Europe, the arena of carnage, the plaything of conquerors!"[168]

The Idéologues, as we have seen, thoroughly approved of the Louisiana Purchase as an extension of representative democratic republicanism and as an example of territorial expansion by peaceful and legitimate means.[169] The Décade spoke of the new advantages the inhabitants of Louisiana would soon enjoy.[170] Lafayette wrote Jefferson, "All will combine to make these adoptive brethren understand, enjoy and forever insure to themselves and their posterity the honors and advantages of such citizenship."[171] In like tones Volney praised this American example of peaceful acquisition of territory.[172] Du Pont de Nemours, who played a minor role in the negotiations, called it "one of the events of my life which have given me the greatest joy."[173]

In 1804 the Décade printed an interesting exchange of letters between Jefferson and Joseph Priestley, the English chemist and clergyman who had emigrated to Pennsylvania. Jefferson had written on March 21, 1801 to Priestley to express his regret for the attacks Priestley had suffered and to say that such religious bigotry was opposed to the principle

---

167 Traité d'économie politique (Paris, 1803) (first edition), I, 393; II, 408-409, 526-527.
168 G. Chinard, Volney et l'Amérique (Baltimore, 1923), p. 139.
169 See Chinard, Jefferson et les Idéologues, pp. 48-49.
170 20 ventôse, an XII.
171 Letters of Lafayette and Jefferson, p. 227.
172 Chinard, Volney et l'Amérique, p. 138.
173 Chinard, Correspondence of Jefferson and Du Pont de Nemours, p. 77.

of the progress of human knowledge.[174] To this Priestley had replied by a dedicatory letter, dated July 1801, prefaced to his *General History of the Christian Church*. In translating this preface the *Décade* was once again using an American example as an oblique but pointed criticism of the newly crowned Emperor. Priestley had said in part: "Many have appeared the friends of liberty while they were subject to the powers of others, and especially when they were suffering by it; but I do not recollect one beside yourself who retained the same principles and acted upon them, in a situation of actual power. You, Sir, have done more than this, having voluntarily proposed to relinquish part of the power which the constitution gave you; and instead of adding to the burdens of the people, you have endeavoured to lighten them, though with the necessary consequence of a proportionable greater diminution of your influence. May this great example, which I doubt not will demonstrate the practicability of truly republican principles . . . be followed in other countries, and at last become universal."[175]

In 1805 Jefferson attracted French attention by two very different achievements. In June he won second prize in a competition held by the Société d'Agriculture of the Department of the Seine for an improved design of the plow. The fifth prize went to a farm laborer, one Pierre Marthe Lecouteux of Maisons. The *Décade* found something profoundly significant in the spectacle of the first magistrate of a great republic attaching his reputation to the perfection of a farm tool and permitting his name to appear on the same list with a humble peasant. It was, the paper said, "a remarkable incident in the history of our century and of the New World."[176] Warden published a letter on the subject,[177] and Du Pont de Nemours wrote Jefferson of the great joy the award brought him. Jefferson, apparently much flattered,

[174] *Décade philosophique*, 30 thermidor, an XII; *Works of Jefferson*, Ford, IX, 216-219.

[175] *Décade philosophique*, 20 thermidor, an XII; Joseph Priestley, *A General History of the Christian Church from the Fall of the Western Empire to the Present Time* (Northumberland, 1802-1803).

[176] June 19, 1805.    [177] *Décade philosophique*, July 29, 1805.

immediately dispatched two models of a new and improved design.[178]

Jefferson's other achievement was his second inauguration. It was Warden who did the translation of the inaugural address published in the *Décade*.[179] The speech—particularly the passages in which Jefferson spoke of his preservation of the freedom of the press in the face of violent personal attacks and in which he attacked the "anti-philosophers"—made a great impression on the *Idéologues*. Joseph Garat wrote him, in introducing a friend: "M. Déforgues will tell you, Mr. President, how many Frenchmen there are for whom your name is a consolation and a hope; he will tell you how much is blessed among us the name of the man who has made the principles of democracy the foundation of the moderation and prosperity of a great people. It was the authority of such an example which the most sublime theories lacked; you have given it to them; and that, I believe, is the greatest contribution that a man could make to the human race. You are civilizing by degrees your savages in spite of their 'anti-philosophers'; our anti-philosophers and savages are apparently more savage and anti-philosophic than yours. There is no way to persuade them that the best laws are those which establish and preserve among men equity and equality, which are really no more than one and the same thing. They refuse to see true civilization except where they see a master and subjects. Oh, Sir, what a place you will occupy in history and, what is worth still more, in the hearts of men."[180]

Of all the *Idéologues*, the one to be most closely linked to Jefferson was the leader of the group, Destutt de Tracy, with whom Jefferson corresponded from 1802 to 1824. The basis of this long friendship was a remarkable intellectual harmony, which is most clearly revealed by the curious story of Jefferson's assistance in the publication of two of Destutt de Tracy's works.

[178] Chinard, *Correspondence of Jefferson and Du Pont de Nemours*, pp. 95, 106.
[179] July 29, 1805.
[180] Chinard, *Jefferson et les Idéologues*, pp. 29-30.

In 1809 Tracy sent his friend the manuscript of his *Commentaire sur l'Esprit des lois de Montesquieu,* which contained political opinions that made impossible its publication in France. Jefferson arranged for its translation and anonymous publication in Philadelphia in 1811.[181] The work was, in effect, an exposition of the fundamental principles of Jeffersonian democracy, and, as Professor Chinard has said, Jefferson could have written whole pages of it without changing a word. In fact so Jeffersonian was its tone that Du Pont de Nemours, unaware of the secret, was convinced that it was the work of Jefferson himself and started to translate it back into French.[182] Scarcely had copies arrived in Paris when Tracy sent Jefferson the manuscript of Part IV of his *Eléments d'Idéologie,* entitled *Traité de la volunté,* likewise unpublishable under French censorship. Various difficulties, however, held up the American edition so long that it did not appear until 1818, three years after Tracy had finally been able to publish the original French text in Paris.[183]

Destutt de Tracy's intellectual agreement was warmed by a deep affection for Jefferson as a person, a respect for him as a statesman and philosopher, and an almost incredulous admiration for a national leader who could write, as Jefferson had in one of his letters, "I have never been able to conceive how any rational being could propose happiness to himself from the exercise of power over others."[184]

Destutt de Tracy saw in the American republic a great example to Europe and the proof that a representative, democratic government insured liberty and thus produced the happiness of the people and the progress of humanity. He did recognize, however, that the American tradition of political moderation and the security from external aggression which the United States enjoyed made the case different

[181] *A Commentary and Review of Montesquieu's Spirit of Laws* (Philadelphia, 1811).

[182] Chinard, *Correspondence of Jefferson and Du Pont de Nemours,* pp. 179-196.

[183] *Eléments d'Idéologie, IVe et Ve parties, Traité de la volunté et ses effets* (Paris, 1815); *A Treatise on Political Economy* (Georgetown, 1817).

[184] Chinard, *Jefferson et les Idéologues,* p. 77.

from that of his own country. He doubted that a single executive or the federal system, both so successful in the United States, would work in France. As an old man, ailing and blind, living under the Bourbon Restoration, he alternately despaired and hoped that the fires of liberty might be rekindled in Europe, and he continued to look across the Atlantic for reassurance. "In my grief," he wrote his old friend, "I say like Dido, *exoriare nostris ex ossibus ultor*; and that avenger I await from America. It is in your nation, Sir, that are concentrated all my affections and all my hopes, as well as all my esteem."[185]

The importance of the Americanism of such thinkers as Destutt de Tracy can scarcely be exaggerated, but it must be recognized that their Americanism was abstract and ideological in the broad sense of the word. It rested entirely on the remarkable consonance between their philosophy and the philosophy of the chief exponent of American democracy, Thomas Jefferson, and on their faith that America represented a justification of their own political creed. It had nothing to do with an understanding of what contemporary American democracy in its practical aspects was really like, or with a sympathy for American life as it was actually being lived.

Certainly no previous period had contained so heterogeneous and uncorrelated a body of opinion on America as that which was expressed during the Consulate and the First Empire. This opinion ranged from the vituperation of Turreau de Linières through the hypocritical flattery of Talleyrand to the wistful idealization of the *Idéologues*. The quality of this opinion is in part explainable by the new relativism born of the Revolution, and by the rise of nationalism, which exaggerated the psychological and historic differences separating the two peoples. But the confusion and diversity arose from the multifarious points of view from which these observers regarded the new republic and from their contradictory faiths, interests, and circumstances. The divisions between their pictures of America were no greater than the division between their minds, and the confusion of

[185] *Ibid.*, p. 179.

the total image was only a reflection of the turbulence within men's spirits in the opening years of the new century.

In this respect, these years demonstrate more clearly perhaps than any others the basic principle which has always governed French opinion of the United States and which has made the image the French have seen as they looked westward not a representation of reality but in a very literal sense a mirage, an illusion. For they always saw not what was there, but what, consciously or unconsciously, they were compelled to see. They discovered each time only a reflection of their own aspirations or of their own fears and prejudices. They were induced to interpret what met their eyes either as a pre-vision of a free, equalitarian, and enlightened France or as an omen of the dangers of their own democratic and materialistic future. The pre-1789 *Philosophes*, by their uncritical universalism, sinned most greatly in this respect, and post-Revolutionary observers, reverting to a more cautious relativism, were, it is true, less ready to apply the example of America *in toto* to France; but the only real change was that the new generation did in a piecemeal fashion what the older generation had done indiscriminately.

French observers have, of course, made invaluable contributions to our understanding of American history both by their records of American manners and by their illuminating and often penetrating interpretations of American society. But even the most clearsighted have, of necessity, regarded America from a special point of view, have made their judgments by a special set of values, and have written under the shadow of European, not American, problems. This has continued to be as true since 1815 as it was before. De Tocqueville, for all his acuity, discovered in America essentially no more than a preview of the "providential democracy" which he saw descending upon Europe; Duhamel sought only a red flag to wave before his countrymen to turn them away from an "ant-hill civilization"; and now Simone de Beauvoir has discovered an Existentialist and Marxian America.

This mirage-vision, this tendency to see in others a refracted reflection of oneself, is of course not peculiar to the French. It is a truism, so obvious that one wonders how it could have been so often missed in high circles, that no matter how hard we work to "implant ideas or facts" (to quote an American Secretary of State), the picture others see of us will be created not by what we are, or what we think we are, or what we wish to be, but instead by what we seem to mean in terms of the private hopes and fears of those we seek to impress. That is why one Russian peace-dove was more effective than a thousand American refrigerators.

It becomes clear that the creation of a climate of understanding between two peoples is an extremely complex problem. But the phenomenon of mirage-vision need discourage only those who think that understanding is merely a matter of setting the record straight and who believe that misunderstanding can be destroyed by a bombardment of facts and sermons. To create understanding it is necessary, first, to appreciate all the complexities of the lives of those whose good will we seek, to learn the structure of their society, the forces governing their thoughts and actions, the ideals by which they live, the fears by which they are beset. Once this is done, the second task is to make clear what our own significance in terms of their lives may be, and to demonstrate (if we can reasonably do so) how our existence may serve to support their efforts, to encourage their aspirations, and to safeguard their treasures.

We shall always be a mirage to the French, and to every people, in the sense that we shall never appear to them either as we stand in the eyes of God, or as we stand in our own eyes. But it is always possible for us to appear in a guise which is at least a part of the total truth and which is that part of the truth which reveals our common humanity and justifies our claim to be fellow men struggling with universal problems.

Voltaire and Franklin understood this. When in 1778 they kissed each other's cheeks, and all France and all America applauded, the two peoples were made to sense, in spite of all their absurd misconceptions about each other, that these two champions of the liberty and dignity of the individual had discovered a ground on which Frenchmen and Americans could stand side by side.

# BIBLIOGRAPHICAL NOTE

A COMPLETE bibliography of all the sources of this study would by itself form a small volume, and such a compilation did not seem necessary. All works cited have been fully identified in the footnotes.

There are a number of good bibliographical guides in the field of French-American relations. Frank Monaghan's *French Travellers in the United States, 1765-1932* (New York, 1933) is remarkably complete, and Charles A. E. Rochedieu's *Bibliography of French Translations of English Works, 1700-1800* (Chicago, 1948) is a valuable aid. The only list of French works on the United States of the eighteenth century is Bernard Faÿ's *Bibliographie critique des ouvrages français relatifs aux Etats-Unis (1770-1800)* (Paris, 1925), but it should be supplemented and corrected by reference to such bibliographies as Sabin's *Bibliotheca Americana* (New York, 1868-1936), George A. Barringer's *Catalogue de l'histoire de l'Amérique* (Paris, 1903), and the *Catalogue* of the John Carter Brown Library (Providence, 1919-1931). Eugène L. Hatin's *Bibliographie historique et critique de la presse périodique française* (Paris, 1866) is very useful in working with French periodicals, and of course Paul L. Ford's *Franklin Bibliography* (Brooklyn, 1889) is essential for a study of the French publications of Franklin's writings. It should be noted that none of these bibliographies, with the exceptions of those of Monaghan and Hatin, can be assumed to be approximately complete. See also the current bibliographies of "Anglo-French and Franco-American Studies" published annually in the *Romanic Review* (1938-1948), the *French American Review* (1949-1950), and the *Bulletin de l'Institut Français de Washington* (1951ff.).

The following studies, a selected list, treat more fully some of the topics discussed in the several chapters of this book:

*Chapter I*. For American exoticism and the Rousseauist concept of America, see Gilbert Chinard's *L'Exotisme américain dans la littérature française au XVIe siècle* (Paris, 1911) and his *L'-Amérique et le rêve exotique dans la littérature au XVIIe et XVIIIe siècle* (Paris, 1913). Edith Philips's *The Good Quaker in French Legend* (Philadelphia, 1932) is also pertinent. On the theory of American degeneration, G. Chinard's "Eighteenth

Century Themes on America as a Human Habitat," *Proc. Amer. Philos. Soc.*, XCI (1947), 25-57, is fundamental. For a discussion of the French relations of the American Philosophical Society, see G. Chinard's "The American Philosophical Society and the World of Science (1768-1800)," *Proc. Amer. Philos. Soc.*, LXXXVII (1943), 1-11. Alfred O. Aldridge's "The Debut of American Letters in France," *French American Review*, III (1950), 1-23, and his "Jacques Barbeu-Dubourg, a French Disciple of Benjamin Franklin," *Proc. Amer. Philos. Soc.*, XCV (1951), 331-392, should also be consulted.

*Chapter II.* Edward E. Hale and E. E. Hale, Jr., *Franklin in France* (Boston, 1887-1888) still contains much of interest, but the best account of Franklin's activities in Paris is in Carl Van Doren's *Benjamin Franklin* (New York, 1938). Gilbert M. Fess's *The American Revolution in Creative French Literature (1775-1937)* (Columbia, Mo., 1941) is valuable. For the influence of American political theory and practice, see G. Chinard's "Notes on the French Translations of the 'Forms of Government or Constitutions of the Several United States' 1778 and 1783," *Year Book Amer. Philos. Soc., 1943*, pp. 88-106, and my "French Publications of the Declaration of Independence and the American Constitutions, 1776-1783," *Papers Biblio. Soc. of Amer.*, XLVII (1953), 313-338. Bernard Faÿ's *L'Esprit révolutionnaire en France et aux Etats-Unis à la fin du XVIIIe siècle* (Paris, 1925) covers French-American relations from the 1770's to 1800.

*Chapter III.* For basic documentation, see Henri Doniol's *Histoire de la participation de la France à l'établissement des Etats-Unis d'Amérique* (Paris, 1886-1892). André Lasseray's *Les Français sous les treize étoiles (1775-1783)* (Paris, 1935) adds many interesting documents. On Lafayette's role in the American Revolution see Louis Gottschalk's *Lafayette Comes to America* (Chicago, 1935) and his subsequent publications, and also G. Chinard's *Lafayette in Virginia* (Baltimore, 1928) and *Letters of Lafayette and Jefferson* (Baltimore, 1929).

*Chapter IV.* The thorough editorial notes in the pertinent volumes of *The Papers of Thomas Jefferson* (Princeton, 1950ff.) contain much information. On the influence of American political theory and practice during this period see Lucy M. Gidney's *L'Influence des Etats-Unis d'Amérique sur Brissot, Condorcet et Mme Roland* (Paris, 1930), G. Chinard's *La Déclaration des droits de l'homme et du citoyen et ses antécédents américains* (Washington, 1945), his "Notes on the American Origins of the 'Déclaration des Droits de l'Homme et du Citoyen,' " *Proc. Amer. Philos. Soc.*, XCVIII (1954), 383-396, and Sherman Kent's essay, "The Declaration of the Rights of Man and Citizen," in *Great Expressions of*

*Human Rights,* ed. R. M. MacIver (New York, 1950). Some special studies of interest are: Kenneth N. McKee's "The Popularity of the 'American' on the French Stage during the Revolution," *Proc. Amer. Philos. Soc.,* LXXXIII (1940), 479-491; Howard C. Rice's *Le Cultivateur américain* (Paris, 1933), on Crèvecoeur; and Robert F. Durden's "Joel Barlow in the French Revolution," *William and Mary Quarterly,* VIII (1951), 327-354.

*Chapter V.* An excellent work on the Emigration in general is Fernand Baldensperger's *Le Mouvement des idées dans l'émigration française (1789-1815)* (Paris, 1925). Concerning the *Emigrés* in the United States, Henri Carré's *Les Emigrés français en Amérique, 1789-1793* (Paris, 1898) contains some interesting material, but the best work is Frances S. Child's *French Refugee Life in the United States, 1790-1800* (Baltimore, 1940). Pierre Martino's "Le Voyage de Chateaubriand en Amérique. Essai de mise au point 1952," *Revue d'histoire littéraire de la France,* LII (1952), 149-164, conveniently sums up the abundant literature on this controversial topic; G. Chinard's *Volney et l'Amérique* (Baltimore, 1923) is important; and there are many publications dealing with Talleyrand's stay in the United States.

*Chapter VI.* For the relations of the Ideologues with Jefferson and the United States see G. Chinard's *Jefferson et les Idéologues* (Baltimore, 1925) and Emile Cailliet's *La Tradition littéraire des Idéologues* (Philadelphia, 1943). On some individual figures, see G. Chinard's *The Correspondence of Jefferson and Du Pont de Nemours, with an Introduction on Jefferson and the Physiocrats* (Baltimore, 1931); my "Antoine Jay and the United States," *American Quarterly,* IV (1952), 235-252; and Richard L. Hawkins' *Madame de Staël and the United States* (Cambridge, 1930), together with G. Chinard's "La Correspondance de Mme de Staël avec Jefferson," *Revue de littérature comparée,* Oct. 1922, pp. 621-640.

A thorough study of a problem complementary to that of this work is Howard Mumford Jones's *America and French Culture, 1750-1848* (Chapel Hill, 1927).

# INDEX

Abington, Mass., 37
Académie de Lyon, 150, 156
Académie des Jeux Floraux, Toulouse, 150, 156
Académie des Sciences, 22, 27, 41, 57, 59-60, 119, 171
Adams, Abigail, 123n
Adams, John, ix, 44-45, 48, 51, 53, 56, 60, 75, 121, 123-24, 126-27, 139, 166, 187, 221-22, 226
Adams, John Quincy, 235
Adams, Samuel, 44, 56, 83, 102, 112, 139, 235
Adet, P. A., 200n
*Affaires de l'Angleterre et de l'Amérique*, 43n, 44, 55-56, 71
Aimé, Denise, 267n
Aldridge, A. O., 25-26n, 35n
Alembert, d', 43, 60, 121
Alexander VI, 6
Alger, J. G., 119n
Alien Acts, 187
Allemagne, d', 136n
*Almanach américain*, 145
Almon's *Remembrancer*, 56
America, *see also* British colonies; United States; foreign relations
American Academy of Arts and Sciences, 111, 121
American Dream, 29, 125, 139-75, 209, 224-25, 254; disintegration of, 182-85
American Philosophical Society, 27-29, 52-53, 75, 89-90, 111, 121, 192, 199-200, 268, 272-74; *Transactions*, 27-28, 30, 121, 219-20, 268
American Revolution, viii, 39-115, 233, 254-56, 264; French enthusiasm for, 39-42
American writings published in French, 19-20, 44, 124-25, 215-17, 233-35
Americanists, 144-45
Americans in France, 20, 22-24, 26, 44-45, 118-25, 210-12, 229-33
*Amérique, L'*, 61

*Amériquiade, L'*, 68n
*Ami de la Révolution*, 164
*Ami du Roi*, 171n
Amiens, Treaty of, 227
Amiable, Louis, 45n
Amis de la Révolution et de l'Humanité, 170
Anburey, Thomas, 116n
Andreani, Count, 177
Angiviller, C. C., Comte d', 121n, 122
Anglomania, 19
*Annales de l'éducation*, 268
*Annales des voyages*, 233, 258n, 259, 264
*Annales du Muséum National d'Histoire Naturelle*, 274
*Annales politiques, civiles et littéraires du 18e siècle*, 62
anti-Americanism, 4-14, 29-30, 62-65, 82-86, 91-93, 95-98, 125-39, 176-78, 180, 182-89, 208-13, 217-19, 227-28, 236-37, 240, 242-44, 247-48, 250-52
anti-colonialism, 6-7, 11-12, 63, 173
anti-slavery movement, 20, 34
Argenson, R. L. d', 21
Armes, Ethel, 92n
Armstrong, Gen. John, 229-30
Arnold, Benedict, 265
*Arrêt du Conseil d'Etat du Roi du 30 août 1784*, 132n
Artaud, J. B., 141
Arthaud, Charles, 121n
Articles of Confederation, 71, 123-24
Asgill, Capt. Charles, 141, 256
Assemblée Constituante, 180
Assemblée des Notables, 268
Assemblée Nationale, 119, 167
Asylum, Pa., 179

Babeuf, F. E., 172
Bachaumont, Louis de, 24n
Bacon, Francis, 5
Bailly, J. S., 59-60, 145, 168
Baldensperger, Fernand, 117n, 156n, 191
Baltimore, Md., 168

INDEX

Durand, of French legation in London, 22-23
Durand, John, 83n
Durand, Fr. M. J., 238
Durand de Dauphiné, 16n
Durden, R. F., 118n, 119n, 211n
Du Rousseau de Fayolle, Pierre, 81, 83-84
Duval, A. V., 143, 215n

Easton, Pa., 85
Echeverria, Durand, 55n, 57n, 72n, 98n, 202n, 256n, 262n
Economistes, see Physiocrats
Edict of Nantes, revocation of, 16
Edinburgh Univ., 113
Emigration, 175-207; "Forced Emigration," 175, 179-80; "Voluntary Emigration," 175-178. See also Emigrés
Emigrés, xii, 179, 212, 248, 250; antipathy to American life, 176-78, 180, 182-93; désaveu des lumières, 191; interpretations of American society, 193-207; nationalism, 186-87, 192, 207; successful adaptation to American life, 180-82. See also Emigration
Empire, First, 225-81
Encyclopédie, 5, 15, 18, 23, 158; Supplément, 10, 37, 43, 55, 64. See also Encyclopedists
Encyclopédie méthodique, 123, 150, 216, 233n, 258
Encyclopedists, 62, 220, 271. See also Encyclopédie
England, constitution of, 19, 163, 256; foreign relations, 228-29; sympathy for American Revolution, 68
Engel, J., 6
English, press, reports on U. S., 126-27; travelers in U.S., 238-39; writings on British colonies, French translations of, 20-21; writings on U.S., French translations of, 44, 116-17, 238-39
Entretiens de Guillaume de Nassau, 62n
Ephémérides du citoyen, 24n, 25, 27, 29n, 30, 33-35
equalitarianism, see United States, equalitarianism
Estaing, Henri, Comte d', 86
Etats Généraux, 147, 161, 268
Eustace, J. S., 118, 211

exoticism, 142, 177-78
Extrait du journal d'un officier de la marine, 104n

Fabre d'Eglantine, Philippe, 164
Fallen Timbers, Battle of, 208
Falls, W. F., 20n
Fauche, Jonas, 210
Fauchet, Claude, 59, 145, 171
Fauchet, J. J. A., 210, 218-19, 224
Faujas de Saint Fond, Barthélemy, 274
Faulcon, M. F., 254
Faulkner, H. U., 243n
Faÿ, Bernard, 57n, 211n, 217n, 222-23n
Federalist, The, 124, 166, 215
Federalist Party, 187, 209, 221-22
federative system, x
Fermiers Généraux, 132
Fersen, H. A. von, 97, 100
Fête de la Fédération, 1790, American participation in, 168
Feutry, A. A. J., 47, 52, 121n
Filson, John, 124
Flaget, Fr. B. J., 238
Florida, 187
Fonferrière, 23
Fontanes, Louis de, 254
Fontenelle, 5
foreign relations, American, 187-88, 208-12, 221, 223-29, 231-32; French, 21, 41-42, 130, 138, 187-88, 208-12, 218, 223-29, 253-56
foreign trade, see French trade with U.S.; U.S., foreign trade; U.S., trade with France
Fouché, Joseph, 262
Fouré Selter, H., 176n
Franklin, Benjamin, ix, xi-xii, 20, 31, 43n, 44-45, 62, 65, 67, 71-72, 74-76, 78, 82, 106, 119, 122, 125, 129, 139-43, 145-46, 160, 163, 165, 168, 172, 210, 215-16, 220-21, 224, 256, 266-67, 275; and Académie des Sciences, 59-60; collaboration in Affaires de l'Angleterre et de l'Amérique, 55-56; and anti-slavery movement, 34; and American Philosophical Society, 27-28, 52, 121; apotheosis in Paris 1790, 170-71; Autobiography, 161, 216, 222; clandestine writings in France, 55-57; in France 1767 and 1769, 3, 22-24, 33; in France 1776-

291

## DATE DUE

| | | | |
|---|---|---|---|
| | | | |
| | | | |
| | | | |
| | | | |
| | | | |
| | | | |
| | | | |
| | | | |
| | | | |
| | | | |
| | | | |
| | | | |
| | | | |
| | | | |
| | | | |
| | | | |

DEMCO 38-297